The poet and his audience

The poet and his audience

IAN JACK

*Fellow of Pembroke College and Professor of English
in the University of Cambridge*

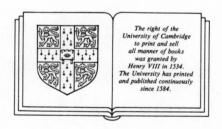

The right of the
University of Cambridge
to print and sell
all manner of books
was granted by
Henry VIII in 1534.
The University has printed
and published continuously
since 1584.

CAMBRIDGE UNIVERSITY PRESS

Cambridge
London   New York   New Rochelle
Melbourne   Sydney

Published by the Press Syndicate of the University of Cambridge
The Pitt Building, Trumpington Street, Cambridge CB2 1RP
32 East 57th Street, New York, NY 10022, USA
296 Beaconsfield Parade, Middle Park, Melbourne 3206, Australia

First published 1984

Printed in Great Britain at the University Press, Cambridge

Library of Congress catalogue card number: 83–26238

British Library cataloguing in publication data
Jack, Ian
The poet and his audience.
1. English poetry – History and criticism
I. Title
821'.009   PR502

ISBN 0 521 26034 5 hard covers
ISBN 0 521 27809 0 paperback

WD

For
ELIZABETH
and
ROWLAND

I doubt if the best work has ever been produced in complete independence of a public . . . The awareness of an audience is an essential discipline for the artist.

Graham Greene

Contents

Acknowledgements

Six scholars have been kind enough to read parts of my book: Dr Richard Luckett, Dr Howard Erskine-Hill, Mr T.A.J. Burnett, Dr Timothy Webb, Professor Edgar F. Shannon and Professor Richard Ellmann. I have benefited from their comments, although I remain responsible for such shortcomings and errors as remain.

I also wish to thank Mr David Foxon for the prolonged loan of valuable bibliographical materials relating to Pope, the late Professor F.S.L. Lyons for answering certain questions about Yeats, and Dr John Miller for his expert guidance on the political affiliations of the subscribers to Dryden's *Virgil*.

A longer version of the first part of the chapter on Pope, which originated as a paper to the Fourth David Nichol Smith Seminar, was printed in *Studies in the Eighteenth Century IV*, ed. R.F. Brissenden and J.C. Eade, in 1979 (Australian National University Press, Canberra). An abbreviated version of the earlier part of the chapter on Tennyson appeared in *The Times Higher Education Supplement*.

I.J.

Introduction

I ORIGINALLY thought of having as a frontispiece to this book the illustration of Chaucer reading to a courtly audience which adorns the manuscript of *Troilus and Criseyde* in the library of Corpus Christi College, Cambridge. There is the poet: there is his book: and there is his audience.

If the illustration were reliable it would provide a clue to a question which must have occurred to many readers of Chaucer. What sort of audience did he write for? Did he (for that matter) write all his major poems for the same audience? Were *The Canterbury Tales* written for the same audience as *Troilus and Criseyde*? Was *The Knight's Tale* written for the same audience as *The Miller's Tale*? If we could give a definite answer to these questions we would be in a stronger position as interpreters and critics of his poetry.

At the moment there is no consensus among Chaucerian scholars, perhaps because the concept of a courtly audience has not been sufficiently analysed. While some experts continue to regard Chaucer as a Court poet, others go so far as to describe *The Canterbury Tales* as 'palpably not a courtly work'.[1] We are left to speculate how far, and in what respects, his poems were influenced by the audience or audiences he had in mind as he wrote.

The question which presents itself so naturally when we read the long poems of Chaucer or Spenser or Dryden may seem less urgent with lyrical poetry. It is still sometimes supposed that lyrics are spontaneous utterances created without thought of an audience – except perhaps, in the case of love poetry, that formed by the poet's beloved. Critics used to praise Marvell's 'To his Coy Mistress' for its sincerity, and I remember one distinguished old scholar assuring me that it could only have been written by a man deeply in love. I wonder. Those of us who are interested in the rhetorical background of seventeenth-century literature may be forgiven for arguing that Marvell's poem tells us more about his audience than about his lady, and concluding that whether or not he had a coy mistress when he wrote it he

1

must certainly have possessed, in the company assembled at Appleton House or elsewhere, an audience of cultivated people who could be relied on to appreciate his art. 'Rare Poems ask rare friends.'[2]

We know that the greatest of Greek lyric poets, Pindar, was so far from writing without thought of an audience that he celebrated public events for a public audience; and the whole history of lyric seems to suggest that his audience frequently exercises a strong influence on a lyric poet. There is no reason why this should imply the absence of strong personal feeling: if ever a poem was inspired by deep personal grief it was *In Memoriam*, and we know that Tennyson told his son that he had begun 'the elegies' without thought of publication: as they multiplied, however, over a long period of years, publication became inevitable, and the nature of the reading public of the day clearly exerted an influence over many aspects of the poem. If Tennyson had made it less 'cheerful' – as he sometimes thought that he should have done – *In Memoriam* would not have proved such an immediate success, and it is unlikely that its author would so soon have found himself Poet Laureate.

Shelley, whose work exerted so profound an influence on Tennyson, once described the poet as 'a nightingale, singing in solitude'. Yet the essay which contains that phrase ends with the proud claim that 'Poets are the unacknowledged legislators of the world', and we have only to read Shelley's letters to find that he was always deeply concerned about the potential audience for his poems. He took a keen interest in the manner of their publication, for example, urging that *Queen Mab* should be printed 'in quarto, so as to catch the aristocrats', and showing a realism which did not always characterise his reflections on the subject by adding, 'they will not read me, but their sons and daughters may'.

Just as the fact that an élite has played a vital part in the history of civilisation is distasteful to many people today, so the fact that the laws of supply and demand have a bearing on the history of poetry may be found disconcerting by readers whose aesthetic is more romantic than they know. They should recall Samuel Johnson's pithy comment on the history of drama –

> The Drama's Laws the Drama's Patrons give,
> For we that live to please, must please to live[3]

– and reflect that the history of European music, painting and sculpture cannot be intelligently studied without reference to the overwhelmingly important part played by the patronage of Church and aristocracy. Dryden's career will no more be understood than will that of Henry Purcell by a critic who ignores the position of a poet or a musician in the reign of Charles II.

Except Shelley, each of the poets with whom I am concerned succeeded in creating for himself a large reading public: a public whose tastes and prejudices inevitably influenced the nature of his poetry. The same is true of most successful poets. It is evident that Dylan Thomas, who proclaimed so eloquently that he did not write for

> the proud man apart
> From the raging moon . . .
> But for the lovers, their arms
> Round the griefs of the ages,
> Who pay no praise or wages
> Nor heed my craft or art[4]

was wholly dependent on those who did heed his art and were prepared to find money to encourage it. If it had not been for the enlightened patronage of the BBC Third Programme he would not have written *Under Milk Wood* in the form in which we know it, a remarkable work which serves admirably to illustrate how the nature of the audience which he envisages helps to determine a poet's choice of genre ('A Play for Voices'), subject-matter, and treatment.

It is my aim to throw light on the careers of six major poets by considering how far the audiences for which they wrote seem to have influenced their poetry. When we read a poem in an anthology, or in the artificial situation required by the demands of 'Practical Criticism', it is reduced to the condition of a cut flower. If we wish to understand the poem it becomes necessary to try to see it, in the manner of an ecologist, in its natural habitat. How *could* Dryden write *Absalom and Achitophel*, how *could* Pope write *The Rape of the Lock*, how *could* Byron write *Don Juan*, how *could* Yeats write the poems in *The Tower*? In each case one clue to the answer is to be found by studying the nature of the reading public for which the poet wrote.

I · DRYDEN
Servant to the King

THE future Laureate of Charles II could not have had a more suitable education than Dryden received as a King's Scholar at Westminster, a school described by the great preacher Robert South as 'so untaintedly loyal, that . . . in the very worst of times (in which it was my lot to be a member of it) we really were King's scholars as well as called so'. He remembered how on 'that black and eternally infamous day of the King's murder . . . the King was publicly prayed for in this school but an hour or two (at most) before his sacred head was struck off'.[1] On that day in January 1649 Dryden was probably one of the boys who were led in prayer by the Master, Dr Richard Busby, a man who was to remain his friend and to become the recipient of a notable compliment from him more than forty years later. The highly rhetorical and linguistic training provided by the curriculum formed an admirable education for a poet. In the first of his critical essays Dryden was to deplore careless poets who 'constantly close their Lines with Verbs; which though commended sometimes in Writing *Latin*, yet we were Whipt at *Westminster* if we us'd it twice together.'[2] If Dryden was never to write a line without being conscious of his audience, the early and forceful presence of Busby may help to explain the fact.

He first reached print as one of the 'divers persons of Nobility and Worth' who lamented the untimely death of the eldest son of the Earl of Huntingdon in 1649. 'Upon the death of the Lord Hastings', which appeared in the company of poems by Denham, Herrick, and Marvell, among others, is the work of a clever schoolboy who was preparing for Cambridge, where John Cleveland was the poet of the day. Like Cleveland, Dryden addresses himself to a self-consciously intellectual and academic audience. When we read such lines as these:

> O had he di'd of old, how great a strife
> Had been, who from his Death should draw their Life?

4

Who should, by one rich draught, become what ere
Seneca, Cato, Numa, Caesar, were:
Learn'd, Vertuous, Pious, Great; and have by this
An universal *Metempsuchosis*

we are reminded of John Evelyn's description of Cleveland as a man who had 'lived long in Universities' and who affected 'words and expressions no where in use besides'.[3] There is a certain piquancy in finding a poet who twenty years later was to censure Cleveland for expressing everything 'hard and unnaturally' himself writing in just such a manner, and for the same reason. As Dryden developed and began to write for a wider and more 'polite' audience the wit which appears so affected in this early poem was refined for Courtly readers.

Since he published only one poem in the next decade, and that an insignificant epistle, Dryden is bound to strike us as one of the least precocious of our poets. The explanation is to be found in the troubled and uncertain times. After his residence at Trinity College, during which his father died and left him a considerable estate, he moved to London and soon came under the protection of his powerful kinsman Sir Gilbert Pickering, a close friend of Cromwell's. It was no doubt under his influence that Dryden wrote the 'Heroique Stanza's, Consecrated to the Glorious Memory of . . . OLIVER Late LORD PROTECTOR', his first considerable poem, and one which was to return to haunt him in his maturity.[4] From the sure tone of the opening to the decisive dignity of the conclusion it is the work of a poet who has cast aside puerilities. Classical allusions and scientific images abound, and the elegy is obviously intended for a highly educated audience; yet we no longer find the ostentation of wit and learning which renders the earlier poem so gauche. As surely as the early work of Milton himself, this is the verse of a young poet who is studying the great masters of his art and aspiring to the highest kinds of poetry. While Dryden's skill in panegyric is already evident he refrains from satire on Cromwell's opponents, so that the elegy may be read as an essentially patriotic composition. As if anticipating his role as the official poet of England, Dryden prophesies a great future, a future enriched by trade due to the nation's foreign conquests.

The same patriotic ardour which led him to eulogise Cromwell inspired *Astræa Redux* (The Return of Justice), in which he celebrated the Restoration. If Dryden changed, as Johnson later observed, 'he changed with the nation'.[5] General Monck made the King's return possible by eventually changing his allegiance: Pepys's cousin, another of the main parliamentary naval commanders, also moved to the King's cause: Locke, Waller and Thomas Sprat were among the numerous poets who had celebrated Cromwell but who now hastened to greet the new monarch in triumphal verses: and Dryden joined the chorus.

On the title-page we find one of the most famous lines in all poetry, the eighth of Virgil's fourth eclogue: *'Iam Redit & Virgo, Redeunt Saturnia Regna'*. As Frances Yates reminds us, for later ages 'The golden age is the Augustan rule, the Augustan revival of piety, the peace of the world-wide Augustan empire.'[6] And so the poem ends on a note of jubilant assurance:

> And now times whiter Series is begun
> Which in soft Centuries shall smoothly run;
> Those Clouds that overcast your Morne shall fly
> Dispell'd to farthest corners of the sky.
>
> . . .
>
> Oh Happy Age! Oh times like those alone
> By Fate reserv'd for Great *Augustus* Throne!
> When the joint growth of Armes and Arts foreshew
> The World a Monarch, and that Monarch *You*.

It is impossible to understand the strange graph traced by Dryden's poetic career if we do not realise that it is the resultant of two very different forces: the pattern of Virgil's career, leading to the culmination of a great patriotic epic, and the hard facts of political and financial circumstances.

If Charles was to be Augustus, and Dryden Virgil, who was to play the essential part of Maecenas? Dryden's first answer is provided by the poem which he wrote immediately after his coronation panegyric, *To My Lord Chancellor*. This eloquent address, thick sown with scientific images which Clarendon can have had no difficulty in understanding, makes it clear that Dryden hoped he would be the English Maecenas, as Richelieu had been the French:

> When our Great Monarch into Exile went
> Wit and Religion suffer'd banishment:
>
> . . .

> At length the Muses stand restor'd again
> To that great charge which Nature did ordain;
> And their lov'd Druyds seem reviv'd by Fate
> While you dispence the Laws and guide the State.

The scientific imagery with which Dryden flattered Clarendon is even more obviously apt in the epistle 'To my Honour'd
Friend, D*ʳ Charleton*, on his learned and Useful Works; and more
particularly this of STONE-HENG, by him Restored to the true
Founders'. As Phillip Harth has pointed out,[7] this poem, written
within a few weeks of Dryden's election to the Royal Society, is
inspired by the same wave of intellectual excitement that is so
unmistakable in other publications by early members and their
associates. Dryden compares the way in which truth had grown
'scarce, and dear, and yet sophisticate' when Aristotle was
regarded as its only supplier to the phenomenon of expensive
quack medicines. He moves on to compliment his friend with a
brilliantly appropriate image from science:

> Nor are *You*, Learned Friend, the least renown'd;
> Whose Fame, not circumscrib'd with *English* ground,
> Flies like the nimble journeys of the Light;
> And is, like that, unspent too in its flight.

Important truths are to be found in Charleton's writings, 'like
rich veins of Ore', while his pen possesses a 'healing virtue ... To
perfect Cures on *Books*, as well as *Men*'. He must be a fine phys-
ician since he is able to 'make *Stones* to live'.

Dryden's interpretation of what may be termed decorum of
audience is further exemplified in the lines 'To the Lady *Castle-
main*, Upon Her incouraging his first Play'. There is nothing difficult about his opening comparison of himself to 'Sea-men ship-
wrackt on some happy shore', or in the lines

> You, like the Stars, not by reflexion bright,
> Are born to your own Heav'n, and your own Light.[8]

We have only to compare this poem with the 'Verses to her *Highness* the *Dutchess*' prefixed to *Annus Mirabilis* four years later to see
that this is a 'prentice piece, yet we notice that Dryden was
already trying to find the proper style for a complimentary poem
to a lady so brilliantly exemplified and defined on that occasion:

Some who have seen a paper of Verses which I wrote last year to her Highness the *Dutchess*, have accus'd them of that onely thing I could defend in
them; they have said I did *humi serpere*, that I wanted not onely height of
fancy, but dignity of words to set it off; I might well answer with that of
Horace, Nunc non erat his locus, I knew I address'd them to a Lady, and accord-

ingly I affected the softness of expression, and the smoothness of measure, rather then the height of thought.

The style of the complimentary epistles brilliantly illustrates Dryden's constant awareness of his audience.

Dryden had good reason to be grateful to the Countess of Castlemaine, the licentious beauty with whom Charles was rumoured to have spent the first night after his Restoration. The King's passion for the theatre made it inevitable that any writer of ambition should attempt the drama, but Dryden's first venture, *The Duke of Guise*, did not seem successful even to his friends, and when the first of his plays to be acted, *The Wild Gallant*, was produced in 1663 the King, according to Pepys, 'did not seem pleased at all'.[9] It was the Countess – whom Pepys described as 'all worth seeing tonight' – who appears to have liked the comedy, and it was no doubt due to her influence that Dryden could claim that it was 'more than once the Divertisement of His Majesty, by His own Command'. When one reads the play it becomes easy to see why Jeremy Collier was to blame Dryden for doing more than any other writer to introduce a strain of profanity into the drama of the time, while the freedom with which religious topics are handled helps to explain Evelyn's remark, three years later, that he very seldom went to 'the publique *Theaters*, for many reasons, now as they were abused, to an atheisticall liberty'.[10]

Whereas Dryden seems to have had little real enthusiasm for writing comedy, the new heroic drama, which was equally popular with the King, aroused his interest as a craftsman and was destined to exert a marked influence on the development of his poetry. It is significant that the first writer to use the term in English, Sir William Davenant when he dedicated *The Siege of Rhodes* to Clarendon, referred scornfully to critics who would 'deny heroique plays to the gentry', so making it clear that the popularity of this new species of drama was due to the taste of the Court and those who took their lead from the Court. Although Dryden does not apply the term to *The Indian Queen*, in which he collaborated with Sir Robert Howard, that play has justly been described as 'the first fully formed heroic play to be acted in London'.[11] It is not surprising that the King was pleased, since the play is full of loyal sentiments:

Rebellion is a greater fault than pride.

'Saucy rebels' receive severe censure, Montezuma turns out to be 'the issue of our murthered King', while Ynca observes that 'Kings best revenge their wrongs when they forgive,'[12] so summing up an essential part of the Restoration settlement.

The dedication of *The Indian Emperour*, which was first performed in 1665, states categorically that 'The favour which Heroick Plays have lately found upon our Theaters has been wholly deriv'd to them, from the countenance and approbation they have receiv'd at Court, the most eminent persons for Wit and Honour in the Royal Circle having so far own'd them, that they have judg'd no way so fit as [rhyming] Verse to entertain a Noble Audience, or to express a noble passion'. The play was dedicated to the Duchess of Monmouth, whom Dryden was later to describe as his 'first and best patroness';[13] and we know that the Duke and Duchess themselves acted in a Court performance three years later. The verse is stronger now, the loyalty still unimpeachable:

> Take heed, Fair Maid, how Monarchs you accuse:
> Such reasons none but impious Rebels use:
> Those who to Empire by dark paths aspire,
> Still plead a call to what they most desire.

In Act V Scene ii Montezuma asks rhetorically, 'Is it not brave to suffer with thy King?' A few lines later his reasoning anticipates that of *Religio Laici*. In the epilogue Dryden shows his usual awareness of his audience, declaring that 'Coffee-wits' should confine themselves to damning the Dutch, permitting 'the great *Dons* of Wit' the privilege 'To Damn all others, and cry up their own', and ends with the assertion that 'the Ladies' should 'have pow'r to save, but not to kill'.

When a severe outbreak of the plague closed the theatres in June 1665 Dryden decided to occupy his enforced leisure by writing a long essay on dramatic poetry. Since he was anxious to canvass various points of view, and so to clarify his own mind, he chose for his form 'a Dialogue sustain'd by persons of several opinions, all of them left doubtful, to be determined by the Readers in general', and discussed the past and future of the English drama in the 'Sceptical' manner of the Ancients, now 'imitated by the modest Inquisitions of the Royal Society'.[14] Before the essay could be published, however, Dryden began to write an ambitious poem celebrating three naval victories against the Dutch in the year 1666.

We may safely assume that the writing of an epic poem had been one of his earliest ambitions, and we note that it was to survive the publication of *Paradise Lost* only a few months later. It is evident that Dryden's epic would at once have been more modern in conception than Milton's, and more traditional: we may juxtapose his comment that he has chosen 'the most heroick Subject which any Poet could desire . . . the motives, the beginning, progress and successes of a most just and necessary War' with Milton's reference to 'Wars, hitherto the only argument Heroic deemed'.[15] Whereas Milton had found himself obliged to abandon the idea of a patriotic epic when his country (as it seemed to him) proved false to itself, deciding to write for 'fit audience . . . though few',[16] Dryden had no such difficulty. The fact that the recent victories had been won at sea (they are now seen by historians to have inaugurated a new era in the history of naval power) rendered them all the more suitable.[17] By a fortunate chance we know that one of the most important men in the history of the Navy, Samuel Pepys, bought a copy and approved of it highly: 'I am very well pleased this night', he wrote on 2 February 1667, 'with reading a poem I brought home with me last night from Westminster hall, of Driden's upon the present war – a very good poem.'[18] To the modern reader *Annus Mirabilis* is likely to appear an odd, baroque sort of work, but it is clear that Dryden had hit on a subject and manner admirably adapted to the audience he had in view.

One of its strange features is that while the first and longer part describes the naval battles, the latter part is concerned with the Fire of London. When the news of this catastrophe reached Dryden he must have reflected that with so large an area of their capital in ruins his countrymen would find less to excite them in a poem dealing exclusively with the war at sea, and it seems a safe conjecture that he decided to add the section on the Fire, another subject of vivid contemporary interest. This meant that the piece could have no pretensions to epic unity; but from the first he had probably intended no more than a brief 'heroic poem' or specimen of his epic manner. With some address he managed to bring the two subjects together in relation to one great theme: following *Astræa Redux* and the coronation panegyric, the new poem celebrated the fortitude and strength exhibited by England under the leadership of the King now providentially restored to her. This enabled Dryden to oppose all those who had interpreted the Fire and the preceding plague (of which virtually nothing is said in his poem) as judgments of God on a nation sunk in immorality and faithless to its trust. We have to realise that such a point of view was widespread, and that even a man like the Earl of Sandwich dreaded the outcome of the year, as Pepys reports, and feared there would be 'some very great revolutions' before he returned to England with the fleet.[19] By adapting the title of three seditious pamphlets published a few years before, *Mirabilis Annus*, Dryden presented an interpretation of recent events highly favourable to the King.

He must have been encouraged by the fact that the behaviour of the King after the Fire provided a most suitable subject for panegyric. 'It is not . . . imaginable how extraordinary the vigilance & activity of the King & Duke [of York] was', Evelyn wrote, 'even labouring in person, & being present, to command, order, reward, and encourage Workemen; by which he shewed his affection to his people, & gained theirs':

> Now day appears, and with the day the King,
> Whose early care had robb'd him of his rest.[20]

The King is the hero of this part of the poem, as he could not be of the earlier part. Stanzas 260–1 describe him as the father of his people, and his prayer, as given in the following stanzas, is in a sense the turning-point of the action. The stanza after the prayer opens with the words 'Th' Eternal heard', just as the conclusion of *Absalom and Achitophel* was to begin 'He said. Th' Almighty, nodding, gave Consent.' Later the City's 'request to the King not to leave them' forms the introduction to the confident stanzas in which the future prosperity and greatness of London are prophesied. The whole is bound together by the common concern with England's future, which is associated above all with trade:

> Thus to the Eastern wealth through storms we go;
> But now, the Cape once doubled, fear no more:
> A constant Trade-wind will securely blow,
> And gently lay us on the Spicy shore.

The resemblances between *Annus Mirabilis* and Sprat's *History of the Royal Society* are so striking that it is tempting to speculate that Dryden may have seen a manuscript of the latter, which appeared only a few months after his poem. Sprat describes how his work had been interrupted by 'the two greatest disasters, that ever befel our *Nation*',[21] yet casts scorn on gloomy fanatics who sought to terrorise the people 'with *Prodigies*, and conceits of *Providences*'. Like Dryden he stresses the courage of the English people, the importance of the Navy – 'now it is rightly understood, that the *English* Greatness will never be supported or increased in this *Age*, by any other Wars but those at *Sea*' – and praises the King for the encouragement he is giving the Society, comparing him to Elizabeth, in whose reign 'it was shewn, to what height the *English* may rise, when they are commanded by a *Prince*, who knows how to govern their hearts, as well as hands'. Like Dryden, he lays great emphasis on the importance of trade: 'It is now most certain that in those Coasts, whither the greatest *Trade* shall constantly flow, the greatest *Riches*, and *Power* will be establish'd.' Sprat's optimism about the future would sound exaggerated if it had not been justified by history. Whether or not Dryden had seen Sprat's work, it is striking how close his attitude was to that of the historian of the Society and of many of its members.

We do not know to whom he would have dedicated *Annus Mirabilis* if it had dealt only with the naval victories: as completed it was dedicated 'To the Metropolis of Great Britain, The most Renowned and late Flourishing City of London, In its Representatives The Lord Mayor and Court of Aldermen, the Sherifs and Common Council of it'. Acknowledging the novelty of such a dedication, he describes London as 'that City, which has set a pattern to all others of true Loyalty, invincible Courage and unshaken Constancy'. The poem was as clearly designed to serve a particular purpose as *Absalom and Achitophel* was to be fifteen years later. He wonders whether any other city has ever submitted with such humility 'to the Judgments of Heaven' and at the same time raised itself with such vigour 'above all humane Enemies': 'I know not whether such trials have been ever parallel'd in any Nation, the resolution and successes of them never can be. Never had Prince or People more mutual reason to love each other, if suffering for each other can indear affection.'[22] With a characteristic flourish of baroque imagery he describes the King and the nation as 'a pair of matchless Lovers', foretells that London will 'stand a wonder to all Years and Ages' – having become 'a *Phoenix* in her ashes, and, as far as Humanity can approach, a great Emblem of the suffering Deity' – and proclaims that 'Heaven never made so much Piety and Vertue to leave it miserable.'

Nothing could have announced more clearly the arrival of a writer with the desire and ability to be an official poet, a man who would rejoice in employing his pen in supporting the Monarch and rallying the People behind him. In 1668 Dryden was created Poet Laureate, a position which he was soon (and revealingly) to combine with that of Historiographer Royal. At the age of thirty-six he must have hoped that he would now be enabled to write the kind of poetry which he had long wanted to write, culminating in a patriotic epic.

His career no more went according to plan than did the rebuilding of London. No clearer evidence of the influence of audience on poet could be desired than the fact that more than a decade was now to elapse before Dryden published another considerable poem. The literary form most in demand was the drama, and the writing of plays was to be his almost exclusive concern until the late 1670s.

One of the speakers in the essay *Of Dramatick Poesie* argues that for forty years English literature has fallen behind the French: 'the Muses, who ever follow peace, went to plant in another country: it was then that the great Cardinal of Richelieu began to take them into his protection; and . . . by his encouragement, Corneille and some other Frenchmen reformed their theatre, which before was as much below ours, as it now surpasses it and the rest of Europe'.[23] Another speaker, Neander, whose views seem closest to Dryden's own, agrees about the harm done to literature by 'a barbarous race of men' but argues that 'We have seen since his Majesty's return many dramatic poems which yield not to those of any foreign nation, and which deserve all laurels but the English.' While the different speakers support different points of view, each of them is emphatic about the influence of the audience, to whose taste (as Crites puts it) 'all your reasons must submit. The unanimous consent of an audience is so powerful that even Julius Caesar . . . when he was perpetual dictator, was not able to balance it on the other side.' Neander insists that the opinion of 'the multitude' is of no account: what matters is the judgment of 'the mixed audience of the populace and the noblesse', and that has emphatically favoured the heroic play.

Dryden's concern about the taste of his audience is even more evident in the 'Defence' of the essay which he published a few weeks later, without the obliquities of dialogue. 'I confess', he wrote, 'my chief endeavours are to delight the age in which I live. If the humour of this be for low comedy, small accidents, and raillery, I will force my genius to obey it, though with more reputation I could write in verse.' As he puts it a little later in the same piece: 'To please the people ought to be the poet's aim, because plays are made for their delight; but it does not follow that they are always pleased with good plays, or that the plays which please them are always good.' When he is driven to admit that since 'The humour of the people is now for comedy' he has written comedies 'rather than serious plays' we realise that we are a far cry from Milton, or even from Ben Jonson.

In the dedication to the Duke of York of *The Conquest of Granada . . . Written by John Dryden Servant to his Majesty*, the Duke is assured that 'Heroic Poetry has always been sacred to Princes, and to Heroes.' Dryden cites Virgil, Tasso and Ariosto but not (needless to say) the great English poet whose epic had recently appeared. The *Second Part* contains a number of speeches precisely calculated to the meridian of the Court, speeches on love, on honour, and on exile:

> Disgrac'd, distrest, in exile, and alone,
> He's greater then a Monarch on his Throne.
> Without a Realm a Royalty he gains;
> Kings are the Subjects over whom he Raigns.[24]

The epilogue to the *Second Part* deals with the subject which had so preoccupied and troubled Dryden, and opens with the statement that

> They, who have best succeeded on the Stage,
> Have still conform'd their Genius to their Age.

It maintains that 'Wit's now arriv'd to a more high degree' than in Jonson's day, and states that it is Dryden's aim 'To please an Age more Gallant than the last'. In the prose 'Defence of the Epilogue' Dryden insists that the English language has improved and that 'the wit of this Age is much more Courtly':

And this leads me to the last and greatest advantage of our writing, which proceeds from conversation. In the Age, wherein those Poets liv'd, there was less of gallantry than in ours; neither did they keep the best company of theirs . . . I cannot find that any of them were conversant in Courts, except *Ben. Jonson* . . . greatness was not, then, so easy of access, nor conversation so free as now it is.[25]

The dedication of *Aureng-Zebe*, some four years later, makes it evident how dissatisfied Dryden was becoming with the theatre. He tells his readers that he had never thought himself 'very fit for an employment' in which many of his predecessors had excelled him 'in all kinds'; and some of his contemporaries, even in his own 'partial judgment', in comedy.[26] As he outlines the heroic poem of which he had spoken to the Earl of Mulgrave some years before, and of which he had been given an opportunity of 'discoursing . . . to his Majesty and his Royal Highness', it becomes clear that he had designed an epic calculated to please 'my king, my country, and my friends' and which would involve in its action 'most of our ancient nobility', with the King and his brother as 'the heroes of the poem'. Nothing could reveal more clearly Dryden's conception of the situation proper to an official poet than the following sentences:

As I am no successor to Homer in his wit, so neither do I desire to be in his poverty . . . The times of Virgil please me better, because he had an Augustus for his patron. And to draw the allegory nearer you, I am sure I shall not want a Maecenas with him. 'Tis for your Lordship to stir up that remembrance in his Majesty, which his many avocations of business have caused him, I fear, to lay aside.

The play is Dryden's masterpiece in the heroic drama. It was designed to appeal to Charles – 'I . . . subsist wholly by his bounty', Dryden wrote in the dedication – and we know that the Earl of Mulgrave recommended it 'to the King's perusal before the last hand was added to it', that the King considered it the best of all his tragedies, and that Dryden 'received the favour from him to have the most considerable event of it modelled by his royal pleasure'. The hero is loyal to his father the Emperor, by whom he is abominably treated, and is contrasted with a villanous younger brother who wishes to make his way to the throne by parricide. Many lines and passages make it clear that the heroic idiom of *Absalom and Achitophel* had been learned in the theatre. Nourmahal's remark that 'Promiscuous Love is Nature's general Law'[27] adumbrates the opening of the great satire, while a speech at I.i.80 is an equally evident anticipation of a later passage on Absalom:

15

> Oh! had he still that Character maintain'd,
> Of Valour, which in blooming Youth he gain'd!
> He promis'd in his East a glorious Race;
> Now, sunk from his Meridian, sets apace.

In *All for Love*, the last play he wrote for the King's Company, Dryden abandons rhyme and explicitly models his style on that of 'the divine Shakespeare': much more successfully (we notice) than the romantics were to do, because unlike them he was an experienced man of the theatre. The dedication contains an almost desperate reaffirmation of the Renaissance belief that 'those who are born for worthy actions, and those who can transmit them to posterity' are natural allies; the fact that it was addressed to the Lord Treasurer who was to fall from power a few months later may serve as an image of Dryden's sheer bad luck at this time. His dramatic career was nowhere near an end, but he had grown weary of the theatre. He was forty-seven and had not yet approached the great poetry which was his lifetime's goal.

While we are bound to share Dryden's regret that the drama occupied so much of his time – until 1682 he was to continue to write about a play a year, and was later to be described by Gerard Langbaine as 'the most Voluminous Dramatick Writer of our Age'[28] – the couplets of *Mac Flecknoe*, the first of his satiric poems to be written, make it evident how much he had learned from the theatre. The animus which inspired this lampoon was probably due to his realisation that he had often cheapened himself during his career as a dramatist. As early as 1669 he must have been wounded by Shadwell's observation that 'it pleases most [theatre-goers] to see Vice incouraged, by bringing the Characters of debauch'd People upon the Stage, and making them pass for fine Gentlemen', and that this 'is contrary to the Customs and Laws of all civilized Nations': 'But it is said, by some, that this pleases the people, and a Poets business is only to endeavour that: But he that debases himself to think of nothing but pleasing the Rabble, loses the dignity of a Poet.'[29] It is usual to say that the prolonged if intermittent hostility between the two men was due to their disagreement 'about Ben Jonson', but in a deeper sense it was about the role and dignity of the poet. What must above all have troubled Dryden was that amidst injudicious and questionable critical judgments his antagonist

16

was pointing to his failure to live up to the high ideal with which he had set out. The poet who had aspired to be England's Virgil had been obliged to devote years of his life to writing plays, many of them comedies which could be condemned by less rigorous moralists than Jeremy Collier. The wound inflicted by the censure just quoted had been exacerbated by recent thrusts, notably in *The Virtuoso* and in *The History of Timon of Athens*, which carries a dedication to Buckingham praising his mockery of Dryden and the heroic play in *The Rehearsal*.[30]

Mac Flecknoe was written to relieve Dryden's own exasperation, for a group of people who were conversant with the theatrical warfare of the time. The reader is expected to pick up references to several of Shadwell's productions, and to other contemporary plays – references so thick sown that they have been used by a recent scholar as evidence for claiming that the poem was written in 1676 rather than 1678.[31] Shadwell's disapproval of the licentiousness of the Restoration stage made him eminently suitable for Dryden's strategy of contrasting such low people as City Poets with gentlemen writers like Sir Charles Sedley and Sir George Etherege. Although Shadwell was no mean dramatist, and was a gentleman whose social status was not greatly below Dryden's own, he is portrayed as a hack whose throne is fittingly placed in a decayed area of London not far from Grub Street. In this gloriously comic poem Dryden not only proclaimed his own maturity as a poet but also provided a model for Pope half a century later.

Meanwhile the nation was becoming more and more preoccupied with politics, and in particular with the Popish Plot, about which Titus Oates had begun to make his lying statements in September 1678. Earlier that year, in the dedication to *All for Love*, Dryden had declared his 'loathing to that specious Name of a Republick' and had warned Shaftesbury and others that 'they who trouble the Waters first, have seldom the benefit of the Fishing . . . Neither is it enough for them to answer that they only intend a Reformation of the Government . . . 'Tis striking at the Root of Power, which is Obedience.'[32] In the dedication of *The Kind Keeper; or, Mr. Limberham*, first performed in the same year though not published until 1680, Dryden complained that literature was being pushed aside by political preoccupations: 'I cannot easily excuse the printing of a Play at so unseasonable a time, when the Great Plot of the Nation, like one of *Pharaoh's* lean Kine, has devour'd its younger Brethren of the Stage.' Few noblemen are now interested in poetry: 'Were it not for two or three instances in Whitehall, and in the town, the poets of this age would find so little encouragement for their labours, and so few understanders, that they might have leisure to turn Pamphleteers, and augment the number of those abominable Scriblers . . . railing against the Government.'

Whether Dryden himself turned pamphleteer during the 1670s, as a result of his position as Historiographer Royal, we do not know; but it is certain that in 1681 he wrote an anonymous pamphlet, *His Majesties Declaration Defended*, in support of 'The Kings late Declaration touching the Reasons which moved him to Dissolve the two last Parliaments'. While he stresses that he has great respect for Monmouth, he suggests that Monmouth is being used by a 'Cabal', and questions whether 'a Prince of his Spirit' would, if he were ever to succeed to the throne, consent 'to be confin'd in the narrow compass of a Curtail'd Mungril Monarchy'.[33] By this time, certainly, Dryden had become involved in the 'violent paper scuffle' which had broken out (as Narcissus Luttrell observed) 'Ever since the dissolution of the last parliament', between two parties of which the one described the other as consisting of 'whigs, fanaticks, covenanters, bromingham protestants, &c.', only to be termed, in their turn, 'tories, tantivies, Yorkists, high flown church men, &c.'[34]

The importance of a poet's intention and his awareness of his audience could not be more vividly illustrated than by the opening of the poem which Dryden may have written at the behest of Charles II and certainly wrote to express the royal point of view on the crisis of the day:

> In pious times, e'er Priest-craft did begin,
> Before *Polygamy* was made a sin;
> When man, on many, multiply'd his kind,
> E'r one to one was, cursedly, confind:
> When Nature prompted, and no law deny'd
> Promiscuous use of Concubine and Bride;
> Then, *Israel*'s Monarch, after Heaven's own heart,
> His vigorous warmth did, variously, impart
> To Wives and Slaves: And, wide as his Command,
> Scatter'd his Maker's Image through the Land.

These lines, with their remarkable sureness of tone, could only have been written during the reign of Charles II, and even so one

is astonished at the suave audacity with which Dryden nego-
tiates the minefield. It is evident that he remembered what the
King would tolerate, and what he would not tolerate, as he wrote
every line. The fine passages of panegyric do something to
balance the satiric characters of Shaftesbury and his followers –
Absalom's praise of his father, for example:

> Whom has he Wrong'd in all his Peaceful Reign?
> Who sues for Justice to his Throne in Vain?   (321–2)

or the lines on the Duke of York:

> His Brother, though Opprest with Vulgar Spight,
> Yet Dauntless and Secure of Native Right,
> Of every Royal Vertue stands possest;
> Still Dear to all the Bravest, and the Best.   (363–6)

Shaftesbury is portrayed as the arch-tempter, the Devil, and we
notice that the only supporters of his to be treated with marked
leniency are his unnamed princely followers,

> Mistaken Men, and Patriots in their Hearts:
> Not Wicked, but Seduc'd by Impious Arts.   (497–8)

The ideological centre of the poem may be found in lines 753–
810 and in David's final speech from the throne, which sum-
marises *His Majesties Declaration Defended*.

The prefatory address 'To the Reader' makes it clear that
Dryden regretted having been obliged to draw his pen 'for one
Party' both because his ambition as a poet soared far beyond
political satire and also for immediately prudential reasons. He
had been happier seeking to unite the nation with *Annus Mirabilis*.
He insists that the best judges will be 'the more Moderate sort',
claims to have rebated the satire, where possible, 'from carrying
too sharp an Edge', and argues that 'there's a sweetness in good
Verse, which Tickles even while it Hurts'. He has treated Monmouth as gently as he could, hoping that he and his father will be
reconciled and even, 'with *Origen*, that the Devil himself may, at
last, be sav'd'.

There are many greater poems than *Absalom and Achitophel*, but
few as perfectly adapted to their occasion and purpose. Its success was almost without parallel. Johnson tells us that the sale
was so large that his father, 'an old bookseller, told [him] he had
not known it equalled but by Sacheverell's trial',[35] and its circulation must very considerably have enlarged Dryden's readership.

19

There is no doubt that it pleased the King. According to Pope, Charles II gave Dryden 'the plan' for *The Medall* and rewarded him with 'a hundred broadpieces for it'.[36] In the 'Epistle to the Whigs' which precedes the poem Dryden abandons the judicial manner which he had attempted in the preface to *Absalom and Achitophel*, and we notice that the later work is called 'A Satyre', whereas the earlier is 'A Poem'. While Dryden refused to write a continuation of *Absalom and Achitophel*, he contributed some powerful passages to Nahum Tate's *Second Part*, and no doubt took an active interest in the whole. Since *Mac Flecknoe* had been published in the meantime it was inevitable that he should now be regarded as a satirist, as he was already regarded as a dramatist, and he implicitly acknowledged his reputation when he permitted the reprinting of the three satires at the beginning of *Miscellany Poems* in 1684.

This explains the rueful reference to himself at the beginning of the preface to *Religio Laici* as a man from whom 'the handling of so serious a Subject wou'd not be expected', a strange comment from a poet who had aspired to be the Virgil of England. Johnson rightly described the poem as 'almost the only work of Dryden which can be considered as a voluntary effusion'.[37] Religion and politics were so closely associated at this time that it is hardly surprising that a poet so much in the public eye should have decided to explain his own religious position. There is a further explanation at the end of the preface, when Dryden tells his readers that his model has been the Epistles of Horace, and that anyone who is 'so lamentable a Critique as to require the Smoothness, the Numbers and the Turn of Heroick Poetry' is failing to understand the decorum of 'a Poem, design'd purely for Instruction', a point repeated at the conclusion of the poem itself, with a characteristic dart of satire:

> And this unpolish'd, rugged Verse, I chose;
> As fittest for Discourse, and nearest Prose:
> For, while from *Sacred Truth* I do not swerve,
> *Tom Sternhold*'s, or *Tom Shadwell*'s *Rhimes* will serve.

Having now won a larger audience, Dryden was all the more eager to remind his readers that a higher style was well within his compass. We are reminded that he may fairly be regarded as the founder of Augustan poetics in England, and that this led to his writing criticism in order to explain his aims in his plays and his poems.

The degree to which he was still the King's Poet is acknowledged on the title-page of *The History of the League*, translated from the French 'According to His Majesty's Command' and published in 1684. In the dedication he remarks that there had never been 'a plainer Parallel than of the Troubles of *France*, and of *Great Britain*'.[38] The fact that Henri IV was Charles's grandfather, and that the French book had been written by royal command, rendered it ideal for the purpose; while Maimbourg's statement of intention, at the end of his address to the reader, is wholly applicable to his translator, 'to give a plain understanding to all such, as shall read this History, that all sorts of Associations which are form'd against lawfull Soverains, particularly when the Conspiratours endeavour to disguise them, under the specious pretence of Religion and Piety, as did the *Huguenots* and *Leaguers*, are at all times most criminal in the sight of God, and most commonly of unhappy and fatal Consequence to those, who are either the Authours or Accomplices of the Crime'.

Only a few months after this, when (in Dryden's words) 'he had overcome all those difficulties which for some years had perplexed his peaceful reign . . . when he had just restored his people to their senses, and made the latter end of his government of a piece with the happy beginning of it', Charles II 'was on the sudden snatched away from the blessings and acclamations of his subjects',[39] leaving his Laureate and Historiographer Royal seriously worried about money. The fact that Dryden's pension was no less than £1,075 in arrears may help to explain his collaboration with Tonson in the two Miscellany volumes of 1684 and 1685, or at least his assent to their publication. And now he unexpectedly found himself obliged to write an elegy calculated to please the new monarch, a Catholic, as surely as he had been in the habit of pleasing his brother. The title, *Threnodia Augustalis A Funeral-Pindarique Poem Sacred to the Happy Memory of King Charles II. By John Dryden, Servant to His late Majesty, and to the Present King*, makes it clear that Dryden was determined to remain Poet Laureate; while the strategy of the poem itself, in which he celebrates the Restoration as the greatest good fortune to have befallen England in his lifetime – an event accompanied by the return of 'Th' officious Muses' – and consoles his readers by assuring them that if Atlas has fallen, Hercules has succeeded him, is evidence of the same determination. The degree of his financial anxiety is curiously indicated by references to the late King's niggardly treatment of poets (with the carefully ambiguous line, 'The Pension of a Prince's praise is great'[40]) and a reminder of the importance of poets to the new monarch.

The tone of the preface to *The Hind and the Panther*, together with shifts of style and emphasis within the poem itself, reflect the uncertain course of events while Dryden was writing it. His affirmation that 'it was neither impos'd on me, nor so much as the Subject given me by any man',[41] is defensive and revealing. One of the aims was of course to defend his own move to Catholicism, another to attack those Anglicans and dissenters who refused to 'come over to the Royal Party' in spite of the Declaration of Indulgence about a fortnight before the poem was published. Dryden knew that his motives were sure to be misconstrued, yet his acknowledgement that in the two episodes he has 'made use of the Common Places of *Satyr*, whether true or false' is remarkably unprepossessing. Of course the poem sold well, and of course it was found a disappointment, for all the brilliance of individual passages of verse. Within a few weeks Matthew Prior and Charles Montague produced *The Hind and the Panther Transvers'd To the Story of The Country-Mouse and the City-Mouse*, a gifted parody which must have been particularly unwelcome to an already harassed poet.

Dryden proceeded to dedicate a translation of a devotional book to the new Queen,[42] in the most flattering terms, and then joined the chorus of poets who celebrated the unexpected birth of a young prince. The baroque manner of *Britannia Rediviva* suits the devoutly Catholic tone of the poem, though we may still be surprised at the assertion that the Trinity did not merely conspire to bring about the birth but also stamped 'their Image on the promis'd Seed'. Towards the end we find the child's recovery from an infant malady compared to Christ's saving of Peter, a satiric passage on the sinful state of the nation, an eloquent but exaggerated panegyric on the Queen, and an address to the King exhorting him to beget at least one further child. It was Dryden's misfortune that such an outburst of 'Prophetick Madness' had been occasioned by the event which, more than any other, led to the banishment of James II and the Revolution of 1688. The child whose birth he had commemorated is known to history as the Old Pretender.

The Revolution did not bring Dryden persecution, but although he was fortunate enough to have received the arrears of his pension just before it, financial hardship and insecurity lay ahead. We now know, on the evidence of a cancellandum leaf discovered by Fredson Bowers,[43] that 'by a particular Favour' the government would have permitted Dryden to remain Poet Laureate if he could have 'comply'd with the Terms which were offer'd' him; but these terms, whatever they were, were unacceptable, and as a result he could no longer dream of royal largess or official encouragement and was obliged to reconsider the nature of the audience he was to address. No one saw more clearly than he that the literature of England was bound to change, as the expression of a changing social order. He would have to resume writing for the theatre: he would have to accept such commissions as came his way (*A Song for St. Cecilia's Day* had recently demonstrated yet again how splendidly he could write to commission); but above all he would collaborate with the publisher Jacob Tonson and develop his skill as a translator to a point which gives him a strong claim to be the greatest practitioner of the art in the English language.

The preface to *Eleonora*, an elegy on the Countess of Abingdon written on commission for her widower, is of particular interest because it points both backwards and forwards. 'They say my Talent is Satyre', Dryden wrote; 'if it be so, 'tis a Fruitful Age; and there is an extraordinary Crop to gather. But a single hand is insufficient for such a Harvest: They have sown the Dragons Teeth themselves; and 'tis but just they shou'd reap each other in Lampoons.'[44] He describes himself as a poet who dares to sing the praises of the Countess

> in a Clime
> Where Vice triumphs, and Vertue is a Crime:
> Where ev'n to draw the Picture of thy Mind,
> Is Satyr on the most of Humane Kind.

He states that his rage, 'Unsafely just', is eager to 'break loose on this bad Age'.[45]

Later he was to write that he had 'wholly renounc'd'[46] satire after the Revolution, but the idea of heading a team of writers to translate Juvenal (whether it occurred to Dryden himself or, as seems more likely, to Tonson) must have been a welcome one. It is interesting, if hardly surprising, to find the poet who had once described Horace's satires as 'incomparably beyond *Juvenals*'[47] now calling the former 'a Temporizing Poet, a well Manner'd Court Slave . . . a Mild Admonisher, a Court Satirist, fit for the gentle Times of *Augustus*'. Nothing could be more appropriate than that Dryden should have turned from the satirist of the in-group to the perpetual outsider – angry and disapproving partly because he is excluded – at this particular crisis in his career.

In the dedicatory *Discourse concerning Satire* Dryden comments that on occasion he and his fellow-translators may make Juvenal 'express the Customs and Manners of our Native Country, rather than of *Rome*',[48] and it is natural that we should enquire how far he himself ventured to write contemporary satire in the innocent guise of translation.

Hardly at all. Although he says that he has translated the first satire 'somewhat largely' we find him retaining the references to the *Theseid* of Codrus and to the tragedies *Telephus* and *Orestes*, and making no attempt to substitute contemporary allusions. The only modern name introduced is that of Shadwell, in the disarming line 'Such woeful stuff as I or *S—ll* write.'[49] In translating the third satire he is almost as circumspect. We can see why he chose it for himself, since the speaker tells the poet 'the Reasons which oblige him to lead a private life, in an obscure place', and takes the opportunity of upbraiding the nobility 'with their 'Covetousness, for not Rewarding good Poets' as well as arraigning the government 'for starving them'; yet Dryden makes virtually no attempt to modernise Juvenal's references. The most that may be said is that at line 39 he tilts the text slightly in his own direction:

> Since Noble Arts in *Rome* have no Support,
> And ragged Virtue not a Friend at Court,
> No profit rises from th'ungrateful Stage,
> My Poverty encreasing with my Age;
> 'Tis time to give my just Disdain a vent,
> And, Cursing, leave so base a Government

but that, like the reference to his own 'too honest Face' (line 51), is a rare self-indulgence. He does not introduce the Fire of London at line 12, where it would be appropriate, and when

24

Juvenal attacks foreigners who arrive in London as poor men yet
end by lording it over their betters Dryden resists all temptation
of a contemporary application. Nothing could be more apt to his
own case than lines 211–12:

> In vain forgotten Services I boast;
> My long dependance in an hour is lost

yet they are extremely close to his original.[50] If his readers chose
to substitute 'London' for 'Rome', that was their own affair.[51] In
the tenth satire explicitly contemporary references are equally
hard to find, while the 'Invective against a standing Army' mentioned in the argument to the sixteenth merely emphasises the
rarity of such allusions, given the opportunities provided by the
original. Much the same is true of the translation of Persius,
which is wholly Dryden's work and which afforded him an
opportunity of paying a fine tribute to 'my *Learned Master*, the
Reverend Doctor *Busby*',[52] so reminding us of the debt of 'our
greatest translator'[53] to his schooling at Westminster.

We may be sure that the sixth satire of Juvenal was not
studied at Westminster – officially, at least – and we notice that
Dryden takes particular pleasure in translating it. While he
observes in his Argument that Juvenal had been ill advised to
make 'one half of his Readers his mortal Enemies' by satirising
women, he himself seems quite unworried by any such danger
when he harks back to the *doubles entendres* of the Restoration and
states that it would be unfortunate if the translation should be
'imperfect and lame . . . without one of the Principal Members
belonging to it'. As one of his colleagues observed, 'The original
has lost none of its shamelessness through him, infamous as it
is',[54] and Tonson seems to have insisted on the omission of a
number of couplets, among them the following:

> The fair unbroaken belly lay displayd
> Where once the brave Brittanicus was layd.
> Bare was her bosome, bare yᵉ feild of Lust
> Eagre to Swallow Evry sturdy Thrust.

Whereas lines 335–6 were printed thus:

> The Panting Stallion at the Closet-Door
> Hears the Consult, and wishes it were o're

the manuscript is much cruder:

> The Panting Stallion in yᵉ closet stands;
> Heares all, & thinks & loves & helps it wᵗʰ his hands.

Even in the form in which it was published the translation must have been strong meat for the readers of 1693, a year after the formation of the first of the Societies for the Reformation of Manners. In lines 432–5 Dryden closely follows Juvenal and must be absolved of any charge of attempting to bowdlerise his original:

> Where the Rank Matrons, Dancing to the Pipe,
> Gig with their Bums, and are for Action ripe;
> With Musick rais'd, they spread abroad their Hair;
> And toss their Heads like an enamour'd Mare

and we notice that his next two lines were disallowed by his publisher. We conclude that while Dryden refrained from introducing anything of significance that could be related to the politics of the day he enjoyed the delicate task of translating Juvenal's 'objectionable' satire and fulfilled it with the indelicacy of a man who had in his prime been Laureate to Charles II.

In spite of the sixth satire it is clear that Dryden was now writing – as he had been in his earlier translations, such as the two published in *Ovid's Epistles* in 1680 – for a less sophisticated audience than that for which he had written his plays and satires. It is remarkable to find him explaining that Horace had been a man 'who wrote Satyrs' (note 15 to the first satire) and feeling obliged to name Patroclus and identify Vulcan (notes 29 to the third satire and 28 to the sixth). It was now his aim to make Latin literature available to a wider public, 'those Gentlemen and Ladies, who tho they are not Scholars, are not ignorant: Persons of Understanding and good Sense; who not having been conversant in the Original, or at least not having made *Latine* Verse so much their business, as to be Critiques in it, wou'd be glad to find, if the Wit of our Two great Authors, be answerable to their Fame, and Reputation in the World'.[55] The mention of 'Ladies' is important, and reminds us of the reference to the translator of one of the epistles of Ovid as being 'of the *Fair Sex*'[56] (it was Mrs Aphra Behn). Addison and Steele were both twenty when the book was published.

'A Discourse concerning the Original and Progress of Satire', like the sixth satire itself, makes it clear that while Dryden was obliged to adapt himself to new circumstances, he remained the same man. Here we find the fullest account of his epic ambitions and of his reasons for abandoning his plan: in the beginning he had been discouraged because Charles II gave him nothing but 'fair Words'; 'and now Age has overtaken me; and Want, a more insufferable Evil, through the Change of the Times, has wholly disenabl'd me'.[57] He must occasionally have reflected on the courage of Milton, who had found himself in a worse situation on the return of the King; but Dryden lacked Milton's patrimony as well as his granitic strength of character, and while he shared his ambition of being read by posterity, for Dryden the immediate applause and support of a contemporary audience was an indispensable preliminary encouragement.

If the fact that he was above all a professional poet was to Dryden a source of weakness as it was of strength, we have reason to rejoice that it led him to produce two masterpieces of translation at the end of his career.

Thanks to surviving letters we know more about the progress of his great translation of Virgil than about that of any of his other undertakings. In 1693 he told Walsh that he was about to publish the third *Georgic* in one of Tonson's Miscellanies, 'as an Essay', and that the complete translation would be published 'by subscription; haveing an hunderd & two Brass Cutts, with the Coats of Armes of the Subscriber to each Cutt . . . besides another inferiour Subscription of two Guinneys, for the rest whose names are onely written in a Catalogue, printed with the Book'.[58] It was all very business-like, at least in intention: half of the subscription-money of the major subscribers was already 'in hande': the engravings were not new, having been made for the earlier translation by John Ogilby and now merely being 'touched up' (as Pope was to observe):[59] while Ogilby was one of a number of predecessors who had published by subscription. Dryden obviously collected the earlier verse translations, which he plundered freely; and his friends hastened to his aid, Gilbert Dolben lending him all the important editions and commentaries, while the Jacobite Earl of Lauderdale sent him from exile the manuscript of his own unpublished translation. Knightly Chetwood wrote the preface to the *Pastorals* for him, and Addison an essay on the *Georgics*. Congreve, Kneller and others seem to have helped him to solicit subscribers. Expectation must have been high by 1697, when the book appeared.

As we turn its pages we find a volume which stands, as surely as Dryden himself, 'betwixt two Ages'.[60] Tonson's desire that Dryden should dedicate it to the King was rejected, though

Dryden noted that 'in every figure of Eneas, he has caused him to be drawn like K. William, with a hookd Nose'.[61] The book has no general dedication, because Dryden held back (as he explained in the letter in which he asked the Earl of Chesterfield for permission to dedicate the *Georgics* to him) 'in hopes of his return, for whom, and for my Conscience I have sufferd, that I might have layd my Authour at his feet'.[62] The *Pastorals* are dedicated to Lord Clifford, whose father had been a patron of Dryden's, with an admission that 'such are my unhappy Circumstances, that they have confin'd me to a narrow choice', and the *Æneid* itself to the Marquess of Normanby, a leader of the Tory opposition to the Revolution who had encouraged Dryden's ambition of writing 'A Heroick Poem . . . undoubtedly the greatest Work which the Soul of Man is capable to perform'.[63]

Although the management of the subscriptions seems unsophisticated in comparison with the intricate manoeuvres of Pope three decades later, and although there was a good deal of friction between Dryden and Tonson, more would-be subscribers at five guineas were eventually found than the number of plates could accommodate. The list begins with the Lord Chancellor, the Lord Privy Seal, the Earl of Dorset, Lord Buckhurst and the Earl of Abingdon, and includes altogether six Dukes, one Duchess (the Duchess of Ormond), a baker's dozen of Earls, and a fair number of other members of the nobility. Important names are those of the future Queen Anne and her husband and son. We also find William Walsh, Edmund Waller, Arthur Manwaring, Sir Godfrey Kneller and the printer William Bowyer. By luck or good judgment there is no clear political preference, since many of the subscribers are hard to classify and the others seem to divide fairly evenly into Tories and Whigs, insofar as the terms are of any use at this time. There are half a dozen Catholics, and one clear Jacobite (Aylesbury), with several other men of fairly definite Jacobite leanings.[64] Very high Tories are absent, as are High Church clergy and also King William's Dutch friends. When we turn to the second subscribers we find a number of aristocrats, as well as Thomas Betterton, Ann Bracegirdle, William Congreve, Dr Samuel 'Gath', Grinling Gibbons, Nicholas Hawksmoor, Samuel Pepys and Thomas Southerne. There are very few churchmen, and no one who is described as a fellow of an Oxford or Cambridge college.

Within a few weeks of publication Dryden was able to tell his sons that the book 'succeeds in the World beyond its desert or my Expectation', and he continued interestingly:

You know the profits might have been more, but neither my conscience nor honour wou'd suffer me to take them: but I never can repent of my Constancy; since I am thoroughly perswaded of the justice of the laws, for which I suffer. It has pleased God to raise up many friends to me amongst my Enemyes; though they who ought to have been my friends, are negligent of me.[65]

There is no doubt that the *Virgil* marks an important point in the history of the financial relations between poet and audience. In John Barnard's words, it 'at once defined and exploited the market for "polite" literature which later supported the *Iliad* and *Odyssey* . . . the new audience, which extended beyond the Court and from the aristocracy to the middle class'.[66] Blackmore was soon to write that while William did little for poets, Tonson did a great deal:

> From thence to both great Acquisitions came,
> To him the Profit, & to them the Fame.

A neat antithesis, but misleading: Dryden would not have undertaken the translation if he had not been assured of profit as well as fame, and it is clear that he earned substantially over £1,000 for the work.

Fables Ancient and Modern, the splendid volume which he published in the last year of his life, is a further collaboration with Tonson and another exemplification of what we may term Dryden's mixed economy. Tonson promised him 250 guineas for ten thousand verses, the sum to be made up to £300 'at the beginning of the second impression'.[67] There can be little doubt that the Duke of Ormond, to whom the volume is dedicated in Dryden's best baroque manner, and whose Duchess is addressed in a fine panegyric, rewarded the poet for his pains, while there is a strong tradition that the epistle 'To my Honour'd Kinsman, John Driden, of Chesterton' was acknowledged by a present of no less than £500.[68] The preface makes it clear that the translation of Homer which Dryden still had in mind would only be feasible if he met with 'Encouragements from the Publick', while a letter to Charles Montague solicits his support for the undertaking.

Like the *Virgil*, this volume as a whole was designed for a wide readership, and Dryden bore the taste of his readers in mind when he chose Ovid and Boccaccio for two of his principal originals. It was no doubt partly for women readers that he made love the central theme: he was now writing for a reading public which may be compared with that with which Byron's Eastern Tales were to enjoy so sensational a success more than a century later. Dryden had already translated a good deal of Ovid, and was well aware that of all the Latin poets it was he who had 'almost all the *Beaux*, and the whole Fair Sex, his declar'd Patrons'.[69] While he describes him and Chaucer (his other main original) as 'well-bred, well-natur'd, amorous, and Libertine', we find a new note in the preface when he writes: 'If there happen to be found an irreverent Expression, or a Thought too wanton, they are crept into my Verses through my Inadvertency.' With an impatient reference to Jeremy Collier, Dryden apologises for anything in his earlier writings which may now be found objectionable: 'I have pleaded Guilty to all Thoughts and Expressions of mine, which can be truly argu'd of Obscenity, Profaneness, or Immorality; and retract them.' At the end he cannot forbear from posing the question, 'Are the Times so much more reform'd now, than they were Five and twenty Years ago?' – a rhetorical question open to the answer that by this time, certainly, a writer had to be more careful what he published, at least in respect of 'morals', than when Fletcher's *The Custom of the Country* had been 'often acted' and when Dryden himself had written *The Assignation* and *The Kind Keeper*.[70] While there are certainly passages in the translations from Ovid which could not have been published when Tennyson was Laureate, yet we see Dryden keeping a vigilant watch on himself because of the changing taste of readers in 'this degenerate Age'.[71] No part of the volume is more valuable than the versions of *The Knight's Tale*, *The Nun's Priest's Tale* and '*The Wife of Bath her Tale*', but we notice that Dryden did not dare 'to adventure on her Prologue; because 'tis too licentious'. He would not have refrained in the 1660s or 1670s.

One of the reasons for Dryden's interest in Chaucer was that he regarded him as his 'Predecessor in the Laurel'.[72] Informing his readers that Chaucer 'was employ'd abroad, and favour'd by *Edward* the Third, *Richard* the Second, and *Henry* the Fourth, and

was Poet, as I suppose, to all Three of them', he went on to medi-
tate on a career which he clearly liked to compare with his own:

In *Richard*'s Time, I doubt, he was was a little dipt in the Rebellion of the
Commons; and being Brother-in-law to *John of Ghant*, it was no wonder if he
follow'd the Fortunes of that Family; and was well with *Henry* the Fourth
when he had depos'd his Predecessor. Neither is it to be admir'd, that *Henry*,
who was a wise as well as a valiant Prince . . . should be pleas'd to have the
greatest Wit of those Times in his interests, and to be the Trumpet of his
Praises.

Augustus and Maecenas make their expected appearance, with
a reminder that the praises of Virgil and Horace 'helped to make
[Augustus] Popular while he was alive, and after his Death have
made him Precious to Posterity'.

Dryden makes a good starting-point for our enquiry because he
is so clear an example of a writer with an instinct to serve as the
official poet of his age. It seemed to him self-evident that the
poet's role was a public one, and that the centre of his audience
should be the King and the Court. His instinct for centrality
assured him of an increasing readership throughout his life, and
even helped him to make the transition to a new order of things
after 1688. We cannot doubt that his inspiration derived in large
measure from his sense of people reading his poems, recognising
the allusions, admiring the wit, and being influenced by what he
wrote.

Throughout his life his choice of genres was principally determined by his sense of what his audience required. The epic
which he wished to write remained unattempted for lack of
patronage. Although he did not regard himself primarily as a
dramatist – still less as a writer of comedy – a large part of his
output consists of plays, as it does of prose writings which are
often devoted to explaining to his readers the nature and intention of his poems and plays. He must have derived a significant
sum of money from his prologues and epilogues, and above all
from the panegyrical epistles, in verse and prose, of which he
became such a master. Moral satire was not something he was
eager to write: the genius which he discovered for satire was
most memorably deployed in two poems which he wrote in
support of the King. The circumstances of his great disciple,
Alexander Pope, were to be very different.

II · POPE
No man's slave

THE key to Pope's career is that he was a Court poet born at a time when the Court was ceasing to be the cultural centre of England. Like Dryden he looked back with veneration to the models of antiquity and cherished the ambition of writing a great epic, and like him he addressed himself to a highly educated and sophisticated audience, a fact to which Swift alluded when he reminded Pope that his epitaph on Gay, 'quite contrary to your other writings, will have a hundred vulgar Readers, for one who is otherwise'.[1]

While one reason why his career could not follow a similar course to that of Dryden was that England had changed so radically, another was that he was born (as Dryden had died) a Roman Catholic, and was therefore a member of a minority subject to legal discriminations and debarred from public appointments. Perhaps it is as well that he did not live in an age which romanticised the rebel, the outsider, the 'under-privileged'. Instead of protesting or yielding to self-pity, he devoted himself to the problem of finding an audience for his poetry with the same astonishing capacity for taking pains which he devoted to the writing of it.

Between 1705 and 1708 his Pastorals circulated in a manuscript as finely penned 'as if he had learned the art of lettering in the best scriptorium',[2] and they can be said to have been published before they were printed: a practice which had been more common in earlier periods. He wished to gain the support as well as the advice of a number of influential readers before he faced a wider audience. He wrote on the manuscript the names of twelve distinguished men through whose hands it had passed, and every one of them (with a single possible exception) seems to have been a friend or acquaintance of Dryden's. As early as this we are bound to notice the skill with which Pope acted as impresario for his own poetry. He not only wrote the words: he was also his own producer and advertising manager. The importance of such assiduity was due to the historical situation in which he found himself, and it is a sign of his fine intelligence that he read the situation so unerringly. The promotion had been flawless, and when the Pastorals appeared in the sixth volume of Lintot's Miscellany their success was immediate. Wycherley told him that 'all the best Judges . . . are Admirers of Yours . . . your Miscellanys, have safely run the Gantlet, through all the Coffee-houses'.[3]

An Essay on Criticism makes it clear that Pope was interested in the way in which a poet's relationship to his audience varies in different periods and affects the poetry which he is at liberty to write. In the reign of Charles II

> The modest fan was lifted up no more,
> And Virgins smil'd at what they blush'd before,

while in the reign of William and Mary 'Pulpits their sacred satire learn'd to spare' and 'the press groan'd with licens'd blasphemies'.[4] We notice the emergence of an independence in moral matters which had not been possible for Dryden. Whereas he had been obliged to cater for his audience, and on occasion to pander to it, Pope was determined to establish a very different relationship with his readers, as the conclusion of *The Temple of Fame* makes explicit:

> Unblemish'd let me live, or die unknown;
> Oh grant an honest fame, or grant me none!

As he could not be a Court poet in the traditional sense, he would explore the possibilities of a novel situation. In this respect, as in others, Pope's career offers an unrivalled example of limitations transformed to opportunities by the power of genius.

Pope's opposition to 'Parties in Wit', powerfully stated in lines 452–7, may remind us of Matthew Arnold's complaint, more than a century later, that in England criticism 'subserves interests not its own. Our organs of criticism are organs of men and parties having practical ends to serve, and with them those practical ends are the first thing and the play of mind the second'.[5] The fact that he was born into a minority rendered Pope peculiarly conscious of the dangers of intellectual provinciality, so that Addison struck a responsive chord when he advised him 'not to be content with the applause of half the nation'.[6] Throughout the first part of his career he went to great lengths to avoid committing himself to either party, though in his later years he has been described, with some justice, as 'Opposition Laureate'.[7]

The *Essay* was highly successful, both in extending the range of Pope's readers and in continuing the task (inherited from Dryden) of educating the Augustan reading public. 'Tonson's printer told me he drew off a thousand copies', Pope wrote to a friend, ' . . . and I fancy a treatise of this nature, which not one gentleman in three score even of a liberal education can understand, will hardly exceed the vent of that number.'[8] Such an estimate of the difficulty of the poem is revealing, as well as surprising. For comparison we may note that the circulation of *The Spectator* early in 1712 has been estimated at between 3,000 and 4,000.[9]

The potential audience for *Windsor-Forest* must have been considerably wider. It is unusual among Pope's early poems in dealing with contemporary affairs, unusual among his poems as a whole in doing so in a manner which is optimistic rather than satirical. The vision of England's future has a buoyancy about it which carries us back to the Restoration, and above all to *Astræa Redux*. But the Peace was welcomed by many who were not Tories, and the fact that a poem by one of them, Thomas Tickell, went into six editions, while the second impression of *Windsor-Forest* was still being advertised in 1718,[10] makes it clear that the latter is merely a milestone on the road to Pope's first spectacular success.

The writing of *The Rape of the Lock* was rendered possible by the existence of the new heroi-comical genre and by the fact that the Petres and the Fermors were reasonably cultivated people. Modern critics have dwelt on the sexual suggestiveness of the poem in a manner which might well have struck Pope and his contemporaries as naive, when one remembers that the avowed subject is a 'rape'. We have only to reflect on the way in which it might have been handled half a century before to appreciate the delicacy of most of Pope's innuendoes. Only a very innocent reader could miss the significance of the 'Hairs less in sight' in Canto IV, or that of the fact that when Sir Plume 'draw[s] *Clarissa* down' he is killed by a frown only to be revived by a smile.[11] When, a few lines later, we are told that he 'sought no more than on his foe to die', we are reminded of Joseph Warton's remark that 'a game

34

of romps was never so well dignified before',[12] while lines 79–80 of Canto V lead us to expect an improper suggestion and then make us ashamed of ourselves – for all the world as if we were reading Sterne. What is most striking is the address with which Pope manages his indelicate suggestions. From this poem we can infer as much about the tone of high civilisation during the reign of Queen Anne as we can about that during the reign of Charles II from *Absalom and Achitophel*.

Pope's determination to do all he could to avoid giving offence to either the Petres or the Fermors is particularly evident in the expanded version of 1714. Condescending as the tone of the dedication may seem to us, it is unlikely to have sounded condescending to Arabella Fermor. As to his audience, Pope claims that *The Rape* 'was intended only to divert a few young Ladies, who have good sense and humour enough to laugh not only at their sex's little unguarded follies, but at their own'. In a sense, but only in a limited and special sense, the poem may be regarded as a satire on women. Pope gave a good account of the matter in a letter:

This whimsical piece of work . . . is at once the most a satire, and the most inoffensive, of anything of mine. People who would rather it were left alone laugh at it, and seem heartily merry, at the same time that they are uneasy. 'Tis a sort of writing very like tickling. I am so vain as to fancy [it] a pretty complete picture of the life of our modern ladies in this idle town.[13]

At first the poem seems to have enjoyed only a *succès d'estime*, as Lintot's Miscellany did not sell well and was re-issued in 1714 with a cancel title-page; but as soon as *The Rape* was expanded and published separately, it was greeted with acclamation. In *A Key to the Lock* Pope drew attention to 'The uncommon Sale of this Book (for above 6000 of 'em have been already vended)',[14] and amusing evidence of its audience may be found in *Trivia*, where Gay, in an account of readers glancing through books displayed for sale, describes 'Pleas'd Sempstresses' who 'the *Lock*'s fam'd *Rape* unfold'. Unlike many of Pope's later poems *The Rape* made a strong appeal to women readers. By 1714 he seems to have come close to the outer circumference of the potential audience for poetry at that time; and the perfect poise of the poem is evidence of the assurance of his attitude to his readers.

A year before this, while he was still on the threshold of establishing himself as the outstanding poet of the age, Pope was already faced by a second challenge, that of ensuring his financial independence. It was natural that he should wish to frequent the best company, to which his genius had gained him the entrée, but that required money; while his Catholicism gave him a sense of insecurity which became particularly pronounced at times of political uncertainty, when the restrictions and penalties of the Clarendon Code were most likely to be invoked – and the Queen's state of health made it only too evident that such a crisis was approaching.

A possibility which he considered only to reject was that of writing for the stage, recently described by John Dennis as 'the only encouragement that we have in these Islands of poetry'.[15] Pope had been persuaded to write a prologue for Addison's *Cato*, and was delighted to be able to report that 'the orange wenches and fruit women in the Park offer the books at the side of the coaches, and the Prologue and Epilogue are cried about the streets by the common hawkers'[16] – yet nothing could atone for the fact that 'all the foolish industry possible had been used to make it a party play',[17] which was the more embarrassing now that he had come within the orbit of Swift and others whose politics were opposed to those of Addison and his friends. But he continued to be fascinated by the theatre, commenting most perceptively on the reactions of the different sections of the audience at *The What D'ye Call It*:

Some looked upon it as a mere jest . . . others as a satire upon the late war . . . Several Templars . . . went with a resolution to hiss, and confessed they were forced to laugh so much that they forgot the design they came with. The Court in general has in a very particular manner come into the jest, and the three first nights . . . were distinguished by very full audiences of the first quality. The common people of the pit and gallery received it at first with great gravity and sedateness, some few with tears; but after the third day they also took the hint, and have ever since been very loud in their clapps.[18]

If the second period of Pope's career reminds us in some respects of the second period of Dryden's it is not because it was devoted to the theatre but because he too had to turn to a form of writing which he adopted only because he was obliged to make money. In Pope's life the period fell a decade earlier than in Dryden's, and no sacrifice to his integrity was involved: he wrote no smutty comedies to amuse the Court, no heroic dramas bordering on absurdity. But he was not doing what he wanted to do, and the frustration which had led Dryden to write *Mac*

Flecknoe had an even more memorable effect when it led Pope to write *The Dunciad*.

When he decided to postpone his plan of writing an epic of his own in favour of translating the *Iliad*[19] Pope was following the example of Dryden, although it was the latter part of Dryden's life which had been principally given up to translation. Pope signed the agreement with Tonson as early as 23 March 1713, and from the first he showed his characteristic flair for promotion. He organised his campaign like a general, stipulating (for example) that the subscribers' copies were to be printed in 'a new Letter' of his own choice with engravings determined by himself, and also that he should have his own 750 copies a month before the book was available to the public.

There is ample evidence of the importance that he attached to the names of the subscribers, and he had no difficulty in persuading his friends to second his own endeavours. We have a description of Swift in a coffee-house in November 1712 informing a 'young Nobleman, that the best Poet in England . . . (a Papist) . . . had begun a translation of Homer . . . for which "he must have them all subscribe;" for, says he, "the author shall not begin to print till I have a thousand guineas for him" '.[20] A letter from Charles Jervas written in the summer of 1714 gives another glimpse of the progress of the campaign: 'Yesterday I gave a Printed Proposal to Lord Halifax & spoke to the Duke of Devonshire to join my Lord Wharton's Interest & move your affair, that we may set 'em agoing about the Counties'[21] – a reference interesting because the idiom associates Pope's 'affair' with the political business of the day. As Jervas realised, Pope was anxious that the *Iliad* should not be regarded as a party venture. Soon Pope was able to tell Caryll that he had 'at least six Tory friends, three Whig friends and two Roman Catholic friends',[22] token figures which serve to underline the point.

In the autumn of 1714, it would seem, he read 'the two or three first books' at Lord Halifax's to an audience that included Addison, Congreve and Garth. In November he told Caryll that he had been 'perpetually waiting upon the great' to solicit their support, adding that as soon as he could 'collect all the objections of the two or three noble judges, and of the five or six best poets', he would retreat to the country for a final revision.[23]

The preface to the first volume makes it clear how conscious he was of his relations with the reading public. He stresses that he has been guided throughout by 'Men of Wit' – Addison, 'the first whose Advice determin'd me to undertake this Task', Steele, Swift, Garth, Congreve, Rowe and Parnell – and that 'the most distinguish'd Patrons and Ornaments of Learning' had been his 'chief Encouragers': Buckingham, Halifax, Bolingbroke, Lansdowne, Carnarvon, Stanhope and Harcourt. He is careful to balance praise of his Whig patron, Halifax, who had recently died, with encomium of Bolingbroke.[24]

What is striking is not so much the number of the subscribers – 575 – as their eminence. The name of the Princess Caroline is followed by those of seventeen Dukes, five Duchesses, forty-eight Earls and many other members of the nobility. There are numerous high officers of state, as well as many eminent writers – Berkeley, Gay, Prior and the Countess of Winchilsea among them. The most celebrated names of all are those of Marlborough and Newton.

Dryden had gone some way towards corralling the Augustan reading public with his *Virgil*: now Pope had consolidated and extended it. While the subscribers were only the van of an army of readers who were to become acquainted with Homer through this great translation, it is important to notice that the enterprise was based on the support of a large section of the élite of the time, men and women whom Pope described, with pardonable exaggeration, as 'almost all the distinguished names of Quality or Learning in the nation'.[25] Among the subscribers, titles are the rule, with 'Esq[uire]' notably more frequent than 'Mr.' or 'Mrs.' '*Mr.* Daniel Gach, *Druggist*', who may be found among the subscribers to Pope's *Shakespear*, is not the sort of person one finds among the subscribers to the *Iliad*.

It was inevitable that Pope should proceed to the *Odyssey*, in the translation of which he employed as assistants William Broome and Elijah Fenton. By April 1723 (if Sherburn is right in his dating) we find Pope launched on his new venture:

I have within these three days . . . given a loose to a few of my commissioned friends, which I judge better than to make any proposal yet to the public . . . I am very certain it is judging right to think that the public will enter much more heartily and readily into any project after the most considerable men in the nation have exalted it into a fashion and reputation to be of the list. Alas! almost every creature has vanity: but few, very few, have either judgment, taste, or generosity.[26]

He asked Harley to help him by taking 'the inclos'd paper . . . to the House of Commons',[27] and by the autumn of 1724 urged Broome to increase the list of subscribers as much as he could, 'particularly at Cambridge, where I want a proper agent'.[28] About the end of the year he proposed to publish his proposals to the town, and wrote in a revealing style to Harley:

I must desire to know in what manner to treat your Lordship & Lady Oxford in the printed List, which I am to annex to this Proposal? If I were to set you down for as many Subscriptions as You have procurd me, half my List would lye at your door . . . I have set down the Duchess & Duke of Buckingham for five Setts; will you allow me to do the same to your self & Lady Oxford? Mr Walpole & Lord Townshend are sett down for Ten, each: I would not deny my obligations: & tis all I owe Them. But to the Duchess & to your Lordship I would keep some measures: I am so much, & ever like to be so much, in hers & your debt, that I will never tell how much, without your absolute command or leave . . . I have kept back my Proposal from the press till I have the honour of your Commands on this subject.[29]

Harley decided that he should be set down for ten sets, his wife for five and his daughter Peggy for one. In his reply Pope acknowledged a degree of vanity in his wish to print his name 'so early, with those of some others', adding that 'there is . . . a worse thing than Vanity, some Interest too, concerned in printing the names of the Subscribers with the Proposalls', since 'They are Incitements to Other men's vanity of being joyned with them.'[30]

When the translation appeared in 1725–6 the list of subscribers, which contained more than 600 names, opened with the King, the Prince, and the Princess, while the Court seems even more prominent than before. There are now twenty-four Dukes and eight Duchesses, and more of the principal officers of state. Clerical representation is not as weak as with the *Iliad*, while the Chancellor and Vice-Chancellor of Oxford University now make their appearance. The names of the first and second masters of Westminster School are worth mentioning; for, as the Prince of Wales was soon to point out in another connection, the gaining of that school was 'worth gaining fifty families'.[31]

When Pope completed the *Iliad*, Gay had welcomed him as an adventurer returned from a long and hazardous voyage.[32] From this second voyage, as from the first, he returned with rich cargo in his hold, and for the remainder of his life he had assured his independence. From now on, as he was to proclaim in the

Imitations of Horace, he would 'live and thrive, Indebted to no Prince or Peer alive'.[33]

Satire has been described as a dry wine that is made from sour grapes, yet such a description can hardly account for *The Dunciad*, the next production of a poet whose works were 'in the hands of every body'.[34] One of his assistants urged him, 'This labour past', to sing of 'heavenly subjects', 'While hovering angels listen on the wing', and Bolingbroke wished him to write something that would 'deserve to be translated three Thousand years hence into Languages as yet perhaps unform'd'.[35] But Pope was not in the mood to write an epic: he was in the mood to write a satire.

The origin of *The Dunciad* is to be found in the Scriblerus Club, in which Pope and Swift joined with Gay, Arbuthnot, Parnell and Oxford to satirise 'The Works of the Unlearned', and Swift's visits to England in 1726 and 1727 exerted an important influence on it. 'The hopes of seeing once more the Dean of St patricks revives my spirits', Arbuthnot wrote, 'I can not help imagining some of our old club mett together like Mariners after a Storm.'[36] One of the results was the publication of the Pope–Swift *Miscellanies*, and originally *The Dunciad* was to have been published in the third volume.

Soon Bolingbroke could report that the poem 'grows and flourishes', commenting that 'the many will stare at it, the few will smile, and all his Patrons from Bickerstaff to Gulliver will rejoice, to see themselves adorn'd in that immortal piece'. There we have three concentric circles, with Swift at the centre as 'all his Patrons'. Some have believed that Pope's account of his indebtedness to Swift in this satire is exaggerated, but a letter from Swift to a Jacobite called Charles Wogan suggests that this is not so. Swift insists that *The Beggar's Opera* is 'a very severe satyr upon the most pernicious Villainies of Mankind' and warns him that because of his distrust for 'Raillery and Satyr' he is

in Danger of quarrelling with the Sentiments of Mr. *Pope*, Mr. *Gay* the Author, Dr. *Arbuthnot*, myself, Dr. *Young*, and all the Brethren whom we own . . . At the same Time you judge very truly, that the Taste of *England* is infamously corrupted by *Sholes* of Wretches who write for their Bread: and therefore I had reason to put Mr. *Pope* on writing the Poem, called the *Dunciad*, and to hale those Scoundrels out of their Obscurity.[37]

The references to 'all the Brethren whom we own' is a singularly explicit description of the inner circle of wits for which, in the first instance, *The Dunciad* was written. Like Swift when he wrote *A Tale of a Tub*, Pope was writing 'to the Tast of those who were like himself'.[38]

Richard Savage tells us that on the day of publication 'a Crowd of Authors besieg'd the Shop; Entreaties, Advices, Threats of Law, and Battery, nay Cries of Treason were all employ'd, to hinder the coming out of the *Dunciad*: On the other Side, the Booksellers and Hawkers made as great Efforts to procure it'.[39] When Curll, with characteristic opportunism, published *A Compleat Key*, he was playing into Pope's hands, as was Swift when he urged the need for annotation;[40] for from the first this poem, directed in the first instance at an in-group, was also (by a paradox with which we become familiar as we study Pope) intended for a wider audience. The second stage of the plan was to equip it with the complicated apparatus with which modern readers are familiar, some of it Pope's own work, some of it the work of his friends. Meanwhile Burlington, Bathurst and Oxford were persuaded 'to owne themselves Publishers of that poem',[41] and with their help copies were distributed before the book had gone on general sale, so that public interest was whipped up while the danger of actions for libel was greatly lessened.

The most revealing part of the new apparatus is the introduction in which Martinus Scriblerus explains 'the occasion and the cause which moved our Poet to this particular work': 'He lived in those days, when (after providence had permitted the Invention of Printing as a scourge for the Sins of the Learned) Paper also became so cheap, and printers so numerous, that a deluge of authors cover'd the land'. While the original model of *The Dunciad* can only have been *Mac Flecknoe*, and while the frustration of a decade spent on work not of his own choosing lies behind Pope's satire, as it does behind Dryden's, we at once become aware of a fundamental difference between the two poems. Unlike Dryden, who confines himself to attacking Shadwell, Pope attacks a host of authors, and does so in such a way as to present a pessimistic picture of the whole literary scene. As we read *The Dunciad* we conclude, as we do not in reading *Mac Flecknoe*, that the bad writing which is being attacked is symptomatic of a general cultural malaise: something is rotten in the state of England. Pope took the high humanist view of literature, and there is no doubt of the sincerity of the dismay he expressed at witnessing its prostitution, often with the support of a government intent on political propaganda.

It may well strike us as paradoxical that an author who had exploited the literary market with such brilliant success should have been more apprehensive about the dangers of the new situation than excited by the possibilities which it offered, yet such was clearly the case. In his *Characteristicks* Shaftesbury had pointed out that a great change had occurred: 'Our modern Authors . . . are turn'd and model'd . . . by the publick Relish, and current Humour of the Times . . . In our Days *the Audience* makes *the Poet*; and *the Bookseller the Author*.'[42] As if in reply, Pope had written in the preface to his *Works* in 1717 that while writers were not justified in fancying 'that the world must approve whatever they produce', neither must readers 'imagine that authors are obliged to please them at any rate': 'the world has no title to demand, that the whole care and time of any particular person should be sacrificed to its entertainment'. The notion of producing poetry, or literature in general, as a vendible commodity seemed to him a dangerous one – in spite of his acknowledgement that 'much better men' than himself had often been driven to it.[43]

One of his motives for writing *The Dunciad* was the desire to dissociate himself from commercial authors. He made no secret of the fact that the *Homer* had been undertaken for money, but while its brilliance might save him from reproach, what about his edition of Shakespeare, a piece of book-making which had been exposed (with a restraint which had made it all the more galling) by a minor poet called Theobald – a man who was obliged to make ends meet by writing the type of farces and pantomimes which seemed to Pope and many others symptomatic of the declining taste of the age?

Which brings us back to the Court. Martinus Scriblerus explains that the action chosen to display the power of Dulness and Poverty is 'the introduction of the lowest diversions of the rabble in *Smithfield* to be the entertainment of the court and town'. A note provides evidence for the statement:

Smithfield is the place where Bartholomew Fair was kept, whose Shews, Machines, and Dramatical Entertainments, formerly agreeable only to the taste of the Rabble, were, by the Hero of this Poem and others of equal

Genius, brought to the Theatres of Covent-Garden, Lincoln's-inn-Fields, and the Hay-Market, to be the reigning Pleasures of the Court and Town. This happened in the Year 1725, and continued to the Year 1728.[44]

The modern reader has to make a historical adjustment. To us it no longer seems surprising that a monarch should be more interested in horses than in poetry. The expectations of an earlier age had been very different. 'A *Prince* without Letters', Ben Jonson had written, 'is a Pilot without eyes. All his Government is groping.'[45] A century later Shaftesbury considered that it would be 'a hard Case indeed, shou'd the Princes of our Nation refuse to countenance the industrious Race of *Authors*': Pope's preface to Shakespeare expresses the same conception of the proper role of a Court. In his early work, he informs his readers, Shakespeare 'writ . . . without patronage from the better sort, and therefore without aims of pleasing them'. Later, however, 'when his performances had merited the protection of his Prince, and when the encouragement of the Court had succeeded to that of the Town, the works of his riper years are manifestly raised above those of his former'.[46] Pope found himself in a very different position, and the fact that George I had subscribed to his *Odyssey* and to his edition of Shakespeare was not sufficient to make atonement. On his death a monarch who could scarcely speak English had been succeeded by a monarch who could, but whose contempt for 'Boetry and Bainting' was never disguised. According to Lord Hervey, 'George Augustus neither loved learning nor encouraged men of letters, nor were there any Maecenases about him':

The King used often to brag of the contempt he had for books and letters: to say how much he hated all that stuff from his infancy: and that he remembered when he was a child he . . . despised [reading] and felt as if he was doing something mean and below him.[47]

'You ought not to write verse', he told Hervey on one occasion, 'Leave such work to little Mr. Pope.'[48] It was natural that it should be under such monarchs that 'the lowest diversions of the rabble' should have become 'the entertainment of the court and town'. It is appropriate that the structure of *The Dunciad* should already remind us of a succession of farces or 'pantomimes', a characteristic which was to become more marked in *The New Dunciad* more than a decade later.[49]

In such an atmosphere covert satire flourished, and the modern reader is often uncertain what precisely is going on. At times we wonder whether it is Theobald who is being satirised, or George II:

> Now Bavius, take the poppy from thy brow,
> And place it here! here all ye Heroes bow!
> This, this is He, foretold by ancient rhymes,
> Th' Augustus born to bring Saturnian times.

Formally, the ghost of Settle is referring to Theobald, yet everything else suggests that the satire is slewing away in the direction of the King, who had succeeded to the throne a year before. As Hervey pointed out some six years later, Pope 'had published several satires . . . in which the King and all his family were rather more than obliquely sneered at'.[50]

This makes it remarkable that the King himself asked for some sort of key to *The Dunciad*. On 17 June 1728 Pope told Oxford that he was preparing 'a thing to gratify you with' – not in fact a key, but *The Dunciad Variorum* itself – adding that he had 'received a Command for the same thing from the Highest & most Powerful Person in this Kingdom'.[51] Nine months later he reported that 'The King & Queen had the book yesterday by the hands of Sir R.W.' At the foot of the first page the King will have found the statement that 'Kings' have been among the readers of the poem, but if he expected any reassurance on lines 5–6

> Say from what cause, in vain decry'd and curst,
> Still Dunce [the] second reigns like Dunce the first?

he did not find it, but merely a reference to Dryden's line 'For *Tom* the Second reigns like *Tom* the first.'[52] In an alternative and presumably earlier version Pope had written 'And when a Settle falls a Tibbald reigns', so it would appear that he deliberately gave the line a political reference 'rather more than oblique' after the accession of George II in 1727.

The only evidence of the King's reaction is at first surprising. Just a week after the royal copy had been presented, Arbuthnot told Swift that 'Mr Pope is as high in favour as I am affraid the rest are out of it', referring to 'your little club'. He added that 'The King . . . Declard he was a very honest Man.'[53] Since the main subject of the letter is a description of the absurd situation in which 'The inoffensive John Gay is now become one of the obstructions to the peace of Europe, the terror of Ministers' – an absurdity which has driven Arbuthnot to begin a piece of bur-

44

lesque historical writing 'which will be printed in the year 1948'
– we can only assume that he is recording the King's reported
comment as yet one more example of the absurdity of the times.

Pope presenting *The Dunciad Variorum* to George II – even more
piquantly, perhaps, Walpole presenting it on Pope's behalf –
this is a picture which may serve as an emblem of Pope's position
in relation to his audience, at this turning-point of his career.
There is an engraving of George Gascoigne presenting *Hemetes*
to Queen Elizabeth: he kneels before the monarch, with a Latin
motto suspended above his head, and the poet's wreath of laurel:
Elizabeth is enthroned, and bears the orb and sceptre of her
authority. Almost a century later, Dryden might have been portrayed in much the same posture, presenting *Absalom and
Achitophel* to Charles II; but one has only to imagine Pope in such
a picture to see that it simply would not do. For a suitable
iconography to represent this relationship, there would have
been need of a Hogarth.

It is not surprising that Pope should, in his letters, frequently
profess his indifference to the Court. 'You use to love what I
hate', he wrote to Swift in 1733, 'a hurry of politicks, &c. Courts
I see not, Courtiers I know not, Kings I adore not, Queens I compliment not.'[54] Yet the Court was seldom out of his mind, and on
occasion it turns up where we would least expect it, as when he
complains (quoting Horace) that he is not the man he used to be,
and adds: 'The climate (under our Heaven of a Court) is but cold
and uncertain: the winds rise, and the winter comes on.' In fact
he shared, if in a slightly lesser degree, the obsession with the
Court which led Swift to add a strange qualification to his high
praise of Pope's Epistles – 'and although in so profligate a world
as ours they may possibly not much mend our manners, yet Posterity will enjoy the Benefit *whenever a Court happens to have the least
relish for Virtue and Religion*'. The bitterness of the Tory satirists
and the exaggerated pessimism with which they viewed the
future were partly due to the fact that they could no more think
of civilisation without a Court than Richardson could think of
morality without Marriage.

This helps to explain the importance to Pope of his powerful
friends, a small group of able men, some of them wealthy aristocrats, who encouraged him by the example of their lives, assisted

him in practical ways, and helped to provide an inner circle of readers who understood his aims and appreciated many (at least) of the subtleties and nuances of his writing. As we study his later work we find him consolidating what might be termed an alternative Court, a Court whose values were not those of practical politics or of the market place.

After Swift's final departure to Ireland in 1727 the friend who influenced Pope most profoundly for some years was the brilliant and enigmatic Henry St John, Viscount Bolingbroke, a man admired by many but by none so inordinately as by Pope, who once went so far as to describe him as 'the greatest man in the world'.[55] Bolingbroke was as anxious as Atterbury and others that Pope should not devote himself wholly to satire, employing all his 'precious Moments, and great Talents, on little Men, and little things: but choose a Subject every way worthy',[56] and it was at his prompting that Pope formed 'a large design for a moral poem',[57] a conception which begins to appear in his letters at this time. It is as important to remember Bolingbroke when we read *An Essay on Man* as it is to remember Coleridge when we read *The Excursion* and *The Prelude*. Pope was no more a philosopher than Wordsworth, but in each case a philosopher friend urged a great poet to attempt 'a long and laborious Work' on 'the Nature and State of Man'.[58]

The most important part of Pope's scheme to be completed was an ambitious poem addressed to a highly educated audience: a work which we know him to have submitted to no less a scrutiny than that of the author of *A Treatise concerning the Principles of Human Knowledge* – since Pope told Spence that he had 'written an address to our Saviour . . . but omitted it by the advice of Dean Berkeley'.[59] When the *Essay* first appeared, anonymously, conjectures on the identity of the author included Bolingbroke himself, as well as Edward Young and a number of other learned divines. It is clear that a competent reader of the poem would be the sort of person (in all probability a man) who was acquainted with such works as John Ray's *The Wisdom of God Manifested in the Works of the Creation* and William Derham's *Physico-Theology*. 'I confess I did never imagine you were so deep in Morals', Swift commented, immediately (and significantly) passing on to Bolingbroke's 'attempt of reducing Metaphysics to intelligible sence & usefullness . . . a glorious undertaking'; while the author

46

of the French translation was to insist that 'Whoever . . . will be [Pope's] Pupil here, must attend only from principles of Reason, a Kind of Attention, which even Philosophers can rarely support without some Struggles and Reluctance.'[60] Only when the *Essay* was included in Pope's *Works*, some years later, was any considerable assistance provided in the form of footnotes. 'You are often obscure', complained Thomas Bentley, 'twice or thrice unintelligible'; while Dr Alured Clarke, who was much better disposed to Pope, and who praised the first Epistle in the highest terms, found the second 'in many places . . . too hard to be understood'.[61]

Yet we must not exaggerate. Whereas Bolingbroke himself had written to Swift, of his own 'Metaphysicks', 'When [Pope] and you, and one or two other friends have seen them, *satis magnum Theatrum mihi estis*, I shall not have the itch of making them more publick', Pope's remark to Fortescue, 'I think myself so happy in being approved by you, and some few others, that I care not for the public a jot', fails to carry conviction.[62] The poem was not written for a small circle, and in fact it sold well even before the French translation made Pope a European celebrity.[63] Anonymity seems to have given him a double advantage: at first people wondered who could have written so brilliant a poem – Pope told Caryll mischievously that there was 'a sort of faction to set up the author and his piece in opposition to me and my little things'[64] – and then they were fascinated to find that a didactic poem on so lofty a subject was the work of the author of *The Dunciad*: 'Mr. *Pope* has . . . struck out a new Scheme of Ethic Poems', the first Oxford Professor of Poetry was soon to observe, in an ill-judged venture into hyperbole, 'in which he has deserv'd as much of the Moral World, as Sir *Isaac Newton* did of the Natural.' The dubious orthodoxy of the *Essay* made it a natural topic of conversation, and readers must have been struck by the modernity of an argument which would, as its author hoped, 'go a great way toward destroying all the school metaphysics'.[65] And of course they would not have missed the political significance of a poem dedicated to Bolingbroke, who had returned from exile yet who was still (and justly) suspected of Jacobitism – a poem containing such lines as iv. 257–8:

> And more true joy Marcellus exil'd feels,
> Than Caesar with a senate at his heels[66]

47

and iv. 265–6:

> Truths would you teach, or save a sinking land?
> All fear, none aid you, and few understand.

'Shocking Words, and almost treasonable!', as Bentley wrote in *A Letter to Mr. Pope*.

Several years before, Pope had told a friend that 'for the future he intended to write nothing but epistles in Horace's manner', and it is noteworthy that he confessed to Swift, shortly after the publication of the *Essay*, that he did not know whether he could 'proceed in the same grave march like Lucretius, or must descend to the gayeties of Horace'.[67] In fact the *Essay* contains far more satire than the *De Rerum Natura*, and this no doubt helped to render it 'more palatable to the generality'.

Satire is even more prominent in the poems which Warburton called the *Moral Essays* and which are closely associated with *An Essay on Man* and the whole shadowy scheme of the *opus magnum*. Pope's own title, *Epistles to Several Persons*, is more appropriate, as a comment of Swift's serves to emphasise: 'I heard you intended four or five Poems addressed to as many friends', he wrote from Ireland; 'and can easily believe they would together make a System with connexion, and a good moral for the conduct of life.'[68] A pointer to the nature of Pope's later work is the number of the poems which are addressed to one or other of his friends. Yet if we compare his Epistles with Dryden's we find that whereas with his predecessor the identity of the person addressed came first, and determined the choice of subject-matter, with Pope it was the subject-matter which led to the choice of a suitable recipient: an indication of the difference between a poet whose patrons were often also his friends, and a poet whose friends were often also his patrons. If we accept Johnson's definition of a patron as 'One who countenances, supports, or protects', then Bolingbroke and Harley (for example) were certainly patrons of Pope, and on occasions he did not hesitate to acknowledge as much.[69]

Nothing could be more appropriate than the fact that the first of the Epistles to be published was addressed to Lord Burlington, a man of great wealth who perfectly fitted Pope's conception of the sort of aristocrat who should be found at a Court forming a focus of civilisation. As early as 1716 Pope told Martha Blount that he was 'to pass three or four days in high luxury, with some company at my Lord Burlington's; We are to walk, ride, ramble, dine, drink, & lye together. His gardens are delightfull, his musick ravishing.'[70] Pope was not alone in his admiration of Burlington. 'Never was protection and great wealth more generously and more judiciously diffused than by this great person', Horace Walpole was to write, and his high estimate of Burlington's importance has been echoed in the present century by the art historian Rudolf Wittkower. In 1750 Berkeley was to write nostalgically from Cloyne in Ireland: 'In this remote corner I am haunted again with a taste for good company and fine arts that I got at Burlington House.' Deeply interested in music, Burlington was an ardent admirer of Italian opera who was also one of the original patrons of Handel, and he was one of those who founded the short-lived Royal Academy of Music in 1719. As a patron of literature, too, he was a figure of importance, subscribing (for example) for no fewer than fifty copies of Gay's *Poems on Several Occasions*, whose author spent a great deal of his time as his guest and made Burlington House the symbolic focus of *Trivia*. The fact that Burlington's greatest enthusiasm of all was for architecture and gardening made him all the more attractive to Pope. 'His Gardens flourish', he had written to the painter Charles Jervas years before, 'his Structures rise, his Pictures arrive, and (what is far nobler and more valuable than all) his own good Qualities daily extend themselves to all about him: Whereof, I the meanest . . . am a living Instance'.[71] The final paragraph of the *Epistle* has an eloquence which springs from Pope's deepest convictions:

> You too proceed! make falling Arts your care,
> Erect new wonders, and the old repair;
> Jones and Palladio to themselves restore,
> And be whate'er Vitruvius was before:
> Till Kings call forth th' Ideas of your mind,
> (Proud to accomplish what such hands design'd),
> Bid Harbors open, public Ways extend,
> Bid Temples, worthier of the God, ascend,
> Bid the broad Arch the dang'rous Flood contain,
> The Mole projected break the roaring Main;
> Back to his bounds their subject Sea command,
> And roll obedient Rivers thro' the Land:
> These Honours, Peace to happy Britain brings,
> These are Imperial Works, and worthy Kings.

In the preface to his *Works* in 1717 Pope had mentioned 'the privilege of being admitted into the best company' as one of the few 'advantages accruing from a Genius to Poetry'.[72] That same year he gave John Caryll an example of what he meant:

After some attendance on my Lord Burlington, I have been at the Duke of Shrewsbury's, Duke of Argyle's, Lady Rochester's, Lord Percival's, Mr Stonor's, Lord Winchelsea's, Sir Godfrey Kneller's (who has made me a fine present of a picture) and Dutchess Hamilton's. All these have indispensable claims to me, under penalty of the imputation of direct rudeness . . . Then am I obliged to pass some days between my Lord Bathurst's, and three or four more.

While we may be tempted to regard him as the prince of all social climbers, the temptation should be resisted. As well as intellectual stimulus, his friends gave him a sense of some measure of security in troubled times, and so helped him to write with a courage which it is easy for us to underestimate. His intimates, certainly, did not regard him as a snob. 'But it is impossible to talk so much of Philosophy, and forget to speak of Pope', Bolingbroke wrote to Swift in 1734:

He is actually rambling from one friends house to another. He is now att Cirencester [Lord Bathurst's seat], he came thither from my Lord Cobhams; he came to my Lord Cobhams from Mr Dormers; to Mr Dormers from London, to London from Chiswick [where Lord Burlington lived]; to Chiswick from my Farm, to my Farm from his own Garden, and he goes soon from Lord Bathursts to Lord Peterborows, after which he returns to my farm again.

Once he told Swift that the 'Top-pleasure' of his life was that of friendship 'with Men much my Superiors', adding: 'To have pleas'd Great men according to Horace is a Praise; but not to have flatterd them & yet not to have displeasd them is a greater. I have carefully avoided all Intercourse with Poets & Scriblers, unless where by great Chance I find a modest one.'

It is not difficult to understand why Horace should have inspired so much of Pope's later work. As a writer in *The Spectator* had put it, the writer of Horatian epistles 'must be guilty of nothing that betrays the Air of a Recluse, but appear a Man of the World throughout',[73] so implicitly referring to the distinction between Horace and Juvenal which Dennis was to sum up when he described Juvenal as writing tragic satire 'more acceptable to Universities and Cloisters, and all those Recluse and Contemplative Men, who pass most of their Time in their Closets', and Horace as a comic satirist 'who owes no small Part of his Excellence to his Experience', and who will probably be 'more agreeable to the discerning Part of a Court, and a great Capital'. Like Horace, Pope had become famous while he was still young; and for all his frequently expressed preference for the tranquillity of private life (than which nothing could, in itself, be more Horatian) he was certainly not a man who wished to 'betray the Air of a Recluse'. What is more, his conception of satire had early been influenced by Shaftesbury's *Soliloquy: or Advice to an Author*, with its insistence that 'Instruction' is 'the Majesty and Life of this kind of writing'. 'You call your satires, Libels', Pope wrote to Swift; 'I would rather call my satires, Epistles: They will consist more of morality than wit, and grow graver, which you will call duller.'

When Bolingbroke suggested that Pope should imitate *The First Satire of the Second Book* he was no doubt thinking mainly of the similarities between Pope's situation and that of Horace, but it was the differences which proved to be of the greatest value to his friend, offering him a theme on which he was to devise many subtle and startling variations. Horace tells the friend to whom the epistle is addressed that he, like his predecessor Lucilius, loves 'to commit all his Secrets to his Papers, as to his intimate Friends':[74] we immediately notice that Pope 'imitates' this statement with a difference:

> In this impartial glass, my Muse intends
> Fair to expose myself, my foes, my friends;
> Publish the present age, but where my text
> Is Vice too high, reserve it for the next.

Whereas Horace contents himself with professing that he lacks the genius 'to describe great Caesar's legions', Pope openly disdains to praise the King and Queen. He makes it clear (with a touch of irony) that he intends to speak out as boldly as 'pension'd Boileau' or 'Laureate Dryden', and we soon find him speaking in a tone very different from that of his original:

> What, arm'd for Virtue when I point the pen,
> Brand the bold front of shameless, guilty men;
> Dash the proud Gamester in his gilded Car;
> Bare the mean Heart that lurks beneath a *Star*;
> Can there be wanting, to defend Her cause,
> Lights of the Church, or Guardians of the Laws?

One of the great attractions of Horace was that he provided a precedent for using autobiographical material in poetry. Pope's delight in this is particularly evident in *An Epistle to Dr. Arbuthnot*, which Warburton aptly termed (with or without Pope's agreement) 'The Prologue to the Satires'. For all the Horatian assertion that he was not 'born for Courts or great affairs', and the dignified simplicity of the passage about his parents, we notice that the Ciceronian motto of the poem – 'You will not attend to the gossip of the vulgar crowd' – accurately indicates that this is the work of a fitting imitator of the poet who had written '*Odi profanum vulgus et arceo*'. If he is asked why he ever became a poet, Pope answers: 'I lisp'd in Numbers, for the Numbers came':

> But why then publish? Granville the polite,
> And knowing Walsh, would tell me I could write;
> Well-natur'd Garth inflam'd with early praise,
> And Congreve lov'd, and Swift endur'd my lays;
> The courtly Talbot, Somers, Sheffield read,
> Ev'n mitred Rochester would nod the head,
> And St. John's self (great Dryden's friends before)
> With open arms receiv'd one Poet more.

It can hardly have been by chance that this poem appeared only a few weeks before Curll's edition of *Mr. Pope's Literary Correspondence . . . being, A Collection of Letters, Which passed between him and Several Eminent Persons*, a supposedly pirated edition which was in fact the culmination of a long-standing ambition and a great deal of ingenious manoeuvring on Pope's part. As we read the carefully-selected and often-rewritten letters in this first collection, with its sub-title 'The Works of Mr. Alexander Pope, in Prose', we find that the autobiographical element now becoming so prominent in his poetry had long been a principal constituent of his letters. Swift, who had always been aware of Pope's desire for 'Epistolary fame',[75] was deeply impressed, assuring him that from his letters 'there might be collected . . . the best System that ever was wrote for the conduct of human life' – a reminder of the tradition of epistolary writing that goes back to Cicero and which was soon to exert so profound an influence on the novels of Richardson; while Ralph Allen of Bath, the future prototype of Fielding's Squire Allworthy, was so delighted by the supposedly unauthorised publication that he helped Pope to bring out the authorised edition of 1737, a handsome book published in both quarto and folio, in which Pope omitted many letters previously published, cut out a few remarks which might have given offence to the pious or prudish, and added between sixty and seventy new letters. Cheaper editions followed, so that most readers of Pope's poems now had access to the image of himself which he wished to promulgate, that of a poet who had 'the good fortune to enjoy many friends, who will be always remember'd as the first Ornaments of their Age and Country'. One is reminded of that characteristically eighteenth-century genre of painting, the conversation piece. Pope himself is portrayed, in a carefully informal pose, pen in hand or negligently thrown aside, surrounded by a few chosen friends, with his tastefully unpretentious 'cottage' at Twickenham and its celebrated garden as a background: Cicero at Tusculum, or Horace on his Sabine farm.

The manner in which the letters were designed to complement the poems is illustrated by a letter from Arbuthnot included in the edition of 1735, the authentic reply from Pope first published by Sherburn, and Pope's reply as printed in the edition of 1737. If it were not for the survival of the manuscript of the authentic version we might be tempted to wonder whether Arbuthnot (who had died in 1735) had ever in fact written with the dying request that Pope should 'continue that noble *Disdain* and *Abhorrence* of Vice'[76] which seemed natural to him (though always 'with a due regard to [his] own safety'): that was, after all, very much what Trebatius had said to Horace, eighteen centuries before. Yet it seems that Arbuthnot did write, and we are left admiring the address with which Pope exploited the fact to produce a longer and very different version of his reply, for publication as the perfect prose commentary on the *Epistle to Dr. Arbuthnot* and *The First Epistle of the Second Book* (published in 1737). 'It is certain', Pope wrote in the published letter, 'much freer Satyrists than I have enjoy'd the encouragement and protection of the Princes under whom they lived. Augustus and Maecenas made Horace their companion, tho' he had been in arms on the side of Brutus . . . You will not suspect me of comparing my self with Virgil and Horace, nor even with another Court-favourite, Boileau: I have always been too modest to imagine my Panegyricks were Incense worthy of a Court; and that I hope will be thought the true reason why I have never offer'd any. I would only have observ'd, that it was under the greatest Princes and best Ministers, that moral Satyrists were most encouraged.'

Once Pope began to imitate Horace it was inevitable that he should turn his hand to *The First Epistle of the Second Book*. 'The

Reflections of *Horace*, and the Judgments past in his Epistle to *Augustus*, seem'd so seasonable to the present Times', he wrote in the Advertisement,

> that I could not help applying them to the use of my own Country. The Author thought them considerable enough to address them to his Prince; whom he paints with all the great and good qualities of a Monarch, upon whom the Romans depended for the Encrease of an *Absolute Empire*. But to make the Poem entirely English, I was willing to add one or two of those which contribute to the Happiness of a *Free People*, and are more consistent with the Welfare of *our Neighbours*.

Since Pope knew very well that Horace had addressed Augustus at the request of the Emperor,[77] the difference between the position of a poet in Augustan Rome and in Hanoverian England presented him with the rich opportunity for irony which is so brilliantly exploited in the opening lines, addressed to a King whose disdain for poetry is openly referred to later in the poem. In the account of the history of English poetry which supplements that in *An Essay on Criticism* we find Pope more interested than Horace in the relation between poets and the audiences for which they write. It had been the misfortune of Dryden to live at a time when it was necessary 'To please a lewd, or unbelieving Court'. Of all the poets of that age

> Roscommon only boasts unspotted bays;
> And in our own (excuse some Courtly stains)
> No whiter page than Addison remains.

Praise of Swift (which brought Pope within danger of arrest) leads to an account of the progress of satire, and of the emergence of that finest type of it which 'heals with morals what it hurts with wit'. While there is real sympathy in the passage in which Pope follows Horace's lead in deploring the difficulties which beset a writer of comedies – above all the fact that he is obliged to please 'The many-headed Monster of the Pit' – we notice that his satire becomes sharper than that of his original when he considers the absurdities into which poets are liable to fall:

> But most, when straining with too weak a wing,
> We needs will write Epistles to the King;
> And from the moment we oblige the town,
> Expect a place, or pension from the Crown;
> Or dubb'd Historians by express command,
> T' enroll your triumphs o'er the seas and land;

> Be call'd to Court to plan some work divine,
> As once for LOUIS, Boileau and Racine.

But it is in the later part of the poem that Pope takes the greatest
liberties with Horace. Whereas Horace's regret that he is not
capable of celebrating 'the Great and Immortal Actions' of
Augustus is followed by a short passage which might be
described simply as an example of *occupatio*, Pope is openly and
audaciously satiric:

> Oh! could I mount on the Mæonian wing,
> Your Arms, your Actions, your Repose to sing!
> What seas you travers'd, and what fields you fought!
> Your Country's Peace, how oft, how dearly bought!

The closing paragraph of his poem is quite different from that of
Horace:

> But Verse, alas! your Majesty disdains;
> And I'm not us'd to Panegyric strains:
> The Zeal of Fools offends at any time,
> But most of all, the Zeal of Fools in rhyme,
> Besides, a fate attends on all I write,
> That when I aim at praise, they say I bite.
> A vile Encomium doubly ridicules:
> There's nothing blackens like the ink of fools.
> If true, a woful likeness; and if lyes,
> 'Praise undeserv'd is scandal in disguise.'

It was no doubt because he had long been aware that the tren-
chancy of his satire rendered it un-Horatian that Pope described
the first of the two Dialogues which constitute the *Epilogue to the
Satires* as 'Something like Horace'. By insisting that Horace 'was
delicate, was nice', claiming that

> His sly, polite, insinuating style
> Could please at Court, and make AUGUSTUS smile,

and urging Pope to 'Go see Sir ROBERT', the Friend gives him a
fine opportunity for speaking out:

> See Sir ROBERT! – hum –
> And never laugh – for all my life to come?
> Seen him I have, but in his happier hour
> Of Social Pleasure, ill-exchang'd for Pow'r;
> Seen him, uncumber'd with the Venal tribe,
> Smile without Art, and win without a Bribe.
> Would he oblige me? let me only find,
> He does not think me what he thinks mankind.
> Come, come, at all I laugh he laughs, no doubt;
> The only diff'rence is, I dare laugh out.

In the Second Dialogue we notice even more clearly Pope's situ-

ation as a poet hostile to the Court who was yet a natural courtier
and friend of courtiers:

> But does the Court a worthy man remove?
> That instant, I declare, he has my Love:
> I shun his Zenith, court his mild Decline;
> Thus SOMMERS once, and HALIFAX were mine.
> Oft, in the clear, still Mirrour of Retreat,
> I study'd SHREWSBURY, the wise and great:
> CARLETON's calm Sense, and STANHOPE's noble Flame,
> Compar'd, and knew their gen'rous End the same:
> How pleasing ATTERBURY's softer hour!
> How shin'd the Soul, unconquer'd in the Tow'r!
> How can I PULT'NEY, CHESTERFIELD forget,
> While Roman Spirit charms, and Attic Wit.

In this proud poem, with its eloquent affirmation about the
'sacred weapon' which is satire, we find a pessimistic interpretation of the state of English civilisation which foreshadows the
sombre eloquence of the conclusion of *The Dunciad in Four Books*.
Aaron Hill praised the work in terms which anticipate the insistence of modern critics that the term 'Horatian' can be a misleading description of Pope's later satires:

I find, in this satire, something inexpressibly daring and generous. It carries
the acrimony of *Juvenal*, with the *Horatian* air of ease and serenity. It reaches
heights the most elevated, without seeming to design any *soaring*. It is raised
and familiar at once. It opposes just *praise* to just *censure*, and, thereby,
doubles the *power* of either. It places the *Poet* in a light for which *nature* and
reason designed him; and attones all the pitiful *sins* of the *trade*, for, to a *trade*,
and a *vile* one, poetry is irrecoverably sunk, in this kingdom.[78]

One day in 1742 Horace Walpole told his friend Richard West
that they lived in 'an age most unpoetical!':

'Tis even a test of wit, to dislike poetry; and though Pope has half a dozen
old friends that he has preserved from the taste of last century, yet I assure
you, the generality of readers are more diverted with any paltry prose
answer to old Marlborough's secret history of Queen Mary's robes. I do not
think an author would be universally commended for any production in
verse, unless it were an ode to the Secret Committee, with rhymes of liberty
and property, nation and administration.

    Wit itself is monopolized by politics; no laugh but would be ridiculous if
it were not on one side or t'other.[79]

Pope himself had to struggle to prevent his poetry from being
'monopolized by politics'. Maynard Mack has pointed out that
these late satires and epistles 'became to an inevitably large
extent exercises in innuendo'.[80] It is revealing that even Swift, in

praising the Second Dialogue, felt constrained to add: 'I live so much out of the world, that I am ignorant of the facts and persons, which I presume are very well known from Temple-bar to St. James's; (I mean the Court exclusive).'

Some of the allusions are obvious enough – line 62 of *The First Epistle of the First Book*, for example, 'Slave to a Wife, or Vassal to a Punk', which alludes to George II, his Queen, and his mistress Mme Walmoden. Lines 99–102 of *An Epistle to Dr. Arbuthnot* are more difficult:

> Does not one Table *Bavius* still admit?
> Still to one Bishop Philips seem a Wit:
> Still Sapho – 'Hold! for God-sake – you'll offend:
> No names – be calm – learn Prudence of a Friend.'

As Mack points out, those who read the passage in the folio or quarto *Works* of 1735 found 'Arnall' in place of 'Bavius', and since Arnall was a government journalist most readers would understand that the 'Table' must be Walpole's; 'but only Pope, or one of his intimates, or one of Walpole's intimates, would have occasion to ask whether the unspoken name which causes the poet's interlocutor to interrupt and urge prudence, and which evidently belongs to a person standing in the same "patronal" relationship to Lady Mary as the Bishop to Philips, as the "one Table" to Arnall, as the "Butchers" to Henley, and as the Free-Masons to Moore, was going to be, once again, that of the Great Man'.[81]

In his later years Pope's antipathy to Walpole and all that he seemed to him (as to many other writers of the day) to stand for, became obsessive, and he forgot his early resolution 'not to be content with the applause of half the nation'. A revealing instance is *One Thousand Seven Hundred and Forty*, a fragment of a poem first published by Warton which is remarkable for lacunae due (as the transcriber stated) to Pope's 'fear of the argus Eye of those who, if they cannot find, can fabricate treason':

> Rise, rise, great W— fated to appear,
> Spite of thyself a glorious minister!
> Speak the loud language Princes . . .
> And treat with half the . . .
> At length to B— kind, as to thy . . .
> Espouse the nation, you . . .
>   What can thy H . . .
> Dress in Dutch . . .

Tho' still he travels on no bad pretence,
To shew . . .[82]

This is merely an extreme example of a tendency with which all readers of the later poems are familiar. Political allusions appear everywhere, and while the scholar welcomes the challenge of explaining them, the ordinary reader may be forgiven for considering them a parasitic growth, a sort of bindweed, intrusive, tentacular, ubiquitous, which is perpetually taking over more and more of the poetic territory.

It is not only a modern objection. An anonymous pamphlet published in 1735, *The Poet finish'd in Prose*, makes it clear that many of Pope's contemporaries were growing impatient. In this dialogue a representative of the taste of the Town claims that 'All the World agrees that his last Writings excell his former as much as can be imagin'd', but a country gentleman who 'lov'd Mr. *Pope* on the Account of his former Writings' quotes the Virgilian phrase *quantum mutatus* and objects strongly to 'that affected Obscurity which runs thro' most of his late Works'.[83] Isaac Watts was of the same mind. Writing to the Countess of Hertford three years later, he asked: 'Can you think, Madam, that if [Horace] had been as obscure in his Satyrs . . . his sense would have been known at fifteen hundred years distance?'

Watts must have encountered far less difficulty in reading a volume by a younger poet, published in 1730, whose subscribers included Pope himself, Martha Blount, Chesterfield, Cowper, Gray and Edward Young, as well as a number of members of the Walpole family: *The Seasons*, published separately from 1726 and then collected. Commenting on the first three poems, a contributor to *The Whitehall Evening-Post* had written as follows:

If an Author, altogether unknown to the World, and unsupported by any thing but the native Force of his own Genius, should make his first Attempt in Poetry, on a Subject which can only please by its genuine Worth and Beauty, without gratifying either the ill Nature, irregular Passions, or Levity of Mankind: if he should venture beyond this, and lay aside the favourite Mode of writing in Rhyme; I think the *general Encouragement* of such a Performance would be a very good Proof of my Assertion [that modern taste is not wholly depraved].

And yet this is exactly true with regard to the Poems of *Winter* and *Summer*, which, tho' introduced into the World under all the Disadvantages I have been supposing, in a little time came to be universally read and approven. The Public, without dwelling on such minuter Faults as they might have found in them, distinguished, with a just Indulgence, that strong and fertile Imagination, which animates the several Representations of Nature they contain . . .

I remarked, with a particular Pleasure, that these Poems were very favourably received by many of the *Fair Sex*.[84]

One has only to remember *The Seasons*, a work of the second rank which came to be more widely read than any poem of Pope's, to realise to what an extent the author of the *Epistles* and the *Imitations of Horace* was a sophisticated poet writing in the last age of the Renaissance tradition. In a most interesting letter written in 1743 and referring to *The Dunciad*, Samuel Richardson comments that Pope 'might employ his Time, and his admirable Genius better than in exposing Insects of a Day', and reminds his correspondent that 'the World, like the Theatre, has its Pit, Boxes, and Upper-Gallery. A Quarles and a Bunyan may be of greater Use to the Multitude who cannot taste, or edify by, the Superlative than Mr. Pope's writings'.[85] It is a shrewd remark which is of the greater interest since it was made by a man who was a successful publisher as well as the author of a novel which marked an era in the development of prose fiction. It is ironical that the final version of *The Dunciad*, with its lament over 'the Restoration of *Night* and *Chaos*', should have appeared not only after the fall of Walpole but also two years after the publication of *Pamela*, and in the same year as that of *Joseph Andrews*. The next decade was to see the publication of remarkable works which would appeal to a wider public than Pope had been accustomed to consider: in prose *Clarissa*, *Tom Jones*, *Roderick Random* and *Peregrine Pickle*, and in verse *The Vanity of Human Wishes* and *An Elegy in a Country Church-yard*.

The extraordinary popularity of *The Seasons*, as the century progressed, was a portent for the future of English poetry. It was not a work which Thomson had designed for the 'Upper-Gallery', and in the first instance he was no doubt aiming above all at the approbation of the 'Boxes'; yet it was the nature of his poem – as of Gray's *Elegy* – to appeal to almost every member of the literary audience. A poem describing the succession of the seasons and the annual occupations of mankind, written in blank verse and in a style accessible to all readers of the Bible and other devotional books, found its way into households which could have had little interest in Pope's later poetry.

Swift once took comfort in the reflection that Pope 'owned

[him] a Cotemporary', remarking that he had become distinguished 'So confounded early' that his 'Acquaintance with great men' – such as Wycherley, Rowe, Prior, Congreve, Addison and Parnell – 'was allmost as antient' as his own.[86] Although he was more than twenty years younger than Swift, and had been only twelve years old when the new century began, Pope remained in many respects a man of the seventeenth century, and by the end of his life he seemed to many a figure from the *ancien régime*.

Yet this conservative poet, who had begun with *Pastorals* and who on his deathbed was found by a friend at work on a patriotic epic, *Brutus*, in which he hoped to immortalise himself as his 'Countrys Poet',[87] was also the man who did more than any other of his age to make possible a new relationship between poet and reader. It would be hard to exaggerate the importance of the remarkable independence which he managed to maintain throughout his career and of the manner in which, in his letters as in his poems, he presents himself as one of the principal subjects of his own writing. While it staggers the imagination to speculate on what he would have thought of Wordsworth, who would, by the end of the century, have essayed a poem of epic length and seriousness on the growth of his own mind, there is no doubt that the emergence of the poet and his development as a major poetic theme owed a great deal to Pope's example, and there could be no more natural transition – for all the differences between the two men and the circumstances of their lives – than that from his satires and correspondence to the satires, the correspondence and the journals of the author of *Don Juan*.

III · BYRON
Too sincere a poet

BYRON is the only major English poet to have grown up in the knowledge that he was destined to be one of his country's hereditary legislators. While he was at Aberdeen Grammar School the headmaster 'had a great notion' that he would 'turn out an Orator',[1] and when he assured his mother that he would 'cut . . . a path through the world or perish in the attempt' it was not of poetry that he was thinking. When she told a friend that she had '*no* doubt of his being a great Man' she was anticipating for him a career embracing politics and public life. 'He is an English Peer', as she wrote on another occasion, 'and has all the privileges of that situation.' For him the word, spoken or written, was always to be a public thing, an instrument of power over his fellow men: it is not surprising that his life, even more than that of 'the little Queen Anne's man' whom he so admired, was to prove 'a warfare upon earth'.

His early poems are the work of a young nobleman marking time, and the preface to *Fugitive Pieces*, the first of the two privately printed volumes which preceded his first publication, states that they are 'printed merely for the perusal of a few friends'. At this early point we already find him in conflict with the standards of the day: before the volume was complete he asked John Pigot to have some stanzas 'printed *separate* from my other *Compositions*, as you will perceive them to be *improper* for the perusal of Ladies'.[2] The poem in question was no doubt 'To Mary', in which the poet mocks prudes who will only make love in the dark:

> Now, by my soul, 'tis most delight
>   To view each other panting, dying,
>   In love's *extatic posture* lying,
> Grateful to *feeling*, as to *sight*.

He had already discovered that it was no longer acceptable to write of the enjoyments of love as it had been in the time of Donne, or Dryden, or of Matthew Prior.

61

When the little book was ready he bowed to the criticism of a clerical friend and burnt most of the copies. The revamped volume, *Poems on Various Occasions*, which he described as '*vastly* correct, & miraculously *chaste*',[3] is considerably less striking than its predecessor; but of course when he sent copies to one or two literary men outside his own circle they thanked him with civil 'Encomiums', and of course he decided to prepare another volume 'for the Public at large'. Byron realised that this collection, from which the 'amatory pieces' were to be 'expunged, & others substituted', would circulate 'fast enough in this County, from mere Curiosity'. He mentioned to his Harrovian friend Edward Long that 'the Cornelian (which *you* & all the Girls, I know not why think my best)' was now omitted: a private joke, since the poem was not addressed to a girl but to John Edleston, the choirboy with whom Byron had fallen passionately in love at Cambridge. In the remarkably infelicitous preface to *Hours of Idleness* he assures his readers that 'It is highly improbable, from my situation, and pursuits hereafter, that I should ever obtrude myself a second time on the Public', and rounds off three paragraphs which might have been designed to set his readers' teeth on edge by quoting Johnson's remark 'on the Poems of a noble relation of mine, "That when a man of rank appeared in the character of an author, his merit should be handsomely acknowledged" ', adding the claim that he himself 'would rather incur the bitterest censure of anonymous criticism, than triumph in honours granted solely to a title': a piece of youthful bravado which was shortly to be put to the test.

He followed the reception of his book with the eagerness of any fledgling author. 'Write soon', he urged Elizabeth Pigot, ' . . . do the Ancients demur? what Ladies have bought? all disappointed I dare say [to find] nothing *indecent* in the present publication'.[4] A few days later he reported that 'many of the London Booksellers have them, & Crosby has sent Copies to the principal watering places. Are they *liked* or *not* in Southwell?' At the beginning of August he brushed aside her intimation that sales were sluggish in Nottingham: 'very possible, in Town things wear a most promising aspect, & a *Man* whose works are praised by *Reviewers*, admired by *Duchesses* & sold by every Bookseller of the Metropolis, does not dedicate much consideration to *rustic Readers*'. He wrote with the high spirits of a young man who sees his name in every bookseller's and enjoys his fame 'in *secret*'. His initial audience was drawn from the fashionable world: 'the Duke of York, the Marchioness of Headfort, the Duchess of Gordon &c &c . . . & Crosby says the circulation will be still more extensive in the Winter, the Summer Season being very bad for a sale, as most people are absent from London'. Byron knew that he would have other groups of readers in Cambridge and at Harrow, which he refrained from visiting because he was embarrassed by a satirical poem, 'Childish Recollections', in which the new headmaster appeared as 'Pomposus'. The omission of this poem and of the dedication were among the changes he intended to make in the second edition. But it was too late: the celebrated review in the *Edinburgh*, written by Brougham but assumed by Byron to be the work of Jeffrey, appeared at the end of February, shortly before the appearance of the renamed *Poems Original and Translated*. 'I am cut to atoms by the E Review', he wrote to Hobhouse, 'it is just out, and has completely demolished my little fabric of fame'. Hobhouse was to recall that Byron 'was very near destroying himself' when he first read the review.

The mood did not last long. 'God help him if he is so easily discouraged he will neither be a statesman or an Orator', his mother commented characteristically, 'in short he will do no good'.[5] His reaction was to extend and rework the satire on which he was already engaged, and which we know as *English Bards and Scotch Reviewers*. A friend who visited Harrow in March 1809 found 'the monitors and upper boys' all engaged in reading it, but by now Byron was aiming beyond Harrow and Cambridge, and he succeeded to a degree which he was later to regret. There is something breathtaking about an unsuccessful poet who has the arrogance to sneer at Wordsworth and Coleridge:

> Let simple WORDSWORTH chime his childish verse,
> And brother COLERIDGE lull the babe at nurse:

a young man who chooses that moment in literary history to deplore, in sentences of a Johnsonian assurance and orotundity, 'the present prevalent and distressing *rabies* for rhyming'. England now had a young satirist who might be erratic in his choice of targets but who was eager to shoot and well provided with the necessary ammunition.

63

Before he left England Byron prepared a second edition. Although some phrases were modified, the fact that he put his name to the poem and added an extended preface and a post-script attacking Jeffrey and a certain Hewson Clarke must have made *English Bards* more controversial than ever. We notice that Byron had committed himself to satire at an earlier age than the Augustan whose work he so admired. If he was going to devote his life to poetry – and about that he still had more than one opinion, according to his mood – he would be a poet whose words would powerfully affect the world. There were to be no more *Hours of Idleness*.

Having gained an audience which grew during his two years abroad, Byron found leisure during his travels to write two satires and another poem which developed spontaneously. The friends to whom he showed the new works expressed a decided preference for the 'great many stanzas in Spenser's measure'[6] which he had begun at Janina and which were the beginnings of *Childe Harold's Pilgrimage*, and though he had a few copies of *Hints from Horace* and *The Curse of Minerva* privately printed neither was to be published in his lifetime. The second publisher approached about *Childe Harold*, John Murray, accepted it, and then made two suggestions. He was opposed to anonymity, as Byron mentioned in a letter to Dallas: 'I don't think my name will answer the purpose, & you must be aware that my plaguy Satire will bring the North & South Grubstreets down on the "Pilgrimage" but nevertheless if Murray makes a point of it, & you coincide with him, I will do it daringly.' Second, Murray suggested as tactfully as he could that certain passages on religious and political matters would cause offence. Byron replied:

With regard to the political & metaphysical parts, I am afraid I can alter nothing . . . even the *Æneid* was a *political* poem . . . and as to my unlucky opinions on Subjects of more importance, I am too sincere in them for recantation . . . I cannot alter the Sentiments, but if there are any alterations in the structure of the versification you would wish to be made, I will tag rhymes, & turn Stanzas, as much as you please. – As for the '*Orthodox*', let us hope they will buy on purpose to abuse.

In fact he was slightly less intransigent than such protests suggest. In Canto I he omitted three stanzas attacking Welling-ton, Holland and others, modified his treatment of the Convention of Cintra, and omitted a stanza on the 'unhallowed' erotic practices of William Beckford.[7] In Canto II he deleted two stanzas on Elgin and other 'classic Thieves' and was persuaded to substitute a 'hypothetical' stanza about an afterlife for his earlier statement that he 'Look[ed] not for life, where life may never be'. He seems to have omitted of his own accord a reference to 'boyish minions of unhallowed love'.

He increased the possibility of himself being identified with the Childe by adding a note naming the friend of I. xci as 'The Honourable I.* W.** of the Guards', whom he had known for 'ten years, the better half of his life, and the happiest part of mine', and pointed out that 'In the short space of one month I have lost *her* who gave me being, and most of those who had made that being tolerable'. Stanzas added at the end of Canto II lament a 'lov'd and lovely one' now known to have been John Edleston. When we remember that in the original edition the first two Cantos were followed by a handful of shorter poems, the last three of them elegiac and intensely personal, we realise that as early as this Byron had rendered it almost impossible for critics to consider his poetry without also becoming involved in a discussion of his life and personality. In spite of all his disclaimers, it is hard to believe that he wished it otherwise.

No actor, certainly, has ever had a better impresario. Murray did well to print the first edition in quarto, so following the example of the publishers of Scott's principal poems and pre-selecting the original readers by price. Gifford, Campbell, Moore, Rogers and others saw the poem in sheets, while Lord Holland (whom Byron had attacked in *English Bards*) was one of the select group who received presentation copies. Three days later the first octavo edition appeared, printed from the same type, to be followed almost immediately by the second. The launch had been spectacularly successful. Dallas found Byron 'loaded with letters . . . all lavish of their raptures',[8] while the Duchess of Devonshire was soon writing to America that the poem was 'on every table' and that the poet was 'courted, visited, flattered, and praised whenever he appears'. During what he was later to call his '*reign*' Byron forgot that he hated society and dined out incessantly. In particular 'Holland House, on which so much . . . of his satire had been directed . . . now [became] one of his most flattering resorts.' To compensate for her difficult status as a divorcée, Lady Holland was 'always *en reine*', as Byron commented (while Lord Holland, for his part, observed that Byron had so far mixed in 'any thing but good society'); but she had 'one merit, and a great one in my eyes ... that in this age of cant and humbug ... she has contrived ... not only to get herself into society, but absolutely to give the law to her own circle'. The Foxite political views current at Holland House were close to his own, and the admiration of a circle so influential that it was sometimes regarded as a sort of alternative government was to stand him in good stead long after he had ceased to frequent it. He found himself at his ease in a society which seems to us now to have been a progressive relic of an earlier age, a natural home for a young writer who had no use for the Lake poets and for a young reformer who found the reformers in general the sort of people with whom he had no desire to mix. So he suppressed the fifth edition of *English Bards*, having gained an impression of 'the *monde*' which was to date rather badly during his years in Italy. Meanwhile the Prince of Wales declared himself an admirer of his poetry, and Byron was amused to imagine himself succeeding Henry James Pye and 'warbling truth at Court'.

His rank was a great advantage. 'When we read the ... sarcasms on the "bravo's trade" ', commented the *Quarterly* reviewer, 'we are induced to ask, not without some anxiety and alarm, whether such are indeed the opinions which a British peer entertains of a British army'.[9] In the *Edinburgh* Jeffrey suggested that there is 'something *piquant* in the very novelty and singularity of that cast of misanthropy and universal scorn'. That was the point: by expressing his own irreverence and scepticism on many matters considered beyond debate by the more stuffy of the readers of the Reviews Byron appealed to the spirit of the time – at least to the spirit of many of its younger and more adventurous minds. More and more readers were ready to turn from the healthy and stirring strains of Scott and Campbell to a more troubling music. It was Byron's good fortune that Scott's Highland outlaws had prepared the way for his 'wild Albanian kirtled to his knee', while his account of 'Spain's dark-glancing daughters' and of the veiled women of the harem added a spice notably absent from Scott's romances. After the Songs of Innocence, the Songs of Experience.

Now Byron was bound to go on. With *The Giaour* he adopted

the device bungled with *Hours of Idleness* and disdained with *English Bards*, that of testing the water before publication. Fifteen copies of the 'disjointed fragments'[10] of the first version were printed and circulated to Lord Holland and others, and then a dozen further copies were shown to suitable persons before the published version appeared in June 1813. When he told Edward Clarke that he would be sent three copies with 'an addition towards the end of nearly 300 lines', Byron added that the copy Clarke already had was 'the first sketch printed off like "the Curse" merely for the "benevolent few" '. Here we see the device of concentric circles in full operation: first the tiny circle of those who saw the poem in manuscript or in a first private printing: then a circle of the same kind who were shown an amended and expanded version: and then the circle of those who could afford to buy that version (more or less revised) – in this case at the 'unconscionable' price of 4s 6d: and finally the wider reading public who bought or borrowed the subsequent cheaper editions – people who had already heard much of the poem and who were eager to read it as soon as they could.

In *The Giaour* and many of the poems which followed it Byron avoided most of the objectionable features of *Childe Harold* and concentrated on the exotic elements which now had a wide appeal. As he described 'the adventures of a female slave, who was thrown, in the Mussulman manner, into the sea for infidelity, and avenged by a young Venetian, her lover',[11] he must have had women readers near the forefront of his mind. In a brilliant anonymous pamphlet Lockhart was later to emphasise Byron's appeal for women: by 1821, he pointed out, 'every boarding-school . . . contains many devout believers' in the romantic young Lord who had written *Childe Harold*, a handsome youth, 'blue-eyed, bare-throated': 'Now, tell me, Mrs. Goddard, now tell me, Miss Price, now tell me, dear Harriet Smith, and dear, dear Mrs. Elton, do tell me, is not this just the very look, that one would have fancied for Childe Harold?' The fact that Byron was now competing with Scott for the suffrages of the female reader was acknowledged by Jane Austen herself in *Persuasion*, where she shows us Captain Benwick and Anne Elliot 'trying to ascertain whether *Marmion* or *The Lady of the Lake* were to be preferred, and how ranked the *Giaour* and *The Bride of Abydos*; and moreover, how the *Giaour* was to be pronounced'. When he claimed that the popularity of *The Giaour* had surprised him, and 'certainly did not raise my opinion of the public taste', Byron referred to it 'and such "horrid mysteries" ', so associating the Tales with the short-lived favourites of the circulating libraries. Yet it was not only women who were carried away by these poems: among their earliest admirers were Hookham Frere, Canning, Richard Heber, Scott, J.H. Merivale and Francis Hodgson.

And of course Gifford, who read *The Bride of Abydos* in manuscript, and then again in its 'probationary state of printing';[12] while Lord Holland was prepared to read a proof overnight. Byron made one important revision, without which the poem could not have succeeded, when he decided that Selim and Zuleika must not remain brother and sister: 'on *second* thoughts', as he told John Galt, 'I thought myself *two centuries* at least too late for the subject; which, though admitting of very powerful feeling and description, yet is not adapted for this age, at least this country'. Whether or not the concession weakened the poem, as he believed, it certainly helped to make it a best-seller. Murray offered him no less than 1,000 guineas for it and its precursor, a sum which Byron rejected as too generous, and we know that 6,000 copies were sold within a month of publication.

In the dedication of *The Corsair* Byron admits that he has 'deviated into the gloomy vanity of "drawing from self" ', and this element, absent from the first two Tales, led to an even greater success. The character of Conrad,

> That man of loneliness and mystery,
> Scarce seen to smile, and seldom heard to sigh,[13]

proved irresistible, above all to women. 'In knowledge of the human heart & its most secret workings surely he may without exaggeration be compared to Shakespeare', wrote one exceptionally intelligent young woman. 'It is difficult to believe that he could have known these beings . . . but from *introspection*.' The future Lady Byron was not the only reader to be deeply impressed, and Gifford reported that he had sold, on the day of publication, 'a thing perfectly unprecedented – 10,000 copies'. Within two weeks 20,000 had been purchased, and in a little over a month 25,000. 'You cannot meet a man in the street who has not read or heard [it] read', Murray reported with pardonable exaggeration.

For all his understandable fears that his work was being over-rated, Byron loved celebrity, and it was only for a moment that he considered a pause and a silence. It is clear that he relished the uproar caused by the inclusion of 'Lines to a Lady Weeping' in the second edition of *The Corsair*. 'Did you ever know any thing like this?', he asked Lady Melbourne: ' – at a time when peace & war – & Emperors & Napoleons – and the destinies of the things they have made of mankind are trembling in the balance – the Government Gazettes can devote half their attention & columns day after day to *8 lines* . . . I really begin to think myself a very important personage – what would poor Pope have given to have brought down this upon his "epistle to Augustus?" '[14] Byron's behaviour after the wreck of his private life which followed his marriage and separation from his wife makes it clear that he found it almost impossible to remain silent about himself. On receiving no reply from Lady Byron when he sent her his poem on their separation, 'Fare Thee Well!', he despatched a copy to Murray with the clear intention that it should be privately printed and shown to the frequenters of his drawing room. He similarly told Murray to print fifty copies of 'A Sketch from Private Life', a powerful lampoon in the Augustan manner on Mary Jane Clermont, Lady Byron's maid and one-time nurse and governess whom Byron considered largely to blame for the separation. Inevitably these poems found their way into print, so that when Byron left England for the last time he was a famous poet whose private life was the subject of more speculation than that of any other English writer had ever been. But two poems to his half-sister Augusta, written near Geneva, were soon to pro-vide even richer pickings for the gossips. Augusta told Lady Byron that she wished one of these, the 'Epistle to Augusta', at the bottom of the sea, and she managed to prevent its publi-cation; but the more revealing 'Stanzas to Augusta' were soon in print, and together the *Poems on his Domestic Circumstances* ensured that interest in the man should be at least as avid as interest in his poetry. The reading public of the time had become Byron's spaniel, and the road to mediocrity lay broad before him. He was saved by his temperament, which preferred the stimulus of an ambivalent response – and by the fact that he did not depend on writing for his living.[15] He would soon be writing the greatest poetry of his career.

Byron was developing his technique, and he had found in Murray and his circle a group of sympathetic admirers. He had come to know as much as anyone about the taste of the reading public, a public for which no one was better equipped to write, and in particular he had discovered that his self-dramatisation was as acceptable to his readers as it was congenial to himself. In an earlier letter he had told Murray that 'people like to be *contradicted*',[16] and he now knew that people liked to be shocked. Few writers have ever exploited these truths with such brilliant panache. The personal and confessional element in his poetry had proved such an attraction that there was no longer any need for him to affect to distinguish between the opinions of the Childe and his own. If he had not allowed himself to become, almost explicitly, the protagonist of his poem, he would have been depriving himself of the most attractive subject available to any writer of the day. Canto III opens with lines addressed to his infant daughter and ends with four stanzas to her which elicited from Lady Byron a remark of some penetration, the remark of a born logician on an instinctive man of letters: 'He is the absolute monarch of words, and uses them, as Bonaparte did lives, for conquest, without more regard to their intrinsic value.'

The superiority of the new Canto, written under the influence of Shelley, was widely recognised, not only by those who shared Byron's political and other opinions. Croker thought that nothing in the poem (as distinct from the notes) could be altered for the better, while Scott commented on the extraordinary fact

that during a period of four years . . . a single author . . . managing his pen with the careless and negligent ease of a man of quality, and chusing for his theme subjects so very similar . . . did, in despite of these circumstances, of the unamiable attributes with which he usually invested his heroes, and of the proverbial fickleness of the public, maintain the ascendancy . . . which he had acquired by his first matured production.[17]

It is remarkable that Gifford saw to the correction of the press. He omitted the political footnotes to *Childe Harold* III, as well as two important lines in *The Prisoner of Chillon*:

> Nor slew I of my subjects one –
> What sovereign hath so little done?

lines vital to Byron's protest against the tyrannical abuse of power. If that was a tax paid involuntarily to political prudence, Byron had reason to be grateful for the tolerance and business acumen of his publisher, who assured him that he believed his own 'connexions' to be 'even more numerous amongst the Whigs than the Tories', a comment that reminds us to what an extent Murray's drawing room at this time fulfilled the functions of a literary club. He was a shrewd man of business, as well as a generous one. Having agreed to Kinnaird's demand that he should pay £2,000 rather than 1,500 guineas for Canto III and *The Prisoner*, he sold 7,000 of each to an assembly of booksellers. If Byron had not been a Lord, if he had not been 'Murray's poet', things would have gone very differently with him, as the case of Shelley sufficiently illustrates. As it is, we are left wondering at the degree of liberty enjoyed by the English upper classes of that age – a liberty unique in Europe. Byron had learned a little more about the art of encroaching, lover-like, on the defences of the reading public.

Before Canto III had been published Byron had written the first two acts of *Manfred*, the other work which (with Canto IV) marks the culmination of the first of the two periods of his poetic career. He was more uncertain about this 'Dramatic Poem' than was his habit, and he rewrote Act III. Gifford thought well of the work, however, and Murray proceeded to publication, although he was understandably worried about the religious tone of certain passages as well as the obviously personal origin of the theme of incest.

When Murray reported that the best critics, such as Frere, were 'in ecstasy with it', he had to admit that it was less popular with 'the general reader'.[18] A newspaper reviewer protested that Byron had 'coloured *Manfred* into his own personal features' by making him guilty of 'one of the most revolting of crimes', yet the more influential Reviews and magazines continued to bear witness to the extraordinary ascendancy Byron had achieved. In *Blackwood's* John Wilson expressed reservations yet stressed that Byron had been 'elected by acclamation to the throne of poetical supremacy', while Jeffrey, in a more discriminating critique, described *Manfred* as 'undoubtedly a work of genius and originality'. Throughout we notice that Byron himself was more anxious to deny any debt to Marlowe than to rebut the imputation of incest.

Although he congratulated himself on having 'at least rendered it *quite impossible* for the stage',[19] we know that he was deeply dissatisfied with his own writing at this time and may conjecture that in different circumstances he might have turned to the theatre and perhaps have developed a new style as a consequence. In his exile in Italy, however, he was 'little aware of the progress of the theatres'. In the preface to *Marino Faliero* he commented that he had been 'too much behind the scenes' to have been greatly attracted to the stage, and we can understand his fury when he heard that the play was to be acted at Drury Lane, in spite of all Murray's efforts. The vehemence of his complaint that he had been 'kept for *four* days . . . in the *belief* that the *tragedy* had been acted & "unanimously hissed" ' is highly revealing, as is his statement that he would not have passed those days again 'for – I know not what'. It is tempting to conclude that he was in a sense a frustrated dramatist, and that if he had been obliged to write for a living he might have returned to England and tried the theatre. As it is, however, his plays are not central to his achievement, nor do they seem to have played an important part in his development as a poet.

It was the composition of *Beppo*, a poem 'in or after the excellent manner of Mr. Whistlecraft . . . on a Venetian anecdote',[20] which enabled Byron to escape from one way of writing and discover another. The previous year he had been given a copy of the *Novelle Galanti* of the Italian poet Giovanni Battista Casti and may well have been struck by the description of the audience for which Casti had written at the beginning of the first tale: not for stern matrons or shy young virgins, nor for strict old religious zealots, but for young men and wives who are virtuous only so far as is reasonable,

> In somma parlo a voi, Donne mie belle,
> Che amate senza smorfia e ipocrisia
> Gl' innocenti piaceri e l'allegria.

Now that he found himself in Venice, Byron was stimulated by Frere's poem to tread in the footsteps of Casti and other informal Italian satirists: 'it will at any rate shew them – that I can write cheerfully, & repel the charge of monotony & mannerism', he wrote, consenting that his name should be placed on the title-page provided that Murray first consulted '*the knowing ones*'.

Towards the end of 1816 Byron had told Kinnaird that he wished to divorce himself as much as possible from England,

and he repeated to more than one of his friends that either he was unfit for England, or England was unfit for him. Such a distancing from his audience vitally affected his relationship with his readers, and as he remained a voluntary exile throughout the second and major phase of his writing it is hard to avoid the conclusion that it suited him admirably. Yet, as he himself said, he 'did not write *to* the Italians, nor *for* the Italians',[21] but for an English audience, and it is important to realise that he was by no means cut off from England, no poet writing in isolation and a void. On the contrary, it was as important for him to keep in touch with '*the knowing ones*' as it was for him to escape from the Constitutional Association and all that it stood for – a cloud on the horizon, no bigger than a woman's hand, which was to reveal itself as the Victorian Age. His letters from Italy are a most important part of his writings, and it is clear that they helped him to form and develop the new persona which had in fact appeared in his earlier letters before he had been able to express it in verse. The letters to Murray and others were not intended to be private. For an account of his doings in Venice he referred Samuel Rogers to his letters to Thomas Moore: on another occasion he told Murray that he might open one of his letters to Moore 'If you want my news': and he even referred Murray to a letter to Augusta for his description of the Bernese Alps. When Murray asked for an account of the beautiful Margarita Cogni, Byron responded at length, describing 'her person – very dark – tall – the Venetian face – very fine black eyes – and certain other qualities which need not be mentioned'.[22] He knew that the select group of men who frequented Murray's drawing room was certain to hear or read his letters. By 1821, in the knowledge that Murray was collecting them, he warned him that Lady Caroline Lamb might send him forgeries. It is clear that Murray's group – which Byron described so variously, according to his mood – formed an inner circle of the readers for whom he was writing: a circle of men of letters who were also men of the world, gentlemen who wrote without getting ink on their fingers, men like Rogers, Moore, Scott and Frere. It was for such an audience that he was now to write, it was such an audience that he had in mind as he composed the early cantos of *Don Juan*, it was such an audience that his nature prompted him to stimulate and shock and drive to the limits of its toleration, and beyond.

The reception of *Beppo* by these sophisticated men, and then by a larger circle also composed of knowledgeable readers, was of great importance to Byron; and it was favourable from the first. Four days before publication we find it under discussion at Devonshire House, from proof-sheets or advance copies. Soon Jeffrey wrote penetratingly on it in the *Edinburgh Review*, and Murray could report that he had sold six times as many copies of Byron's poem as of *Whistlecraft* itself, in a sixth of the time. 'If *Beppo* pleases you shall have more in a year or two in the same mood',[23] Byron had written from Venice. Now he had received the signal for which he had been hoping.

Having found how far he could go without antagonising the more liberal section of the reading public, he characteristically went further. Uncertain whether *Don Juan* was 'too free for these very modest days', he resolved to try the public pulse anonymously. In November he told Hobhouse (who, with Scrope Davies, at this point constituted the innermost circle of all) that he was sending him Canto I of a poem 'as free as La Fontaine – & bitter in politics – too', adding that 'the damned Cant and Toryism of the day may make Murray pause'. Byron explained that he wrote with the same freedom as Ariosto, Boiardo and Voltaire, and Pulci and Berni – 'all the best Italian & French' writers, as well as Pope and Prior; 'but no improper words nor phrases – merely some situations – which are taken from life'. He realised that the bitter stanzas on Brougham which he had added to Canto I were unacceptable. Meanwhile he moved on to Canto II, as he eagerly awaited news from England of the reception of Canto I.

Murray's natural eagerness to advertise at once a new poem by the most celebrated poet of the day was quickly dashed by the views of his advisers, particularly Hobhouse and Scrope Davies. Hobhouse was worried by 'the blasphemy and bawdry and the domestic facts'.[24] Frere objected because a 'friend of freedom should be a friend to morality', because the attack on Lady Byron was unfair, and because he thought the satirical passages on Southey and others were most likely to damage Byron himself. 'If we had a very Puritan court indeed', he observed, 'one can understand then profligacy being adopted as a badge of opposition to it, but the reverse being the case, there is not even that excuse for connecting dissoluteness with patriotism.'

Kinnaird was more favourably disposed to publication, but even he stipulated that it 'must be *cut* for the *Syphilis*'. In a carefully composed letter Hobhouse set out to tell Byron the verdict of his friends. He reminded him that he had 'by far the greatest reputation of any poet of the day', so that he had a great deal to lose, and insisted that he could not print his attack on Castlereagh unless he were available to meet him in a duel. The general objections to publication were 'drawn from the sarcasms against the Lady of Seaham, from the licentiousness, and in some cases downright indecency of many stanzas, and of the whole turn of the poem; from the flings at religion, and from the slashing right and left at other worthy writers of the day'. Byron was bound to be identified with his hero. And the greatest difficulty of all was that the most objectionable parts of the poem were undoubtedly also the best. This letter is the fullest verdict of '*the knowing ones*' that we possess on any poem of Byron's. It makes it clear that they were shrewd and sympathetic critics who were anxious that he should not completely antagonise the reading public of the time.

Byron was disappointed if not surprised, telling Murray that he had wanted an informed opinion on 'poetical merit – & not as to what they may think due to the Cant of the day – which still reads the Bath Guide, Little's poems – Prior – & Chaucer – to say nothing of Fielding & Smollett'.[25] The only excisions to which he agreed were those of the stanzas on Castlereagh 'and the two concluding words (Bob-Bob) of the two last lines of the third Stanza of the dedication'. If in the end Murray should refuse to publish the poem, even anonymously, Byron wished him to print fifty copies for private distribution, a strategy which had served him well in the past and which he knew would inevitably lead to publication. He claimed indignantly that 'half Ariosto – La Fontaine – Shakespeare – Beaumont – Fletcher – Massinger – Ford – all the Charles second writers – in short, *Something* of most who have written before Pope . . . and much of Pope himself' would be liable to similar objections:[26] a reminder that the Regency period had something in common with the Restoration, and that Byron had something in common with Dryden and Rochester and other poets of that era. It was often noticed that he retained many of the characteristics of a Regency dandy after the fashion had passed: Trelawny tells us that 'The character he most commonly appeared in was of the free and easy sort, such as had been in vogue when he was in London, and George IV was Regent.'

Soon he made up his mind that *Don Juan* must be published, though anonymously, and instructed Kinnaird to make the best bargain with Murray that he could. One letter makes a particularly clear statement about his attitude to his audience:

The poem will please if it is lively – if it is stupid it will fail – but I will have none of your damned cutting & slashing . . . I have not written for their pleasure [that of the English]; – if they are pleased – it is that they chose to be so, – I have never flattered their opinions – nor their pride – nor will I. – Neither will I make 'Ladies books' 'al dilettar le femine e la plebe' – I have written from the fullness of my mind, from passion – from impulse . . . but not for their 'sweet voices'.

He half despised himself for having made 'Ladies books' when he wrote the Tales, and half despised the 'sweet voices' whose acclamation he had so fully enjoyed. Having moved to a greater realm of poetry, he was impatient of restraint.

It is not surprising that he fought vigorously to defend *Don Juan*, arguing that it was 'the most moral of poems'[27] and powerfully deploying the Argument from Snobbery: 'are you all *more* moral [than Pulci]? . . . No such thing, – *I* know what the World is in England by my own proper experience – of the best of it – at least – of the loftiest'. As Moore recognised, Byron had lived abroad so long that he had 'forgotten that standard of decorum in society to which every one must refer his *words* at least, who hopes to be either listened to or read by the world'. He had always been something of an outsider in English society: he remembered Holland House during his 'reign' and ignored the more staid men and women who constituted the great majority of the aristocracy, to say nothing of the upper middle class whose opinions were now becoming more and more influential. He was amused by the thought that *Don Juan* 'must set us all by the ears'.

In fact he made more concessions in Canto I than he was to make in any other. He now agreed to the omission of the dedicatory stanzas to Southey and of the attack on the late Sir Samuel Romilly.[28] In spite of his insistence that there must be 'no gelding' of Canto II he finally agreed to the omission of certain words which 'ladies may not read', though he rejected other suggestions with scorn. Even his friends often failed to understand that he was stimulated by uncertainty as much as he was by praise. He was a gambler who had to go on gambling, a surf-rider who was impelled to continue until he met the wave which threw him, a tightrope-walker who was driven to demand more and more of his own courage and agility. It was not that the public reception of his work was a matter of indifference to him, as he often claimed: it mattered intensely: but it mattered with a difference, just as he was determined to wear his laurel with a difference.

When the book appeared the less knowledgeable of the purchasers of the expensive quarto were puzzled to find a printer's name, but no publisher's. While there was of course no indication that the introductory stanzas to Southey had been omitted, certain typographical features – the fact that stanzas xv and cxxxi consist of nothing but two rows of asterisks, the rest of the page being blank, and the asterisks in stanzas cxxix and cxxx – merely drew attention to omissions and served to stimulate the imagination of the reader. Whether this had been Murray's intention, or whether he had acted in simple fear of Byron's anger, the effect is as piquant as that of similar typographical devices in *Tristram Shandy*.

In Canto II the reference to 'my grand-dad's Narrative'[29] reminds readers that the poet is the grandson of a famous seaman, and (while the shipwreck was and remains strong meat) the romance of Juan and Haidee was nicely calculated to appeal to readers who had been delighted by the Tales. At the end of Canto I the poet had promised his readers that they would 'meet again, if we should understand Each other', and at the end of II he makes his bow,

> Leaving Don Juan and Haidee to plead
> For them and theirs with all who deign to read

very much in the manner of the epilogue of a play. We are reminded of the special relationship which obtains between author and reader when a literary work appears in parts.

A week after publication Kinnaird reported that the poem had '*failed*', with the interesting comment that 'the quarto edition has disgusted people, & has announced a pretension it never was meant to put forth'.[30] Three months later only 12,000 of the 15,000 quarto copies had been sold: a triumph for an ordinary poet, but for Byron a comparative failure. 'There has been an eleventh commandment to the women not to read it', he grumbled, ' – and what is still more extraordinary they seem not to have broken it.' The courtesan Harriette Wilson took the poem to bed with her, then wrote to urge Byron not to 'make a mere *coarse* old libertine' of himself. 'What harm did the Commandments . . . ever do you or anybody else . . . ?' she asked, in a remarkable rhetorical question. A writer in the *Eclectic Review* described *Don Juan* as a poem 'such as no brother could read aloud to his sister, no husband to his wife', so anticipating a common and troublesome Victorian criterion. For the moment it appeared that Byron had overreached himself, and that the poet who had so instinctive an understanding of the importance of his readers had encroached too far. 'Why will Lord Byron write what we may not read?', asked Jane Waldie, on behalf of her sex.

The initial circulation seems to have been principally in London, a point made by the author of an article in *Blackwood's* which acknowledged that the power and genius of Byron had never been more evident than in this profligate work.[31] Blackwood himself had told Murray that it was a book he 'could not sell on any account whatever'. A copy reached Wordsworth, who regretted the failure of the *Quarterly* to chastise the poem: 'every true-born Englishman will regard the pretensions of the Review to the character of a faithful defender of the institutions of the country, as *hollow*', he wrote, 'while it leaves that infamous publication . . . unbranded'.

For all his professions that he was not writing for women and the common people, Byron was by no means satisfied with the assurances that the 'best Judges &c.' praised his poem, and he admitted that he was 'in a damned passion at the bad taste of the times'. He took pleasure in telling Murray that the pirated Paris edition was being read 'in Switzerland by Clergymen and ladies with considerable approbation': later he was to boast that he cared 'but little for the opinions of the English – as I have long had Europe and America for a Public'. When Murray asked whether the poem was to be continued he replied splendidly, like a great tennis-player disposing of a weak return of service: 'You ask me for the plan . . . I *have* no plan – I *had* no plan – but I had or have materials . . . If it don't take I will leave it off where it is with all due respect to the Public – but if continued it must be in my own way . . . Why Man the Soul of such writing is it's licence? – at least the *liberty* of that *licence* if one likes.'

The outcry over the first two Cantos worried Byron, who feared that his paternal rights over Ada might be threatened if the work were denied copyright. He complained that 'the *Cant* is so much stronger than *Cunt* – now a days'.[32] Murray and his 'parlour boarders' (or his 'Utican Senate', the phrase varying with Byron's mood) were understandably hesitant about further publication, and just when they had decided in favour of it another voice seems to have exerted a decisive influence. 'At the particular request of the Countess G[uiccioli] I have promised *not* to continue Don Juan', Byron wrote on 6 July 1821. 'She had read the two first [Cantos] in the French translation – & never ceased beseeching me to write no more of it . . . from the wish of all women to exalt the *sentiment* of the passions – & to keep up the illusion which is their empire. – Now D.J. strips off this illusion.' It is ironical that he had just read *John Bull's Letter to Lord Byron*, in which the author, now known to have been Lockhart, points out that in *Don Juan* Byron is no longer writing for young women, but for the best judges and for immortality. He mentions that by this time 'pirated duo-decimo [is] competing it all over the island with furtive quarto', and compliments Byron on a poem 'written strongly, lasciviously, fiercely, laughingly' which 'sells, and will sell to the end of time', whether Murray 'honours it with his *imprimatur* or . . . not'. He tells Byron that he is the only man (thanks in part to the privileged position which had kept the *Quarterly* silent) 'who has any chance of conveying to posterity a true idea of the *spirit* of England in the days of his Majesty George IV', adding: 'You know the society of England, – you know what English gentlemen are made of, and you very well know what English ladies are made of.'

It is an excellent joke, though it may be a joke partly of his own contriving, that Byron should have abandoned so ostentatiously masculine a poem on the insistence of a woman: a woman who was not his wife, who was not strait-laced or middle class, who was not English, and who (relying on a bad translation) agreed with the view transmitted to him by his half-sister that the poem was considered '*execrable*'.[33] Such was the 'Free masonry' of women, as he told Hobhouse. It is thoroughly characteristic of Byron to have sent Murray the Contessa's note acknowledging his promise not to proceed with the poem. We can only conclude that he wanted the reason which he had given for the cessation broadcast by the frequenters of Murray's drawing room.

In Canto IV, published with III and V at the end of the year, he complained that he had been 'accused . . . of a strange design Against the creed and morals of the land' and that his publisher had told him that

> Through needles' eyes it easier for the camel is
> To pass, than those two cantos into families.

The fact that Canto IV was written above all for women ('who make the fortunes of all books!', as he acknowledged in line 857), helps to explain the strong element of the romantic in the continuation of the love story of Juan and Haidee. Canto V contains more wit, but we know that an amusing stanza about Queen Caroline was omitted, with Byron's permission, and another about Wedlock and Padlock, without it. Unlike the first two Cantos, these sold well from the first. We are told that 'booksellers' messengers filled the street in front of the house in Albemarle Street, and the parcels of books were given out of the window in answer to their obstreperous demands'.

In the preface to his Laureate elegy on George III Southey took the occasion to deplore the 'lewdness and impiety, with which English poetry has, in our days, first been polluted'. He claims that 'For more than half a century English literature has been distinguished by its moral purity', and invokes the Victorian criterion by claiming that 'A father might . . . have put into the hands of his children any book which . . . did not bear . . . manifest signs that it was intended as furniture for the brothel.' Half a century takes us back to a time when poetry had lost the vigour of the early part of the century and was deeply influenced by the Sentimental movement. When Southey refers to those 'who are still to be called gentle readers, in this ungentle age', we sense that a term which had formerly referred to men and women indiscriminately had come to refer principally to women, and above all to young ladies. We recall that Bowdler's *Family Shakespeare* was a recent book.

Byron had intended to bring Don Juan to England at some

point, where he was to be 'cause for a divorce'[34] and rich occasion for satire, but when he read *A Vision of Judgement* he was moved to write *The Vision of Judgment* 'to put the said George's Apotheosis in a Whig point of view, not forgetting the Poet Laureate for his preface and his other demerits'. Whether he could fairly expect Murray to publish the poem was questionable. *Cain*, published with *Sardanapalus* and *The Two Foscari*, proved anything but a bargain for the unfortunate publisher, who had unwillingly paid £2,710 for the three works, and he also had *Werner* on his hands. At this point the conflict of interest between poet and publisher becomes irresistibly comic. 'As to "a poem in the old way to interest the women" ', Byron wrote in March 1822, ' . . . I shall attempt of that kind nothing further. – I follow the bias of my own mind without considering whether women or men are or are not to be pleased.' Shelley commented that Murray's suggestion was 'very good logic for a bookseller, but not for an author', adding that 'the shop interest is to supply the ephemeral demand of the day': to which Byron replied, according to Trelawny, 'John Murray is right . . . all I have yet written has been for women-kind; you must wait until I am forty, their influence will then die a natural death, and I will show the men what I can do.'

At one point Byron told Kinnaird that if he could not find a publisher for *The Vision* he was to have fifty copies privately printed for him, the same device which he had considered for the first two Cantos of *Don Juan*.[35] Later he urged Murray to print the poem without a publisher's name, the very ruse which had angered him with *Don Juan*. Now he even suggested the use of 'some other bookseller's name' or the pretence that it was 'a *foreign* edition'. When Murray continued to drag his feet Byron sent *The Vision* to John Hunt for publication in *The Liberal*, so seeming to many to throw in his lot with the radicals and putting at risk the astonishingly privileged position *vis-à-vis* the Establishment which he had enjoyed as a member of the Upper House and indeed as 'Murray's poet'. What made matters worse was that Murray, whether from malice or inadvertence, gave Hunt a copy of the poem without a number of important corrections, and without the preface which was designed to make it clear that Southey and not the King was the principal object of the attack and which also contains a defence of the 'supernatural personages' in the poem and an insistence that 'the Deity is carefully withheld from sight, which is more than can be said for the Laureate'. Hunt published an announcement blaming Murray for the omission of the preface, while most copies of *The Liberal* include a list of 'Errata' which succeeds only in drawing attention to certain of the most objectionable jibes against the monarch in the text of the poem.

Byron was justifiably furious. The fact that he had made no attempt to publish *The Irish Avatar*, a blistering satire written at the same time, shows that he knew there were limits to what one could publish in political satire: in that case he had contented himself with telling Moore to have twenty copies 'carefully and privately printed off'.[36] Now he had the mortification of seeing a masterpiece published in a periodical with which he had already severed his connection, in an inaccurate text which rendered him liable to prosecution. *The Literary Register* probably spoke for the common reader when it described the poem as a 'profligate and outrageous insult . . . to the . . . majority of mankind' and commented (predictably) that it did not contain a line which could be read 'for a wife, a child, or a mother'. The corrected second edition did little or nothing to set matters right, and at the beginning of 1824 the publisher was to be brought to trial.

But that is to anticipate. In July 1822 Byron told Kinnaird that he had obtained permission from the Countess to continue *Don Juan* 'if I will make it more sober – that is – dull'.[37] In October he told Murray that he had begun Canto XI and had brought his hero to England: 'how do you like that? – I have no wish to break off our connection.' He recalled nostalgically that Murray had once offered him 1,000 guineas a canto for as many as he might choose to write. It is not difficult, therefore, to imagine the feelings with which he read Murray's letter of 29 October telling him of the outcry occasioned by *The Liberal* and deploring his association with 'such outcasts from Society'. Of Cantos VI–VIII, which he had read in manuscript, Murray wrote that they were so 'outrageously shocking' that he could not publish them on any account:

For Heaven's sake revise them – they are equal in talent to any thing you have written . . . My company used to be courted for the pleasure of talking about you – it is totally the reverse now – and by a re-action even your former works are considerably deteriorated in sale.

In fact Cantos VI and VII, at least, hardly seem to account for such an attitude. Canto VI would appear to have been written for women – women (admittedly) sophisticated enough to enjoy being shocked. The description of Juan's adventures in the seraglio are risqué in a manner calculated to appeal to boudoir readers; while neither the mischievous allusion to the Queen's trial in stanza lxxviii nor the description of Catherine the Great as 'greatest of all sovereigns and w——s'[38] is likely to have shocked Murray and his senate. In VII Byron acknowledges that he is accused of 'A tendency to under-rate and scoff' and defends himself characteristically by referring to a host of earlier writers. The satire on jingoism and the military art of butchery will have offended many readers, while Canto VIII, which opens with the words 'Oh, blood and thunder!' and becomes more and more 'unsound' as it continues, must have given widespread offence. One of the examples of a man fighting a just war is George Washington: Byron glances satirically at Wordsworth's 'Carnage is God's daughter', and deploys his irony at the expense of 'Glory', while he also refers to Wellington's enormous pensions and reveals his own republican sympathies. He describes bigamy as a 'false crime', refers pointedly to the famine in Ireland and to the weight of George IV (twenty stone), and reveals his hatred of tyranny and indeed of monarchy.

Most offensive of all is the preface to these three Cantos: if it reached Murray with the manuscript that would help to explain the vehemence of his disapproval. It contains a violent attack on Castlereagh, who had recently committed suicide, uses two quotations from Voltaire in defence of the poem, and launches a broadside against 'the degraded and hypocritical mass which leavens the present English generation':

Socrates and Jesus Christ were put to death publicly as *blasphemers*, and so have been and may be many who dare to oppose the most notorious abuses . . . But persecution is not refutation, nor even triumph: the 'wretched infidel', as he is called, is probably happier in his prison than the proudest of his assailants.

While it is inevitable that Byron and Murray should have parted, few divorces have occasioned more unhappiness. There is an amusing letter from Leigh Hunt describing Murray 'in a deplorable state'[39] writing to tell Byron 'how delighted he should be, if his Lordship would but be "*so nobly generous*" as to let him publish works of his "former glorious description" '. He describes Murray sitting for hours in front of a picture of Byron: 'Imagine the languishing bookseller.' Having suppressed a most unfair letter in which he compared Murray to Edmund Curll, Byron wrote recalling that he and Shelley 'used to laugh now & then – at various things – which are grave in the Suburbs' and hinting that he might continue *Childe Harold's Pilgrimage* – Murray's dearest wish.

He now found that he could no longer expect the privileged treatment accorded to an aristocratic Whig rebel courted by Holland House and published by the proprietor of the *Quarterly Review*. 'He complains bitterly of the detraction by which he has been assailed', Jeffrey wrote in the rival *Review*, pointing out that on the contrary, 'we cannot recollect a single author who has had so little reason to complain . . . From the very first, he must have been aware that he offended the principles and shocked the prejudices of the majority . . . Yet there never was an author so universally and warmly applauded, so gently admonished.'[40] He went on to point out that Byron sometimes seems 'inclined to insinuate, that it is chiefly because he is a *Gentleman* and a *Nobleman* that plebeian censors have conspired to bear him down!', and observed that '*The party* that Lord B. has offended, bears no malice to Lords and Gentlemen. Against its rancour, on the contrary, these qualities have undoubtedly been his best protection; and had it not been for them, he may be assured that he would, long ere now, have been shown up in the pages of the *Quarterly*.' Byron's debt to Murray and his advisers was even greater than Jeffrey knew, and nothing could be more revealing than the fact that at the very time when he had broken with his publisher Byron insisted that the copy of *Heaven and Earth* which was to be printed in *The Liberal* should be the proof marked by Murray or Gifford to indicate a passage to be omitted. For all his protests, Byron's association with Murray had given him an inner circle of readers, and a sense of only slightly shocked acceptance by 'the best judges', which he was not to enjoy again.

The letters of this period are the letters of a worried man whose faith in *Don Juan* never wavered. At times Byron became suspicious of Murray, saying that he was 'bullied by the priests and the Government'; yet he was anxious to reassure the publisher that there was little or no 'community of feeling – thought

– or opinion between L[eigh] H[unt] & me', and insisted that his poem 'will be known by and bye for what it is intended a *satire* on *abuses* of the present *states* of Society –and not an eulogy of vice'.

As if to reassure himself, he wrote two poems of a much less sophisticated sort. *The Age of Bronze* was 'calculated for the reading part of the Million – being all on politics &c. &c. &c. and a review of the day in general', while *The Island* was intended to be only 'a little above the usual run of periodical poesy'.[41] He told Leigh Hunt that his opinion of the average reader was lower than his and bet him that 'the most *stilted* parts of the political "Age of Bronze" – and the most *pamby* portions of the Toobonai Islanders will be the most agreeable to the enlightened Public'. In fact it was *Don Juan* which was beginning to circulate most widely, however, so fulfilling the prophecy of a contributor to *Blackwood's* who had written that 'a book of real wickedness and real talent' like this was 'pretty sure to find its way into every house that has any pretensions to be *"comme il faut"* ', while a young man who worked for Galignani in Paris delighted Byron by telling him that it was 'by far the most popular' of all his poems, 'especially with the women – who send by hundreds slily – for copies' and added that when Galignani printed his poems they always printed an extra number of copies of the satire.

Cantos IX–XI reveal Byron's growing awareness of the shocked response of a large part of the English reading public. Canto IX opens uncompromisingly with an attack on Wellington, 'the best of cut-throats', originally intended for Canto III, the gravamen of the charge being that the man who had had it in his power to free Europe from the tyranny of Kings had sunk to restoring Legitimacy. Acknowledging that he will 'offend all parties', the poet then returns to Juan and his adventures with Catherine the Great. In Canto XI the emergent subject of the whole poem, Hypocrisy, is rendered explicit,[42] and by bringing his hero to England Byron not only fulfils a promise but also plays his trump card. Readers of the 'Fashionable Novels' must have found a great deal to their liking in the description of the 'mighty Babylon' and its social scene: the leaders of the 'beau monde', 'drapery misses', fortune-hunters, and profligates of every kind. Soon Byron admits that he is no longer 'The grand Napoleon of the realms of rhyme', having fallen on evil days. Southey is attacked again, while a bitter stanza on 'Sporus'

(Henry Hart Milman, whom Byron suspected of having turned Murray against his poem) appears in the first edition as eight lines of asterisks. The young Juan is advised to be a hypocrite, and the poet addresses his audience directly:

> You are *not* a moral people, and you know it
> Without the aid of too sincere a poet.

When we read Cantos XII–XVI, the only part of the poem written after the break with Murray, we find no falling off in vigour or technique, but we sense that the poet is marking time, as if uncertain which direction to follow. As he writes of the fashionable world, 'The twice two thousand, for whom earth was made',[43] Byron has a retrospective tone:

> For I was rather famous in my time,
> Until I fairly knocked it up with rhyme.

While there is plenty of the sort of social scandal which he knew would be acceptable to his readers – since 'no one has succeeded in describing The *monde*, exactly as they ought to paint' – we notice that he cannot always bring himself to bowdlerise his language: while a slightly risqué reading is revised at one point, we hear that Lord Henry 'in . . . Love or war Had still preserved his perpendicular', and are informed elsewhere that 'There's pretty picking in those "petits puits".' The most revealing remark in the whole poem occurs at XIV. xii:

> I think that were I *certain* of success,
> I hardly could compose another line.

While Canto XVI ends strongly, with a description of a Norman Abbey based on Newstead and the delightful appearance of 'the fair Fitzfulke', and while we have a few stanzas of a further Canto, it may be that by the spring of 1823 the element of uncertainty had become too strong. In any event, Byron then laid the poem aside for the last time.

His career as a poet was virtually at an end, but two postscripts form an appropriate conclusion to the story of his relations with the reading public of his day.

Three months after Byron's death John Hunt was tried for publishing a work 'calumniating the late king, and wounding the feelings of his present Majesty'.[44] When counsel for the prosecution asked for passages from *The Vision of Judgment* to be read out in court, his opponent shrewdly insisted that the poem must be read in its entirety. This off-beat recreation of a scene which had been familiar five centuries earlier – when the setting would have been the royal Court or the hall of some great nobleman, and the reader the poet himself – must have constituted a remarkable spectacle. When the lines in which Southey offers to write the Life of Satan were read out we are told that there was 'great merriment in Court'. Although Hunt was found guilty and subsequently fined, Byron may be said to have won this round of the contest.

He lost the other when his Memoirs were burnt in the grate of Murray's room, a month after his death at Missolonghi. When he gave Moore the manuscript Byron had given him permission to allow 'the "Elect" ' to read it, much as he had arranged for a small circle to see preliminary printings of so many of his poems. We know that at least twenty-four people read the Memoirs, among them Lord and Lady Holland, Kinnaird, Lord John Russell, Henry Luttrell, Gifford and Lady Caroline Lamb: Moore actually had a copy made, because he was afraid that the manuscript might become worn out 'by passing through so many hands'. Of the eleven men who were present when the final decision was taken, however, only Moore and Luttrell acknowledged that they had read the Memoirs, and both were against their destruction. As the papers were fed into the fire the spirit of Byron must have watched with a sense of irony as he witnessed the final triumph of Murray's 'cursed puritanical committee'.

Byron's end had been implicit in his beginning. He had never regarded poetry as his vocation, and while he worked hard on many of his poems Scott's remark that he 'manag[ed] his pen with the careless and negligent ease of a man of quality' was precisely the sort of compliment that he most valued. Lady Blessington tells us that 'he seemed to think that the bays of the author ought to be entwined with a coronet to render either valuable, as, singly, they were not sufficiently attractive; and this evidently arose from *his* uniting, in his own person, rank and genius'.[45] As early as 1813 he had written in his journal: 'no one should be a rhymer who could be any thing better', adding that he was annoyed 'to see Scott and Moore, and Campbell and Rogers, who might have all been agents and leaders, now mere spectators'. So far as he was consistent about anything, he was consistent about this. Towards the end of his life he used to say that 'a man ought to do something more for mankind than write verses', and he told Count Pietro Gamba that 'Poetry should only occupy the idle.' In 1821 he reflected that he had 'at least had the name and fame of a Poet – during the poetical period of life (from twenty to thirty)', and added: 'whether it will last is another matter'. Deeply as he admired Pope, he did not envisage for himself a poetical progress, in the Virgilian-Renaissance manner, from the less demanding genres to the final assault on the epic, the poet's Everest. When James Hamilton Browne expressed the wish that he would attempt an epic, Byron remarked that even Milton was little read at the present day, adding, 'I shall adapt my own poesy, please God! to the fashion of the time, and, in as far as I possess the power, to the taste of my readers of the present generation; if it survives me, *tanto meglio*, if not, I shall have ceased to care about it'. His willingness to allow others to modify the phrasing of his poems, so long as they did not alter the political and moral sentiments, marks him off from the most dedicated of poets.

'The end and aim of his life is to render himself celebrated', Lady Blessington recorded in 1823: 'hitherto his pen has been the instrument to cut his road to renown, and it has traced a brilliant path; this, he thinks, has lost some of its point, and he is about to change it for the sword, to carve a new road to fame'.[46] Nothing could have been more natural, granted his attitude to public affairs, on the one hand, and to poetry on the other. From his early days his heroes had been statesmen, not poets:

> For the life of a Fox, of a Chatham the death,
> What censure, what danger, what woe would I brave?

The difficulty came when he considered how such ambitions could be realised:

If I had any views in this country [he once wrote], they would probably be parliamentary. But I have no ambition; at least, if any, it would be 'aut Caesar aut nihil' . . . To be the first man – not the Dictator – not the Sylla, but the Washington or the Aristides – the leader in talent and truth – is next to the Divinity! Franklin, Penn, and, next to these, either Brutus or Cassius – even Mirabeau – or St. Just.

As he realised, however, he was quite unsuited to the realities of English political life: it was partly because he needed to distance himself and be his own man that he spent the greater part of his adult existence abroad.

It was only in some great crisis or convulsion that he could visualise himself on the political scene: at some moment when the political and the martial had become one. His view of history was essentially operatic. Conscious to an exaggerated degree of being a patrician, he found 'such fellows as Bristol Hunt' little if at all preferable to Castlereagh; but if, as he often hoped, a revolution were approaching in England – 'which won't be made with rose water' – then he would return to play his part. A man of greater genius than his own considered him 'capable . . . of becoming the redeemer of his degraded country'; but that man was Shelley, whose approach to the practicalities of politics will be touched on in the next chapter. In 1822 Byron told Moore that he would have gone to South America or Greece long ago, but for his liaison with the Countess Guiccioli. The suggestion that he should become King of Greece, which is unlikely to have had much weight behind it, must have appealed to the author of *Childe Harold* as much as it no doubt amused the author of *Don Juan*.

He was a role-player before he was a poet, and his yearning for a vast audience preceded his desire for poetical fame. When he set out for Greece he had no illusions about the modern Greeks, but he reflected that, at the worst, he had found 'the means of making a dashing exit from the scene of this world' where he found the part he 'was acting had grown excessively dull'.[47] He immediately became a hero in England, and his death at Missolonghi provided the perfect final scene. Although he died at thirty-six he was more famous by the end of his life than any earlier English poet had been. Critics with the ambition of evaluating his work in purely literary terms are forever destined to an honourable defeat. It was not only as a poet that Byron made the world his theatre and his audience mankind.

IV · SHELLEY
The unacknowledged legislator

'**M**y father is in parliament', Shelley wrote in his first letter to Leigh Hunt, 'and on attaining 21 I shall, in all probability, fill his vacant seat'.[1] Although he was not a nobleman like Byron, Shelley too was born into the ruling class, proceeding from Eton to Oxford as Byron had gone from Harrow to Cambridge. He belonged to a wealthy family, and never seriously regarded writing as a means of earning a living. From first to last, indeed, he considered poetry 'very subordinate to moral & political science', and this is the clue to a career which can never be understood by those whose knowledge of his work is confined to a selection of the better-known lyrics.

A poet with a message is a poet in search of an audience, and even before he made his first attempt to publish verse we find him keenly interested in the technique of publication. 'Robinson will take no trouble about the reviewers', he wrote from Eton, for all the world as if he were an experienced author, 'let every thing proper be done about the venal villains . . . We will all go then in a posse to the booksellers in Mr. Groves barouche & four – shew them we are no grub street gareteers . . . Send the reviews in which Zastrozzi is mentioned to Field Place, the British review is the hardest, let that be pouched well.'[2] The truth that he knew very little about the market for books is revealed by his conviction that his second Gothic romance, *St. Irvyne, or The Rosicrucian*, was sure to circulate, 'as it is a thing which almost *mechanically* sells to circulating libraries, &c'. He had no hesitation about publishing the book at his own expense, and was soon asking whether the public was not 'captivated' by the title-page. It was not, and more than four years after Shelley's death the unfortunate publisher reckoned that, allowing for interest, he was at least £300 out of pocket.

A similar excess of optimism had accompanied the publication of *Original Poetry; by Victor and Cazire* in September 1810.

Most of the large printing of 1,500 copies had to be pulped when Shelley discovered that one of the poems supposedly by his sister Elizabeth ('Cazire') had in fact been plagiarised from 'Monk' Lewis. While the original verse in the volume is of little interest, we are struck by the degree to which Shelley's revolutionary sympathies are already in evidence: 'you see I mingle metaphysics with even this', he wrote to a friend, 'but perhaps in this age of Philosophy that may be excused'.[3] 'Metaphysics' may also be detected in *The Wandering Jew*, a narrative poem in tetrameters in the manner of Scott, perhaps written with the assistance of Thomas Medwin, in which Shelley was almost certainly aiming at a wider audience. It is not surprising that Ballantyne declined the poem, which was to have been dedicated to Sir Francis Burdett, a Member of Parliament whose battle for freedom of speech had led to his imprisonment in the Tower of London. Ballantyne's letter of rejection is a model of tact in which the modern reader may be at fault in suspecting an element of irony. He did not doubt the poem's success, he wrote, but considered it 'perhaps better suited to the character and liberal feelings of the English, than the bigoted spirit which yet pervades many cultivated minds in this country [Scotland]'. He added that Scott himself was under attack in 'our Scotch spiritual and evangelical magazines and instructors, for having promulgated atheistical doctrines in *The Lady of the Lake*'. Shelley then submitted the poem to R. and J. Stockdale of Dublin, enclosing Ballantyne's letter and commenting on the absurdity of the imputation of atheistical principles to his own work; but the Stockdales were equally unwilling to publish, and *The Wandering Jew* did not appear until after Shelley's death: a portent of things to come.

The same fate befell the poems in the Esdaile notebook, written between the ages of sixteen and twenty. Shelley was on safe ground when he assured Thomas Hookham that at least they could not be accused of being 'a volume of *fashionable literature*': while much of the verse was of the requisite mediocrity, the ubiquitous political and anti-religious opinions rendered the collection unsuitable for the library table or the boudoir. The French Revolution is celebrated in a translation of the 'Marseillaise', a poem 'To the Republicans of North America' addresses them as 'Brothers!', while the Irish struggle against

England is the inspiration of the stanzas 'On Robert Emmet's Tomb'. Freedom is the goal, Tyranny the enemy, and there are no shadings or hesitancies. A footnote to one of the poems includes in a list of legal murderers Julius Caesar, Moses, Mohammed, Napoleon, Wellington and Nelson. Religion is the daughter of Falsehood, the Christian God is the 'bloodstained King of Kings'. One of the longer pieces, a narrative called 'Henry and Louisa', anticipates *The Revolt of Islam* in describing a conflict between 'the injured and the brave' on the one hand and 'the Tyrant of the World' on the other. Shelley hoped that his poems might circulate among the well-to-do and provide him with funds with which he would be able to help the poor, particularly in Ireland.

The very title of the second volume of his verse to attain publication vividly demonstrates the difficulty which Shelley was always to experience in coming to terms with any section of the reading public. According to Thomas Jefferson Hogg the poems were in proof when he persuaded Shelley that the book must be pseudonymous, and it was published with an extraordinary title, *Posthumous Fragments of Margaret Nicholson*: as the work (that is) of a woman who had attempted to assassinate George III in 1786 and had then been consigned to Bedlam. In an Advertisement which anticipates that of *Epipsychidion* Shelley describes the first poem as 'intimately connected with the dearest interests of universal happiness', adding: 'much as we may deplore the fatal and enthusiastic tendency which the ideas of this poor female had acquired, we cannot fail to pay the tribute of unequivocal regret to the departed memory of genius'. While the pretence that the volume was published by the woman's nephew somehow adds a further element of absurdity to the whole affair, we cannot doubt that the poems themselves had been written in all seriousness: throughout we find Shelley's characteristic sympathy with the French Revolution, and attacks on the 'Oppressors of Mankind'. At first he believed that the book was selling well: 'Nothing is talked of at Oxford but Peg Nicholson', he wrote in a letter, 'I have only printed 250 copies & expect a second edition soon.'[4] He was convinced that the Epithalamium of Francis Ravaillac and Charlotte Corday, part of which he described as 'the production of a friends *mistress*', would make the volume sell 'like wildfire'; but nothing was ever to be heard of a second edition.

Neither his poetic career nor his attitude to his audience can be understood without attention to the polemical works in which he sought to address the public directly in prose, eager to elucidate and justify the views which are so evident in his early poetry. The first of these was *The Necessity of Atheism*, written while he was still contemplating *Queen Mab*, in the Christmas vacation after his first term at Oxford.

That December he told Hogg, who was seeking a publisher for a novel containing many 'free notions',[5] that Stockdale would no longer publish for him, and that he greatly doubted whether he would be well disposed to Hogg: 'booksellers possess more power than we are aware of, in impeding the sale of any book whose opinions are displeasing to them'. Although he gave it out to all but his closest friends that he was not contemplating any further publication, however, Shelley was in fact writing a novel 'principally constructed to convey metaphysical & political opinions by way of conversation', and he seized with avidity on the arguments against Christianity with which Hogg presented him, a series of telling points extracted from Locke and Hume. Instead of writing a prize poem on 'The Parthenon', as his father desired, he used Hogg's work as inspiration for *The Necessity of Atheism*.

On a first reading one is astonished to find that this celebrated pamphlet is only about a thousand words long, between two and three pages of the present book. Written with studied lucidity, it argues that the existence of God cannot be logically proved: a conclusion which now seems as unanswerable to agnostics as it is unworrying to convinced Christians. Instead of bearing an author's name it is subscribed '*Thro' deficiency of proof,* AN ATHEIST'.

It may be doubted whether any publication has ever been exposed for sale for a briefer period. Twenty minutes after it appeared in Slatter and Munday's bookshop in the Oxford High Street, a Fellow of New College entered, glanced through the pamphlet, and ordered that all copies in the shop should immediately be burned, but for one which was to be retained as evidence of a serious offence. Presentation copies had already been despatched to all bishops and heads of colleges, however, although Shelley's plan to have the pamphlet advertised 'in 8 famous papers'[6] in London had to be abandoned because of the possibility of a prosecution for blasphemy. He was summoned before the governing body of University College, was foolish enough to refuse to acknowledge authorship, and was sent down. Having been bullied at Eton, he had now made a voluntary martyr of himself at Oxford.

Like many other men and women of the age he believed that a revolution in England was essential, and he hoped by his writings to play a part in guiding the course of events. This had an important bearing on the audience for which he wished to write. In deploring unnecessary luxuries, he described 'expensive printing' as 'that worst of all',[7] and soon we find him trying to imitate Tom Paine's success as a polemicist and publicist. Since he was determined 'to lose no opportunity to disseminate truth and happiness', the wide circulation of cheaply published material was obviously an important goal. When he went to Dublin in 1812, with the primary object of supporting Catholic emancipation, he accordingly took with him *An Address to the Irish People* for distribution 'throughout Ireland'. Fifteen hundred copies were printed on cheap paper and in small type, and sold at 'The lowest possible price . . . because it is the intention of the Author to awaken in the minds of the Irish poor, a knowledge of their real state' and to suggest 'rational means of remedy'.[8] He even hoped that extracts might be printed as Paine's works were, 'in large sheets to be stuck about the walls of Dublin'. A letter to Elizabeth Hitchener differentiates sharply between the audience he had in mind for his pamphlet and for his verse. The *Address* 'shall be printed very cheap, and I shall wilfully lose money by it. I shall distribute throughout Ireland, either personally or by means of booksellers.' On the other hand he intended to squeeze money 'out of the rich; the poor cannot understand and wd. not buy my poems, therefore I shall print them expensively.' He intended to differentiate similarly between two books which were never completed, a novel which was to be printed cheaply, and a volume of essays on philosophy or 'Metaphysics', to be printed 'expensively – the first edition that is (I am vain enough to hope for a second)'. He congratulated himself on having 'vulgarized the language' of the *Address* ' . . . in order to reduce the remarks it contains to the taste and comprehension of the Irish peasantry', but in fact it is the work of a young idealist who knew nothing whatever of the people whose cause he had volunteered to espouse, and there is a revealing absurdity in the opening of the postscript: 'I have now been a week in Dublin . . . ' While the simplicity of the style is often telling, at times we feel that we are reading a stylish translation from the Latin, and even such members of 'the peasantry' as were literate – a tiny minority – must have found the pamphlet far too long. *Proposals for an Association of . . . Philanthropists* was intended for 'a different class . . . the young men at Dublin College', so that he was free to write in his own 'natural style tho in the same strain'.

The distribution of his writings was his first care. In February 1812 he told Elizabeth Hitchener how he had set about 'disseminating the doctrines of Philanthropy and Freedom': 'I have already sent 400 of my little pamphlets [*An Address*] into the world, and they have excited a sensation of wonder in Dublin . . . Copies have been sent to 60 public houses.'[9] His methods were unusual. Every day he sent a man out to continue distribution, while he himself stood on the balcony of their lodging and waited until he saw a passer-by who struck him as '*likely*', to whom he would throw a copy. It is hardly surprising to find Harriet adding a postscript in which she describes herself as 'ready to die of laughter'. 'Percy looks so grave', she adds. 'Yesterday he put one into a womans hood of a cloak.' In spite of his hope of soon having a newspaper at his disposal Shelley's experiences in Ireland were not encouraging, and by 18 March he had withdrawn both the *Address* and the *Proposals* from circulation, resolving no longer to write for the illiterate and looking forward to an influence to be exerted after his own death in a mood which anticipates that of the 'Ode to the West Wind'.

While still in Dublin he had composed a concise *Declaration of Rights* as a broadside poster to be displayed on walls as opportunity offered, and on his return to England he hoped it might also prove 'useful in farm houses' there.[10] Had not Benjamin Franklin found such methods effective? In August his Irish servant was arrested for posting the *Declaration*, however, and Elizabeth Hitchener had to be warned against allowing copies to fall into the hands of 'priests or aristocrats'. When he printed *A Letter to Lord Ellenborough*, in which he protested against the sentencing of the publisher of the third part of Paine's *Age of Reason*, Shelley told Hookham that while copies should be distributed to 'any friends who *are not informers*' he had now decided not to publish it and intended to limit himself to 'gratuitous distribution'.

The most extraordinary example of Shelley's attempt to reach the common reader, as emblematic as Don Quixote's tilting at the windmills, was his use of balloons and bottles to convey his message through the elements. One might expect the sonnets 'To a Balloon laden with *Knowledge*' and 'On Launching some Bottles filled with *Knowledge* into the Bristol Channel' to be mock-heroic in tone, yet their intention seems to be serious, and they make strange reading. Swift himself could not have devised a more impracticable mode of communication for his Laputians.

Before he left for Ireland Shelley had been contemplating a poem which would be 'by anticipation a picture of the manners, simplicity and delights of a perfect state of society',[11] and soon after his return we find him hard at work on *Queen Mab*. On 18 August he sent Hookham a specimen of this work on 'The Past, the Present, & the Future', commenting that he had enough material for a further six cantos and adding, significantly: 'I have not attempted to temper my constitutional enthusiasm . . . a Poem is safe, the iron-souled Attorney general would scarcely dare to attack "genus irritabile vatum" '. In January 1813 he wrote that the notes would be 'long & philosophical', with the interesting comment that he would 'take that opportunity which I judge to be a safe one of propagating my principles, which I decline to do syllogistically in a poem'. Although he also stated that 'A poem very didactic is I think very stupid', he told Hogg a few days later that the 'didactic' part of the poem was in one metrical form (pentameters) and the 'descriptive' in another: a revealing admission. 'As I have not abated an iota of the infidelity or cosmopolicy of it, sufficient will remain . . . to make it very unpopular. Like all egotists I shall console myself with what I may call if I please the suffrages of the chosen few.' 'The chosen few' anticipates his use of the Pindaric συνετοί in relation to *Epipsychidion*, and it is noteworthy that he first uses the word on the title-page of *A Refutation of Deism*.[12] In March Shelley told Hookham that he was determined to give the poem to the world, if only Hookham had the courage, and revealed a definite notion of the public he was hoping to address: 'I expect no success. – Let only 250 Copies be printed. A small neat Quarto, on fine paper & so as to catch the aristocrats: They will not read it, but their sons & daughters may.'[13] It is of interest that he would apparently have contemplated a larger edition if Daniel Eaton had not been in prison and therefore unavailable to help in selling the book. Still, as he reflected, 'Small Christmas or *Easter offerings* of a neat little book have frequently a surprising effect.'

Shelley soon became aware (as he had not been initially) that the 'Anti Christian'[14] tendency of the notes could not possibly escape attention, and he cannot have been surprised that Hookham decided not to add his imprint to a book which had Voltaire's 'ECRASEZ L'INFAME!' as its first motto. In May Harriet told a friend that the poem 'must not be published under pain of death, because it is too much against every existing establishment', but that it was to be privately distributed to friends, a few copies also being despatched to America. 'Do you know any one that would wish for so dangerous a gift?', she asked. The poem bore the simple legend: 'Printed for P.B. Shelley'.

During the summer some seventy copies were circulated, while almost a third of the poem was reprinted in 1815, presumably at Shelley's own instigation, in an obscure periodical, *The Theological Inquirer, or, Polemical Magazine*.[15] By this time he was coming to dislike *Queen Mab*, however, and he reprinted only one passage (as 'The Dæmon of the World') in the *Alastor* volume in 1816. The poem's wider circulation, which was to owe nothing to his own actions or wishes, remained in the future.

By the age of twenty-one, therefore, Shelley had printed more than most aspiring poets; but a good deal had been printed at his own expense, several of the poems had not been published, and those which had been published had attracted the minimum of attention, much of it satirical. The extreme scarcity of his early poems and pamphlets, satirised in the passage in Peacock's *Nightmare Abbey* in which Scythrop receives 'a letter from his bookseller, informing him that only seven copies had been sold, and concluding with a polite request for the balance',[16] is a vivid reminder of his failure to find an audience. While these early difficulties were largely due to his revolutionary views on religion, morality and politics, it is misleading to suggest that the verse of the early periods contains much of real merit. To regard *Queen Mab*, as do both Neville Rogers and Richard Holmes, as Shelley's first major work,[17] is to invite misconception. It is a work of great importance to anyone who wishes to understand the development and continuity of his thought, but the best place to study these is not the poem itself but the notes, a number of which constitute brief essays on such diverse topics as the arguments for the existence of God, the history of Christianity, necessity, chastity and prostitution, and 'the unnatural craving for dead flesh'. It seems to have been after writing *Queen Mab* that Shelley began to be seriously concerned with the art of poetry. The interest of the early verse, in which we find anticipations of the themes of most of his later work, derives from the greatness of the poems which he was soon to write.

We first hear of *Alastor . . . and other Poems* in a letter from Shelley to John Murray telling him that he has had 250 copies printed and sending for his consideration 'all the sheets' of the volume 'but the last'[18] – all (that is) except sheet 'H', or perhaps sheets 'G' and 'H', 'The Dæmon of the World' being partially or wholly omitted either for reasons of prudence or more probably because it was not yet ready. If Murray had accepted the volume, as the example of Byron may serve to suggest, the story of Shelley's career might have been very different. But Murray refused it, and it was the much less celebrated firm of Baldwin, Cradock and Joy that published the first important collection of poems by Shelley in 1816. The title-poem is not an easy one, and the apparent discrepancy between the preface and the poem itself has exercised critics ever since: even so, the failure of the Reviews to notice the high promise of *Alastor* is remarkable, and Shelley had every reason to be deeply disappointed. It is true that Leigh Hunt yoked him with John Hamilton Reynolds and Keats as one of the 'Young Poets' of the day, but all that he said of him was that he was 'a very striking and original thinker'; while the few words of qualified praise vouchsafed by the *Monthly Review* and the *Eclectic* were outweighed by censure. 'I do not say that I am unjustly neglected', Shelley wrote to Leigh Hunt in December, with remarkable restraint, 'the oblivion which overtook my little attempt of Alastor I am ready to acknowledge was sufficiently merited in *itself*; but then it was not accorded in the correct proportion considering the success of the most contemptible drivellings', the final words no doubt referring to such members of 'the illustrious obscure' as those later listed in the preface to *Adonais*: the authors of '*Paris*, and *Woman*, and a *Syrian*

Tale, and Mrs. LeFanu, and Mr. Barrett, and Mr. Howard Payne'.

He remained uncertain whether he possessed 'powers deeply to interest, or substantially to improve, mankind'.[19] In August 1817 he was to comment to Charles Ollier, 'the sale I believe was scarcely any thing', as if echoing the *Monthly* reviewer's satirical reference to his 'readers (if he has any)'. Immediate praise would have mattered infinitely more to him than that to be awarded by the *Quarterly* three years later.

Shelley was now swiftly reaching his astonishing maturity as a poet, and his visit to Switzerland stimulated him to write the 'Hymn to Intellectual Beauty' and 'Mont Blanc'. But the suicide of Fanny Godwin in October and that of Harriet in December were profoundly depressing, and in his anxiety for the custody of Harriet's children he found himself 'dragged before the tribunals of tyranny and superstition'. It is a sign of his deter-mined courage that he resolved to make another attempt to influence a section (at least) of the reading public. Today *A Proposal for Putting Reform to the Vote throughout the Kingdom* seems remarkably moderate, with its opposition to immediate univer-sal suffrage because it could only 'place power in the hands of men who have been rendered brutal and torpid and ferocious by ages of slavery';[20] yet whether or not Richard Holmes is right in his belief that Shelley's views were 'much further left than he admitted' (and I believe that he is), even the proposals which he did advance would have proved unacceptable to most members of the governing class of the day. 'Do not advertise sparingly', Shelley wrote to Ollier, instructing him to send twenty or thirty copies to Hookham and twenty to Leigh Hunt and expressing the hope that William *Hone* (underlined) and Stockdale would sell the pamphlet. Presentation copies were to be despatched to Sir Francis Burdett, Mr Brougham, Lord Holland, Mr Cobbett, Mr Curran, Douglas Kinnaird (Byron's friend), Francis Place, Robert Montgomery, Thomas Creevey, and a score of other individuals. Ten copies were to go to the London Hampden Club, five to the Birmingham Hampden Club, and five to 'Mr. Hallet of Berkshire'. The editors of the *Statesman*, the *Morning Chronicle* and the *Independent Whig* were also to receive copies. Soon Shelley was asking how the remainder of the printing of five hundred were selling.

In the spring of the following year he began a poem which occupies a key position in the pattern of his poetic life, a poem he was later to describe as being 'in the style and for the same object as "Queen Mab" ':[21] Hunt was very flattering, and Shelley was determined to publish, against advice from Byron about the need for caution as to 'religion, &c.' We have only to read the preface to *The Revolt of Islam* to see the importance of this new work in relation to Shelley's search for an audience. After *Alastor*, he was seeking reassurance with 'an experiment on the temper of the public mind, as to how far a thirst for a happier condition of moral and political society survives, among the enlightened and refined, the tempests which have shaken the age in which we live'. The poem is addressed to the highly educated 'in the cause of a liberal and comprehensive morality'. Although he rejects 'methodical and systematic argument' in favour of a narrative form, the poet is intent on attacking 'all the oppressions which are done under the sun'. 'How far I shall be found to possess that more essential attribute of Poetry, the power of awakening in others sensations like those which animate my own bosom', he expects to learn from 'the effect which I shall produce upon those whom I now address'.

Nothing could be more rational or lucid than the preface, yet good sense could hardly be ascribed to the first step which Shelley took towards finding a publisher. On 13 October he wrote a letter, probably to Longman, enclosing 'the 4 first sheets of my Poem, entitled "Laon & Cythna, or the Revolution of the Golden City" '.[22] He describes it as 'a tale illustrative of such a Revolution as might be supposed to take place in an European nation, acted upon by the opinions of what has been called (erroneously as I think) the modern philosophy, & contending with antient notions . . . It is a Revolution of this kind, that is, the *beau ideal* as it were of the French Revolution.' As a specimen of a narrative poem, endowed with the usual complement of hero and heroine, he sent the publisher Canto I only: a canto quite different from the poem as a whole, a canto of obscure and perplexed allegory which might have been designed to 'throw' any publisher's reader. He actually commented that 'if it were all written in the manner of the first Canto, I could not expect that it should be interesting to any great number of people', and went on to ask whether Longman would publish it at the author's expense, if he should be unwilling to undertake the risk of publication himself.

When Longman refused the poem Shelley came to an agreement with James and Charles Ollier, who had already published *A Proposal for Reform*, and this small firm became his publisher for the rest of his life, a fact which did little to help him in his quest for an audience.

The final paragraph of the preface to the poem in its original form drew attention to the fact that the lovers were brother and sister, a 'circumstance which was intended to startle the reader from the trance of ordinary life'. Shelley explained that he wished 'to break through the crust of those outworn opinions on which established institutions depend', and stated it as his belief that 'the exhibition of a practice widely differing from their own' has a tendency to promote among men 'charity and toleration', an optimistic view which was not to be confirmed in practice. The first person to object was the printer: 'That McMillan is an obstinate old dog', Shelley wrote indignantly in December, 'as troublesome as he is impudent. 'Tis a mercy as the old women say that I got him thro' the poem at all – Let him print the errata, & say at top if he likes, that it was all the Author's fault, & that he is as immaculate as the Lamb of God.'[23] He adds that he would be glad to have news of the reception of the poem, claiming that he is 'tolerably indifferent as to whether it be good or bad'. Perhaps the printer's objections served to confirm reservations on the part of the Olliers themselves, since they seem to have refrained from publication, and only a very few copies (though more than the three mentioned by Peacock) found their way into circulation. In a powerful and understandably indignant letter Shelley stated that 'if the book was quietly and regularly published' he did not believe that the government 'would touch anything of a character so refined and so remote from the conceptions of the vulgar', adding: 'They would hesitate before they invaded a member of the higher circles of the republic of letters', an argument by no means without force. He emphasised that 'the fruit of reputation (and you know for *what purposes* I value it) is within my reach'.

In the event Shelley was persuaded to make the relatively slight revisions which the Olliers considered necessary, and almost at once we find him recovering two copies from Ebers's

British and Foreign Circulating Library in Old Bond Street, where one must suspect that he had placed them himself. He was soon 'extremely desirous'[24] of having all the copies recalled: the account of the matter which he gave Thomas Moore was not altogether candid:

The present edition of 'Laon & Cythna' is to be suppressed, & it will be republished in about a fortnight under the title of 'The Revolt of Islam', with some alterations which consist in little else than the substitution of the words *friend* or *lover* for that of *brother* & *sister*. The truth is, that the seclusion of my habits has confined me so much within the circle of my own thoughts, that I have formed to myself a very different measure of approbation or dis-approbation for actions than that which is in use among mankind; and the result of that peculiarity, contrary to my intention, revolts & shocks many who might be inclined to sympathise with me in my general views. –

As soon as I discovered that this effect was produced by the circumstance alluded to, I hastened to cancel it – not from any personal feeling of terror, or repentance, but from the sincere desire of doing all the good & conferring all the pleasure which might flow from so obscure a person as myself.

In fact only thirteen lines of the poem, and the final paragraph of the preface, were omitted or revised on account of the theme of incest, while another fifty lines were changed for other reasons, in particular to avoid the charge of blasphemy. Line 4,714, for example, 'How Atheists and Republicans can die', was revised to 'How those who love, yet fear not, dare to die'.

Early in 1818, impatient at not having received copies of *The Revolt of Islam*, as the poem was now re-titled, Shelley asked for six copies, stressed that he ought already to have substituted them for copies of the earlier printing, and urged the need for advertisements in which *Alastor* should also be mentioned. A few days later, disappointed by the poor initial response of the book-sellers, he asked Munday to stock the book and advertise it in Oxford, so harking back to his tiny original readership there. Inevitably he became deeply discouraged. 'I suppose at present that it scarcely sells at all', he wrote on 22 January, ' – If you see any reviews or notices of it in any periodical paper pray send it me, – it is part of my reward – the amusement of hearing the abuse of the bigots.'[25]

In fact the first review was all that any young poet could hope for. Having quoted seventy-two lines from the poem in the *Examiner* of 30 November, Hunt again quoted liberally from it on 25 January and then devoted no fewer than three notices in sub-sequent issues to an account of this 'extraordinary production'.[26] He gives an account of the story, explaining the allegory of Canto I as he does so, and is explicit about the poet's moral and political objectives. 'If the author's genius reminds us of any other poets', he remarks at one point, 'it is of two very opposite ones, Lucretius and Dante.' This long review, which exemplifies Hunt's almost clairvoyant skill as a critic of new poetry, is the more telling because it acknowledges the poem's faults, 'obscurity, inartificial and yet not natural economy, violation of costume, and too great a sameness and gratuitousness of image and metaphor, and of image and metaphor too drawn from the elements, particularly the sea'. 'The book is full of humanity', it continues, 'and yet it certainly does not go the best way to work of appealing to it, because it does not appeal to it through the medium of its common knowledges . . . We have no doubt he is destined to be one of the leading spirits of his age, and indeed has already fallen into his place as such; but however resolute as to his object, he will only be doing it justice to take the most effectual means in his power to forward it.' Hunt's is the only review which Shelley can have seen before he left England for the last time in March of the same year. It is appropriate that he should have spent his final evening with its author, yet one phrase in the review must have sunk into his mind, as the answer to the question he had put to the reading public: 'the work', Hunt had written, 'cannot possibly become popular'.

Few contrasts could be more striking than that between the reputation of Shelley as he left for Italy and that of Byron two years before. While the personal life of each of them had been disastrous, Byron's notoriety merely served to whet the public's interest in his poetry, so that anything he wrote, in verse or prose, was certain of the widest circulation. For all his genius, he had more of the ordinary man about him than Shelley: he had captured the public with the first two Cantos of *Childe Harold's Pilgrimage* and the Eastern Tales, and in John Murray and his '*knowing ones*' he had strong and influential advisers and backers. Charles and James Ollier, on the other hand, for all the credit they deserve as the publishers of the *Poems* of Keats and of important work by Hunt and by Charles Lamb, carried little weight in the worldly world of publishing: they had no Review, their premises were not a literary centre. In September 1819 Shelley was to instruct the Olliers to send a copy of any work of his to Hunt, Godwin, Hogg, Peacock, Keats, Moore, Horace Smith and Lord Byron '(at Murrays)'.[27] The last address is peculiarly revealing: while Shelley could look to a remarkable circle of friends and acquaintances as an inner circle of readers, it was a group of men less influential than that to which Byron had access. Shelley's letters make it clear that his sense of failure was sharpened by the inevitable contrast with Byron, while his new wife's *Frankenstein* was soon to be selling as no volume of his was ever to sell, in his lifetime.

It would have been understandable if Shelley had relapsed into silence, but the escape from his troubles in England and the beauty of Italy provided new stimulus and encouragement. 'The bright blue sky of Rome', as he wrote in the preface to *Prometheus Unbound*, 'and the effect of the vigorous awakening spring in that divinest climate, and the new life with which it drenches the spirits even to intoxication, were the inspiration of this drama.' Although he did not believe himself endowed with dramatic talent, he had been reading the Greek dramatists and thinking about the drama more intensely than before. Having begun a tragedy on the madness of Tasso, and considered Job as a tragic hero, he decided to take as his protagonist Prometheus, 'the Champion . . . of mankind', and to show his conflict with Jupiter, the Oppressor, in a new light. He describes Prometheus as 'the type of the highest perfection of moral and intellectual nature, impelled by the purest and truest motives to the best and noblest ends'. Fully to understand the work and its meaning we must recall that Shelley believed that the writers of his age were the forerunners of a great revolution, 'some unimagined change in our social condition or the opinions which cement it'. Acknowledging what one of his critics had termed 'a passion for reforming the world', he wrote this lyrical drama 'to familiarise the highly refined imagination of the more select classes of poetical readers with beautiful idealisms of moral excellence'. While he knew that he had written a masterpiece, he also knew that in taking Æschylus as his original he was depriving himself of any possibility of a wide readership. In the words of Mary Shelley, 'The father of Greek tragedy does not possess the pathos of Sophocles, nor the variety and tenderness of Euripides; the interest on which he founds his dramas is often elevated above human vicissitudes into the mighty passions and throes of gods and demi-gods: such fascinated the abstract imagination of Shelley.'[28]

After *Prometheus*, which he described as 'written only for the elect', as a work which 'if I may judge by its merits, . . . cannot sell beyond twenty copies', and even (almost two years later) as 'never intended for more than 5 or 6 persons',[29] Shelley decided to make an attempt at the acting drama. In July 1819 he told Peacock that *The Cenci* was based on a story well known in Italy which seemed to him eminently dramatic, and expressed the hope that its turning on a father's incestuous passion for his daughter would not militate against its representation on the stage, as he had been at pains to treat the subject with 'peculiar delicacy'.[30] The following month he assured Hunt that this new play was 'totally different' from anything that might have been expected of him, 'of a more popular kind', words echoed in a letter to Ollier in September. He asked Peacock 'to procure . . . its presentation at Covent Garden', pointing out that the principal role of Beatrice was 'precisely fitted for Miss O'Neil, & it might even seem to have been written for her' and confessing that he would have liked Kean to have played the part of Count Cenci, had that been possible. 'I think you know some of the people of that theatre', he wrote rather vaguely, 'or at least some one who knows them, & when you have read the play, you may say enough perhaps to induce them not to reject it without consideration'. He believed that, if the play was accepted, it would help to have an account of the historical Count Cenci published in the press, to make it clear that he himself was not responsible for 'the unexpected horror of the story'. He brushed aside, as having arrived too late, certain suggestions about the handling of the subject which Peacock sent him, and had the play printed in Italy to make it easier for the people at the theatre to read it and appreciate its full merit.

No one but Shelley would have based a drama intended for popularity in the theatre of that day on the subject which he chose. For all his towering imaginative and intellectual powers, he never sufficiently grasped that everything has a context, and that part of the context is human nature at a given time and in a given place.

If the belief that *The Cenci* was written 'without any of the

peculiar feelings & opinions which characterize my other compositions'[31] was characteristic of Shelley in its lack of self-
knowledge, the dedication to Hunt was characteristic in its
generosity of spirit and its lack of all tactical sense. Shelley's
reference to the 'patient and irreconcilable enmity with
domestic and political tyranny and imposture' which the two
men shared prepares the reader for the discovery that this new
work differs less completely from its precursors than the poet
himself seems to have supposed. While he states in the preface
that he has tried to represent the characters as they must
actually have been, and has sought 'to avoid the error of making
them actuated by my own conceptions of right or wrong, false or
true', it is obvious that he gives the incidents an interpretation of
his own, as we are presented with yet another account of the conflict between the forces of Tyranny and those of Liberty. The
most striking alteration is that he makes Count Cenci a devout
Catholic, whereas he had commonly been represented as an
atheist. It is relevant to remember a remarkable comment he had
made to Thomas Hookham in 1812: 'I am determined to apply
myself to a study that is hateful & disgusting to my very soul, but
which is above all studies necessary for him who would be
listened to as a mender of antiquated abuses. – I mean that
record of crimes & miseries – History.'

Although it is a sign of remarkable poetic versatility to have
been able to write in an idiom so different from that of *Prometheus
Unbound* (to say nothing of *Julian and Maddalo*)[32] at the same point
in his life, there is a further respect in which *The Cenci* differs less
than Shelley supposed from his other writings. While it is true,
as he claimed, that he had 'avoided with great care . . . what is
commonly called mere poetry',[33] and while the style was calculated to cause little difficulty to any reader or theatre-goer
familiar with Shakespeare and his contemporaries, who are
echoed only too frequently, the subject of incest, delicately as it
may be handled, here takes on a more repulsive form than it had
in *Laon and Cythna*. It is easy to see why the story of Cenci and his
daughter appealed to Shelley, and it would no doubt have
appealed to Webster or Tourneur; but as Jeffrey had pointed out
in relation to *Manfred*,[34] incest was no longer an acceptable
dramatic theme. It is yet another sign of Shelley's inability to
understand the public that he persisted in believing that *The*

Cenci had 'all the capacities for being popular'.[35] In December 1819 he asked Ollier if it had been accepted for production, telling him to publish the play if it had not. His friends (he told him in a later letter) had great hopes that it would succeed 'as a publication'. He wrote to Leigh Hunt that it had been written 'with a certain view to popularity a view to which I sacrificed my own peculiar notions in a certain sort by treating of any subject the basis of which is moral error'. He was astonished that it had been refused at Drury Lane,[36] 'although expressly written for theatrical exhibition' and (in his own view) 'singularly fitted for the stage'.[37] More than a century was to elapse before the first public performance took place.

Hunt immediately saluted *The Cenci* as 'undoubtedly the greatest dramatic production of the day'[38] and later gave a great deal of space in the *Indicator* to the story on which the tragedy was based, and to the work itself. While the *Monthly Magazine* and the *Literary Gazette* attacked it, *The Cenci* received much more favourable treatment in other periodicals, and proved more successful than any of Shelley's earlier productions. Alone of his publications, *The Cenci* reached an authorised second edition in his lifetime; yet we have only to remember that the first edition consisted of a mere 250 copies to realise that he had achieved no more than a *succès d'estime*. It may be recalled that Murray had sold 10,000 copies of *The Corsair* on the day of publication, and 25,000 in a little over a month.

It is remarkable that Act IV of *Prometheus* was written after *The Cenci*, as if Shelley reacted from the strain of dealing with realities by adding a more abstract conclusion to a 'Lyrical Drama' which was already sufficiently abstract. He had been wounded by the *Quarterly*'s review of *The Revolt of Islam*,[39] while Ollier's depressing account of his sales led him to comment that he was inclined to think he wrote 'less for the public than for myself'. Certainly Act IV, described by Mary Shelley as 'a sort of hymn of rejoicing in the fulfilment of the prophecies with regard to Prometheus',[40] is a work which only the συνετοί could be expected to comprehend. There are (of course) no human characters, and while the blank verse spoken by Panthea and Ione contains wonderful lines – 'Sweet as a singing rain of silver dew' – and scenes that Blake might have been able to illustrate, the lyrical passages sung by 'unseen Spirits', 'A Train of dark

Forms and Shadows', and a 'Semichorus of Hours' frequently soar beyond the normal range of the human ear. Hunt was shrewd when he described it as an *'odi-profanum . . . poem'*, a masterpiece which even he despaired of rendering 'at all recommendable to readers in general'.[41]

Shelley's letters are full of contrasts between his two dramatic works. On 6 March 1820 he told Ollier that *Prometheus Unbound* was his 'favourite poem', adding: ' "Cenci" is written for the multitude, and ought to sell well.'[42] On 20 July, commenting that he was not sure whether it was wise 'to affect variety in compositions, or whether the attempt to excel in many ways does not debar from excellence in one particular kind', he told Medwin that *Prometheus Unbound* was 'of a totally different character' from *The Cenci*, a point he repeated in a letter to Keats a week later. The following year, when he told Peacock that he was 'devising literary plans of some magnitude' and complained that 'nothing is so difficult and unwelcome as to write without a confidence of finding readers', he added: 'if my play of "The Cenci" found none or few, I despair of ever producing anything that shall merit them'. 'For "Prometheus" I expect and desire no great sale', he wrote to Ollier the next day. ' "The Cenci" ought to have been popular.'

In November 1819 Shelley had told Hunt that *The Mask of Anarchy*, 'Written on the Occasion of the Massacre at Manchester', was of 'the exoteric species',[43] a description which explains why it was intended for the *Examiner* and not the *Indicator*. Whereas the latter periodical was intended to have 'nothing temporary . . . in it, political or critical',[44] the former was essentially political, supporting parliamentary reform, 'freedom from superstition', and liberal views in general: in 1812 Bentham had calculated that it sold between 7,000 and 8,000 copies.

Shelley was an excellent classicist, and he could not have used the word 'exoteric' without reference to the commentators on Aristotle who had divided his writings into the esoteric and the exoteric – those for insiders (his own pupils) and those for outsiders (a wider public).[45] Whereas almost everything that Shelley had hitherto written in verse, apart from *The Cenci*, had been esoteric, and published expensively, the verses in which he expressed his indignation on receiving 'the terrible and important news of Manchester',[46] which he regarded as 'the distant thunders of the terrible storm which is approaching', were written (as Mary Shelley was to point out) 'for the people', and in a style admirably suited to a large audience:

> I met Murder on the way –
> He had a mask like Castlereagh –
> Very smooth he looked, yet grim;
> Seven blood-hounds followed him.

It is a characteristically Shelleyan irony that Hunt did not dare to print the poem, which remained unpublished until the year of the Reform Act.

In his search for a wider audience Shelley turned again to prose. He wrote a long and powerful letter to Hunt, as editor of the *Examiner*, protesting against the outcome of the trial of Richard Carlile, a disciple of Tom Paine who had been severely punished for 'blasphemous libel'; but Hunt did not dare to publish it.[47] A similar fate awaited *A Philosophical View of Reform*, which Shelley described as 'a commonplace kind of book' that was intended to be 'instructive and readable . . . appealing from the passions to the reason of men'.[48] A century was to elapse before this, his clearest statement of his mature philosophical views, was to find its way into print.

Hunt was no longer the only critic to praise Shelley's work, and while reviewers were apt to censure his opinions even as they praised his poetic genius, the example of Byron proved that a mixed reaction was compatible with the extreme of celebrity.[49] It is not surprising that Shelley became more and more dissatisfied with Ollier,[50] more and more regretful that there was 'no other bookseller, upon whom I can depend for publishing any of my works'; but his comment that publishers were 'all rogues', understandable as it is, was unfair to a small firm that was losing money by publishing his poems. In the same letter he asked Hunt whether he knew of any bookseller who would 'publish a little volume of *popular songs* wholly political, & destined to awaken & direct the imagination of the reformers. I see you smile' – he added – 'but answer my question.' He was essaying poems of very different kinds. He told Ollier that if *Julian and Maddalo* were to be published, it must be without his name, and 'in some unostentatious form', because it was an attempt of a new kind which would not 'harmonize'[51] with *Prometheus Unbound*. *The Witch of Atlas*, written in relief at escaping from the realities of *The Cenci* and in spite of Mary's urgings to remember the reading public and its interests, is in another style again, making no direct contact with reality. As for *Œdipus Tyrannus or Swellfoot the Tyrant*, a *jeu d'esprit* published anonymously by a certain J. Johnston of Cheapside (with the baffling imprint 'C.F. Seyfang'), that had to be withdrawn immediately under threat of prosecution from the Society for the Suppression of Vice. It is said that seven copies were sold. 'I wonder why I write verses', Shelley wrote to Peacock in July, 'for nobody reads them.' Six months later he was a little more optimistic, as a result of the reception of *The Cenci*, and we find him telling Ollier that if he wrote more his next attempt would be a drama (*Charles the First*), in which he would attend to the advice of his critics 'to a certain degree'; but he immediately adds that he is uncertain whether he will write more: 'I could be content either with the Hell or the Paradise of poetry; but the torments of its purgatory vex me, without exciting my power sufficiently to put an end to the vexation.'

While he had not abandoned the ambition of writing poetry which many people would read, we are not surprised to find Shelley, early the following year, producing a poem 'to be published' (as he told Ollier) 'simply for the esoteric few', in an edition of 100 copies: 'it would give me no pleasure that the vulgar should read it'.[52] The introductory lines, which are almost a literal translation from a canzone of Dante's, are peculiarly appropriate:

> My Song, I fear that thou wilt find but few
> Who fitly shall conceive thy reasoning.

No comment on the audience he envisaged for this poem could be more apt than that in a letter to John Gisborne: 'The Epipsychidion is a mystery . . . I desired Ollier not to circulate this piece except to the Σύνετοι, and even they it seems are inclined to approximate me to the circle of a servant girl & her sweetheart.' Shelley was of course concealing the 'flesh & blood' reality of Emilia Viviani – 'As to real flesh & blood, you know that I do not deal in those articles, – you might as well go to a gin-shop for a leg of mutton, as expect any thing human or earthly from me' – yet the word from Pindar is highly significant. He was classing himself with the poets who write for a small audience of 'Understanders'.

It was about this time that he planned and wrote his reply to Peacock's provocative essay, 'The Four Ages of Poetry'. No one has ever written more nobly, or more justly, of the importance of poetry in human life than the author of 'A Defence of Poetry', and we are bound to notice that this very importance, and the wide interpretation which he gives the word 'Poetry' (without in any way derogating from the centrality of poetry written in verse) must have made his own failure to reach an audience all the harder to bear. The 'Defence' was intended as the first of two or three parts of a longer essay, but the second number of *Ollier's Literary Miscellany*, for which it had been written, failed to appear, and the 'Defence' itself remained unpublished until 1840.

While he was failing to reach the public with poetry and prose in which he had attained the maturity of his genius, Shelley had the disagreeable experience of hearing that William Clark, 'one of the low booksellers in the Strand', had republished – or rather published – *Queen Mab*, against his wishes and consent.[53] He wrote to Ollier to say that he had not seen the poem for some years, and that so far as he could remember it was 'villainous trash', and he directed an attorney to apply for an injunction to restrain the sale, though he had no expectation of success. The *Examiner* for 15 July carried a letter in which he protested against this unauthorised publication, 'not so much from literary vanity, as because I fear it is better fitted to injure than to serve the cause of freedom'. It is revealing that he should have exaggerated his youth at the time of composition, saying that he was eighteen, whereas he had been nineteen or twenty. While he may have felt some natural pleasure at the report that one of his poems was said to be 'selling . . . by thousands' (an absurd exaggeration), recent scholars who welcome this unauthorised publication as a political gesture have paid too little attention to its immediate effect on Shelley's reputation at a critical moment in his career. It is true that his position was very different from that of Dryden when his enemies had republished his 'Heroique Stanza's' on Cromwell, or that of Southey when an unauthorised edition of *Wat Tyler* made its appearance: Clark did not act from malice: Shelley had not radically altered his views and was not open to the charge of having become a turncoat. On the contrary, the views which he was now expressing in great poetry were so close to those which he had expressed a few years before in 'prentice work that Clark's action not merely drew attention to a poem which he had long put behind him but was also likely to encourage a reductive reading of his mature work as simply that of a revolutionary writing in verse. In the event Clark was obliged to withdraw the edition after some fifty copies had been sold, as a result of a prosecution by the Society for the Suppression of Vice; but in the following years Richard Carlile, the man in whose defence Shelley had written in the *Examiner*, a courageous publisher who occupies an honourable place in the history of the struggle for the liberty of the press, proceeded to publish several cheap editions. Whatever political influence these piracies may have had it is difficult to avoid the conclusion that their immediate influence on Shelley's reputation as a poet must have been unfavourable.

By the time news of Clark's edition had reached Italy Shelley had completed one of the masterpieces for which we now remember him, his elegy on a 'great genius whom envy & ingratitude scourged out of the world'.[54] While Shelley is wrong in his account of the reason for the death of Keats, this subject of 'human interest and passion' led to his writing one of the poems in which an actual event enabled him to build a bridge between the world of everyday experience and the universe of his own imagination and intellect. While he was still at work on *Adonais* he described it as 'a highly wrought *piece of art*, perhaps better in point of composition than any thing I have written', adding that the Gisbornes were among 'the very few persons who will be interested in it and understand it'. He considered the poem 'little adapted for popularity', and wrote revealingly to Horace Smith: 'I am glad you like "Adonais", and, particularly, that you do not think it metaphysical, which I was afraid it was ... I wrote, as usual, *with a total ignorance of the effect that I should produce.*'

By this point in the chapter the words I have italicised will be less surprising than they would otherwise have been, yet we have only to recall the traditional Art of Poetry, as understood from the days of classical antiquity onwards, to realise how astonishing it is that such a remark should have been made by a great

112

poet in the plenitude of his powers. As we have seen, Dryden never wrote a line without considering the effect it would have on his readers, and much the same was surely true of Chaucer, as it was of Pope – and indeed of Byron. Shelley never came to terms with the elementary fact that it is part of a poet's task to be constantly aware of the likely reactions of his audience. 'The poetry of your "Adonais" is very beautiful', Peacock wrote; 'but when you write you never think of your audience. The number who understand you, and sympathise with you, is very small. If you would consider who and what the readers of poetry are, and adapt your compositions to the depth of their understandings and the current of their sympathies, you would attain the highest degree of poetical fame.'[55] It is a penetrating remark, however strange it may seem when made by the author of an essay in which it is stated that modern poets must write for an audience which is not only continually diminishing in size but also sinking 'lower and lower in the comparison of intellectual acquirement'. A similar pessimism about the position of the nineteenth-century poet had been expressed by Peacock in a letter which reached Shelley before the essay itself. 'Considering poetical reputation as a prize to be obtained by a certain species of exertion', Peacock had written, 'and that the sort of thing which obtains this prize is the drivelling doggrel published under the name of Barry Cornwall, I think but one conclusion possible, that to a rational ambition poetical reputation is not only not to be desired, but most earnestly to be deprecated.'

During the last year of his life Shelley was frequently assailed by doubts. 'I despair of rivalling Lord Byron', he wrote shortly after completing *Adonais*, ' . . . and there is no other with whom it is worth contending'.[56] A few days later he told Peacock that it offended him to see himself 'classed among those who have no name': 'If I cannot be something better, I had rather be nothing, and the accursed cause to the downfall of which I dedicated what powers I may have had – flourishes like a cedar.' 'I have no confidence', he complained in December, 'and [to] . . . put forth thoughts without sympathy is unprofitable vanity.'

He showed considerable determination by continuing to write. In September he had told Ollier, from whom he had lost all hope of breaking away, that he was 'full of great plans', one of them a tragedy on Charles I.[57] He also intended to 'write a Symposium', while in November Ollier received *Hellas*, with a letter in which Shelley explained that its success must depend on immediate publication: the hope that it might be out by Christmas was an extraordinary manifestation of optimism, even for Shelley. Ollier must have hesitated more than once over a work which contains so clear a statement of atheism. It is no wonder that he omitted the penultimate paragraph of the preface, which begins with the words 'Should the English people ever become free' and continues by describing the age as that of 'the war of the oppressed against the oppressors, and every one of those ringleaders of the privileged gangs of murderers and swindlers, called Sovereigns'. Yet he had the courage to publish the work, which appeared as early as February 1822, and Shelley was pleased with the production, though he realised that this 'sort of imitation of the Persae of Æschylus, full of lyrical poetry',[58] could not possibly appeal to a large audience.

He was now in full command of the technical skill to express his profound imaginative vision, as we know from 'The Triumph of Life' and other poems and fragments which Mary was to include in the *Posthumous Poems*. What he lacked was the impulse which would have been provided by a more considerable degree of public acknowledgement. 'I try to be what I might have been', he wrote to John Gisborne. 'I can write nothing', he confessed to Hunt in January 1822, '& if Adonais had no success & excited no interest what incentive can I have to write?' In May he told Horace Smith that 'the sun has extinguished the glowworm': for all his admiration for *Don Juan* – and no poet of the age was a more generous or discerning critic of his rivals – Shelley knew very well that he too was a great poet. But he had no encouragement except that provided by his wife, by Hunt, and by a tiny band of friends and appreciative reviewers. 'I write little now', he told Gisborne three weeks before his death. 'It is impossible to compose except under the strong excitement of an assurance of finding sympathy in what you write . . . Lord Byron is in this respect fortunate. He touched a chord to which a million hearts responded, and the coarse music which he produced to please them disciplined him to the perfection to which he now approaches.'

A careful study of the reviews and other evidence strongly suggests that Shelley would have had less reason for despair if he had lived a few years longer. A good deal of understanding was shown by certain of the reviewers of the *Posthumous Poems* in 1824 and of the Galignani edition five years later, and very soon his work was exerting an important influence on two young poets as different from each other as Tennyson and Browning. While he was the only one of the six poets considered in this volume not to have attained celebrity during his lifetime, it must be remembered that he died younger than the others, and that it is very rare for a poet in his twenties to attain the celebrity which Pope had attained by the end of his third decade – to say nothing of the instant fame which came to Byron when he published the first two Cantos of *Childe Harold's Pilgrimage* at the age of twenty-four.

We know from his letters that Shelley, like almost every poet, hoped to be famous after his death. 'I *will* live beyond this life', he had written to Elizabeth Hitchener as early as 1811.[59] The following year he told Godwin that he would 'look to events in which it will be impossible that I can share, and make myself the cause of an effect which will take place ages after *I* shall have mouldered into dust'. Later he wrote to Byron, with reference to Canto III of *Childe Harold*, 'Is there nothing in the hope of being the parent of greatness, and of goodness, which is destined, perhaps, to expand indefinitely?' – a clear echo of his own aspiration. He had told Godwin that he had written *Laon and Cythna* with a sense of the precariousness of his own life, 'resolved to leave some record of myself', adding: 'Much of what the volume contains was written with the same feeling, as real, though not so prophetic, as the communications of a dying man', a description particularly apt in relation to the urgent speed of the verse in many of his poems. In a despondent letter he once told the Gisbornes that 'The seeking of a sympathy with the unborn and the unknown is a feeble mode of allaying the love within us; and even that is beyond the grasp of so weak an aspirant as I', but later he remarked to them that 'The decision of the cause whether or no *I* am a poet is removed from the present time to the hour when our posterity shall assemble.'

No poet has ever given more eloquent expression to the hope that his thoughts might be driven 'over the universe' after his death than the author of the 'Ode to the West Wind'. It was ironical, however, that Shelley's thoughts were first scattered widely in the immature form in which they are expressed in *Queen Mab*, while readers who were primarily interested in his poetry tended to concentrate on the lyrics which had often been written in moments of depression – solitary utterances composed with little thought of any audience: poems which illustrate his description of the poet as 'a nightingale, who sits in darkness and sings to cheer its own solitude with sweet sounds.'[60] It is true that he goes on to assume that the nightingale has auditors, but they do not seem to be numerous, or near at hand, or in any way encouraging to the singer. While it is astonishing that Shelley achieved so much, we are bound to agree with Mary that though he did not – at least latterly – 'expect sympathy and approbation from the public . . . the want of it took away a portion of the ardour that ought to have sustained him while writing':

Chameleons feed on light and air:
Poets' food is love and fame.

V · TENNYSON
Laureate to Victoria

WHEN Tennyson was persuaded to compete for the Chancellor's Gold Medal at Cambridge, and won it with 'Timbuctoo', he refused to recite the poem in the Senate House, as was customary, but persuaded a friend to read it for him. He was always to be in two minds, he was always to hate publishing, he was always to owe a great deal to his friends, he was always to be worried about the reactions of his audience.

He belonged to a family of poets, and his first audience had been his family. His father, 'who was a sort of Poet himself',[1] had a deep interest in classical metres which he transmitted to his son. Two of Alfred's brothers published volumes of their own: when old Mrs Tennyson boasted that she was the mother of the Laureate she would often add that she had two other sons who had also 'written some very beautiful verses'.[2] Their sisters too were passionately interested in poetry: they formed a circle of friends who called themselves 'The Husks' and talked and wrote about it incessantly. When we read of the unhappy side of their family life, the perpetual worry about their father, the inherited tendencies to epilepsy and melancholy, the overcrowding at the rectory and the occasional financial stringencies, we should also remember the supportive influence of being one of a close family group constantly concerned with poetry. The fact that the first admirers of Tennyson's verse heard him reciting it aloud does a good deal to explain the remarkable importance of the auditory element in his work, and his morbid sensitivity to outside criticism.

In the introductory lines to 'Morte d'Arthur' he describes the 'Deep-chested music' of the poet 'mouthing out his hollow oes and aes', and the memoirs of eminent Victorians are full of accounts of what his wife was to term 'the glamour of his reading'.[3] His grandson described it as 'a deep-voiced swinging chant in which rhythm and vowel sounds were emphasized at the expense of the ordinary dramatic emphasis and inflexion'.

Tennyson would never admit that anyone but himself could read his poems as they were meant to be read. Once he told William Allingham that he wished there were 'some fixed way of indicating a poet's intention as to the pronunciation of his verses. "It doesn't matter so much (he said) in poetry written for the intellect – as much of Browning's is, perhaps; but in mine it's necessary to know how to sound it properly" '[4] – so voicing a desire shared by many poets but also involuntarily suggesting something curious about his view of the nature of poetry. He was particularly given to reading – or performing – *Maud*: Jane Welsh Carlyle claimed that he read it to her three times in succession, and on another occasion he read it to a young woman and then assured her (as he sat her on his knee) that 'Many may have written as well as that, but nothing that ever sounded so well.'[5] He did not believe that one of his poems had been communicated if it had not been heard in his own voice.

One has only to recall the early illustrations of Chaucer reading his work to an aristocratic audience, and to reflect on the ubiquitous irony and the wealth of subtle allusions in his verse, to become aware of the possibility of a very different relationship between poet and audience. Tennyson's audience was expected simply to listen and to admire, in the manner of his father's congregation as he rolled out the sonorous periods of one of his sermons. One of his fears about publication was that those who could not hear his voice would miss an all-important element of the poetry. He would have been delighted to be able to record his readings, as a modern poet can do: in fact he was one of the first poets to make the attempt, but the old voice of the ruined recordings can give us only the faintest impression of the powerful harmonies of the poet at his best.

It is appropriate that his first publication was a family affair, *Poems, By Two Brothers*, in which he and Frederick were joined by Charles. It is not surprising that he omitted work which we now find more interesting than anything he included because he considered it 'too much out of the common for the public taste'. He viewed the public with apprehension, describing it to his uncle as 'a many-headed Monster'.[6]

For a young man who had seldom been more than twenty miles from home the transition to Cambridge might well have proved traumatic; but Tennyson was fortunate in having been preceded by the gifted Frederick, who had already won a prize for a Greek ode, and while we know very little about his first terms at Trinity he was soon to make his mark there. Nothing could reflect more credit on the College than the fact that this diffident, gifted, awkward, arrogant young man, so striking in appearance and so unconventional in manner, was soon welcomed into a group which regarded itself as the élite of the most distinguished college in the greatest of all universities. The essential seriousness of the Apostles, a club to which he belonged only briefly but whose members continued to be the closest of his friends, suited Tennyson, while their questing intellects served admirably to broaden the horizons of a youth brought up in a provincial rectory. They were highly characteristic of their time, members of the upper middle class which was to dominate the country throughout the Victorian period. As one or two poems bear witness, Tennyson felt himself intellectually inferior to several of his new friends. Like Keats, he was not 'a consequitive Man':[7] in a university devoted to mathematics he believed, in words he was later to put into the mouth of an 'Ancient Sage', that 'nothing worthy proving can be proven': and he completely lacked the quick wit of the debater. Yet by 1830 one of the Apostles described him as 'truly one of the mighty of the earth'.

Such support was of particular importance because poetry was at a discount at this time. In *England and the English* Bulwer Lytton was shortly to write of 'the more than natural distaste for poetry that succeeded the death of Byron': 'With a sigh we turned to the actual and practical career of life: we awoke from the morbid, the passionate, the dreaming, "the moonlight and the dimness of the mind", and by a natural reaction addressed ourselves to the active and daily objects which lay before us'.[8] It was Tennyson's good fortune that his friends, deeply concerned as they were with 'the actual and practical career of life' in the period immediately preceding the Reform Act, were also deeply interested in poetry. Like his own family, they loved to listen to him reading or reciting his poems: like his family, they clearly sensed that a little criticism would go a long way with him. This second audience, like the first, encountered his poetry as an auditory experience: 'it is necessary to hear him read it before you can perceive the melody', as one of them commented.[9]

While all poetry of course exists to be read aloud, as all music exists to be played, it remains true that the element of sound in Tennyson's verse is exceptionally important: perhaps too important at times. As far as we know none of the men to whom Pope showed his *Pastorals* had an opportunity of hearing him reading them, and the beauty of the manuscript makes it evident that he had prepared them for reading by others. Tennyson, on the other hand, often refrained from writing his poems down at all, and if he lost what he had written he had no difficulty in recalling it. When he recited the first version of 'The Lotos-Eaters' – no doubt hanging 'sleepily over the syllables'[10] – Arthur Henry Hallam sat behind him and tried to jot it down.

The meeting with Hallam was the most important event in Tennyson's life. The whole family took to him: Frederick was later to comment that 'Never was there a human being better calculated to sympathize with and make allowances for those . . . feelings to which we are liable.'[11] It is as appropriate that he and Tennyson should have proposed to publish a joint volume of poems, 'as a sort of seal of our friendship'[12] (so that *Poems, By Two Brothers* would have been followed by *Poems, by Two Friends*) as that Hallam should have become the accepted suitor of Emily Tennyson. When Hallam's poems were already in print his father exercised his veto, but nothing could prevent his son from being the greatest influence on Tennyson for the brief remainder of his own life and the long decades of Tennyson's.

While Hallam's poems circulated privately, Tennyson's *Poems, Chiefly Lyrical* were published in 1830. If we did not know that many of these had been written during his time at Trinity it would be tempting to explain the weaknesses of the collection by saying that Tennyson had not yet escaped from the troubled womb of the rectory. While two or three of them, notably 'Supposed Confessions of a Second-Rate Sensitive Mind', have an obvious connection with Cambridge, for the most part the verses and the Apostles seem to belong to different worlds. Here is part of the opening poem, 'Claribel':

> Her song the lintwhite swelleth,
> The clearvoiced mavis dwelleth,
> The fledgling throstle lispeth,
> The slumbrous wave outwelleth,
> The babbling runnel crispeth,

> The hollow grot replieth
> Where Claribel low-lieth.

What *are* we to make of 'The fledgling throstle lispeth'[13] and all those spitting terminations in 'eth'? The fact that this poem, 'Claribel', is sub-titled 'A Melody', shows that Tennyson knew what he was doing; but why was he doing it? When he began another poem 'Thy tuwhits are lulled, I wot' did it not occur to him that while the tone of his recitation might have made it clear to his listeners that this was no more than a light-hearted *jeu d'esprit*, his readers could only find it absurd? In general these pieces are far too 'poetical' to be poems. They are spangled with poetical words as a cheap dress may be spangled with *diamanté*. Adjectives are ubiquitous and intrusive: in ten lines of one stanza[14] the single verb 'are' is weighed down with 'diamonded', 'griding', 'starry', 'troublous', 'sheeny' and half a dozen more. It is true that poetry is the use of language in which the sound becomes part of the meaning, but here we find a marked hypertrophy of sound and a corresponding atrophy of total meaning.

The contrast between 'Claribel' and the last poem in the volume, with its Greek title and its embarrassingly facetious footnote,[15] makes it evident that Tennyson had no clear idea of the audience for which he was writing. John Stuart Mill, who recognised the merit of 'Mariana', had no doubt that 'The May Queen' was 'fitted for a more extensive popularity'.[16] Many of the poems differ from the ordinary Album verse of the day in little but their greater metrical sophistication. There is nothing in the volume to shock the most genteel of readers: at a time of life when Donne had written the earliest of his *Songs and Sonnets* and Byron had so recently been recommending the pleasures of making love by daylight, Tennyson's Muse is almost embarrassingly chaste. Of the women he describes or writes about the only one with any reality is 'Isabel', in a poem we now know to have been inspired by his mother.

While W.J. Fox and Leigh Hunt both wrote enthusiastically about *Poems, Chiefly Lyrical*, the most important review was that by Hallam.[17] It is best understood as a skilful piece of rhetoric calculated to achieve three objectives: to place Tennyson in the appropriate tradition of English poetry: to flatter readers with the conviction that if they admired his poems they would become members of a distinguished avant-garde: and above all to encourage a poet whom he loved, and in whose genius he unquestioningly believed. It is no more a simple puff than it is a piece of impartial criticism. It could not have been written by a man who know only the poems in the book. It is the work of a friend who had often heard Tennyson reciting his verse, a critic (himself a poet) who had more than a shadowy notion of the direction in which the new poet was moving.

It is not surprising that John Wilson was provoked by such exaggerated praise. Writing in *Blackwood's* (as 'Christopher North') he recognised that 'Alfred Tennyson is a poet' but rightly (if a little unkindly) described him as 'the Pet of a Coterie'.[18] Where he was wrong was in describing his friends as his worst enemies. Tennyson's friends must have been well aware of some at least of his limitations; but they knew, as the reviewer did not, that any attempt at trenchant criticism would be more likely to silence him than to assist in his development.

But for Hallam, Tennyson would not have taken the continental journey which was to have such memorable results for his poetry, nor would he have published another volume within three years. The nature of the inspiration he derived from his travels is of particular interest: whereas Hallam returned 'brimful of adventures and anecdotes of a satirical description',[19] Tennyson said little, contenting himself with playful reflections on the accuracy of his friend. He brought back memories of his own feelings and of the Pyrenaean scenery which was to prove so important to both 'Œnone' and 'The Lotos-Eaters'. It is easy to understand why Hallam wanted to see such poems in print as soon as possible: whether a longer period of preparation would have been advisable must remain an open speculation.

Unlike the previous volume, *Poems* has obvious links with the Apostles. It opens with the sonnet 'Mine be the strength of spirit fierce and free',[20] and contains three sonnets on political affairs which are obviously the work of an admirer of Milton's 'On the late Massacre in Piedmont'. 'The Palace of Art' was inspired by Trench's observation that 'we cannot live in Art' and seeks to embody Tennyson's belief 'that the Godlike life is with man and for man'. The lines 'To J.S.' have a restrained eloquence which anticipates *In Memoriam*. We also find a number of narrative poems calculated to appeal to a wide range of readers, from 'The

Lady of Shalott' (an expression of the poet's own dilemma which can so readily be taken simply as a narrative) to 'Mariana in the South' and 'The Miller's Daughter'. At the last moment Tennyson withdrew 'The Lover's Tale', remarking that 'though I think it might conduce towards making me popular, yet to my eye it spoils the completeness of the book and is better away': a decision which drove Hallam to protest that he must be 'point-blank mad'.[21] As well as one or two absurd poems – above all 'O darling room', which gave Croker so easy an opening[22] – the volume also contains a handful of singularly unconvincing love-poems of the Album sort. The love-poems supposed to be spoken by women make a very different impression. 'O Love, Love, Love', 'The Sisters', 'The May Queen' and above all 'Œnone' itself might have for their motto two lines from 'A Dream of Fair Women':

> Beauty and anguish walking hand in hand
> The downward slope to death.[23]

Moxon cannot have been hopeful, since he printed only 450 copies, as against the 600 copies of *Poems, Chiefly Lyrical* too optimistically printed by Effingham Wilson. When almost a hundred were sold in the first two days things looked promising; but then Croker's attack appeared in the *Quarterly Review*. Its effect on Tennyson was as shattering as that of Brougham's review in the *Edinburgh* had been on Byron twenty-five years before, and Tennyson lacked the pugnacity which led his predecessor to immediate and effective counter-attack. The pain was still vivid when he wrote 'Merlin and the Gleam' in his old age, remembering how, 'at the Croak of a Raven', he had been snarled at and cursed by 'A barbarous people, Blind to the magic, And deaf to the melody'.

To understand the effect of Croker's review we have to recall that Tennyson had still reached only two circles of readers, circles which overlapped: that formed by his family and a few friends, and that formed by the Apostles and a few further friends. Before Croker's onslaught the only real breath of cold wind from outside had been Christopher North's review of his first volume. It was now necessary for him to break the sound barrier, to reach a wider audience consisting of people who had not heard his voice. In 1850 Charles Kingsley wrote of certain readers who looked back on Tennyson's early volumes as 'an era in their lives',[24] but they were very few: the question now was whether he could develop from a coterie poet to a poet with an established position in the literary world. Croker's review seemed to answer with a resounding negative the question which Hallam had prompted Tennyson to put to the public a little prematurely. Two full years were to pass before three hundred copies of *Poems* had been sold.

One might have expected the sudden news of Hallam's death in Vienna to have reduced Tennyson to silence; yet while it removed the friend who had acted as his constant supporter it also concentrated his mind – or rather his imagination – wonderfully. An old biographer might have said that Hallam left his friend a valuable legacy, the legacy of tears; but Tennyson's heart had always been full of tears, and what seems to have happened was that he was now provided with a focus for his deep instinctive pull towards the elegiac. Paradoxically, Hallam's death acted as a sort of release, by providing an overwhelming justification for Tennyson's hereditary and personal melancholy. Within a few months he began 'the elegies' (the future *In Memoriam*), and wrote or drafted 'Ulysses', 'Tiresias', the 'Morte d'Arthur' and several other important poems. Very soon Edward FitzGerald reported that his friend had been 'making fresh poems . . . finer, they say, than any he has done', and added, significantly: 'But I believe he is chiefly meditating on the purging and subliming of what he has already done: and repents that he has published at all yet.'[25] We can only admire the patience, the intelligence and the humility which led Tennyson to study the reviews of his first two volumes, and to revise his poems when he felt that the strictures of the reviewers were justified.

It is not to be supposed that the interval of nine years before his next collection was due to any plan, or to a determination to follow the prescription of Horace.[26] Tennyson grumbled frequently, 'accusing the baseness of his lot in life and looking to outward circumstances for more than a great man ought to want of them', as Spedding complained.[27] He thought of publishing again, but decided against it; and when he heard that Mill was writing a belated review of his last volume he said that he did not wish '*to be dragged forward again in any shape before the reading public at present*'. It was with great difficulty that his friends persuaded him to publish 'St. Agnes' Eve' in *The Keepsake* at the end of 1836, and the lyric which was to become the germ of *Maud* in a memorial volume the following year. Yet he was beginning to be known to a slightly larger circle. Elizabeth Barrett was enquiring about him, while his poems were circulating in manuscript in America and were admired by Emerson. In 1841 William Davis Ticknor paid him £150 for a collection of his work, reputedly the first occasion on which an American publisher observed the proprieties to the extent of paying for English poetry, and this seems to have been decisive. The following year, when the proofs of the two-volume *Poems* had been sent him, he wrote to FitzGerald characteristically: 'Not for my sake but yours did I consent to submit my papers to the herd – d—m'em!'[28]

'*Odi profanum vulgus et arceo.*' It was one thing for Horace to write in such a tone at the court of Augustus, another for young Alfred Tennyson five years after Victoria had become Queen. Nor was it appropriate: conditions were not altogether unpropitious. Coleridge, Crabbe, and the admired Mrs Hemans and Letitia Elizabeth Landon were all dead, while Wordsworth and other senior poets had ceased to publish. Browning had severely damaged his tender reputation with *Sordello*, a poem then universally regarded as unreadable. The greatly expanded reading public of the day was prepared to be interested in poetry, so long as it was poetry within its range. Jeffrey had written on the subject twenty years before, in an essay he was now on the point of reprinting. Praising Crabbe for addressing his poems to 'the middling or humbler classes of the community', he defined them as 'almost all those who are below the sphere of what is called fashionable or public life' and estimated that there were 'not less than two hundred thousand persons who read for amusement or instruction' in their ranks, as against fewer than twenty thousand in 'the higher classes'. In 1844 he revised his figures to fewer than thirty thousand in the higher classes and 'not less than 300,000 persons' in the middling classes, but came to the same conclusion:

It is easy to see . . . which a poet should chuse to please for his own glory and emolument, and which he should wish to delight and amend out of mere philanthropy. The fact too we believe is, that a great part of the larger body are to the full as well educated and as high-minded as the smaller; and, though their taste may not be so correct and fastidious, we are persuaded that their sensibility is greater.[29]

A remarkably perceptive observation.

Of the three reviews of the *Poems* of 1842 written by Apostles, that by Monckton Milnes in the *Westminster* is particularly interesting. He asserts that 'Poetry is . . . now more respectable than it has ever been before in this country', adding that 'no man, of whatever gravity of station or character, would be ashamed of having written good verse'.[30] However deficient his knowledge of the history of poetry – were not Chaucer, Spenser and Milton men of some 'gravity of situation'? – it is noteworthy that he insists that 'Among the large and intelligent middle classes . . . there is much poetry read and enjoyed' and that 'It is on this broad basis, not on the clatter of a coterie . . . that the fame of Wordsworth rests. Poetry every day becomes more human, more true to the common heart of man . . . The imaginative power may at other periods have been more deeply concentrated in individuals, but it has never been so widely diffused and so freely cultivated as now.' He argues that Tennyson is well on the way to placing himself at the head of the poets of the day by teaching 'still more than he delights . . . and suggest[ing] still more than he teaches'. In the *Quarterly* John Sterling justly praised 'Ulysses' and 'Locksley Hall' but preferred above all such 'English Idyls' as 'Dora' and 'The Gardener's Daughter'. He was afraid, however, that the moral was too often '*obtruded*'. Spedding, writing in the *Edinburgh*, sympathetically considered Tennyson's development and urged him now to look for 'a subject large enough to take the entire impress of his mind'. These long reviews in the most influential periodicals of the time were the work of a loyal Praetorian guard, Apostles who belonged to the second circle of Tennyson's readers, and who were now recommending his work to a wider public. The following year, in R.H. Horne's *A New Spirit of the Age*, Elizabeth Barrett proclaimed that 'The name of Alfred Tennyson is pressing slowly, calmly, but surely, – with certain recognition but no loud shouts of greeting, – from the lips of the discerners of poets, of whom there remain a few, even in the cast-iron ages, along the lips of the less informed public'. When Gladstone urged Tennyson's claim to a civil list pension, the following year, it was probably not only for tactical reasons that he described him as a great poet who 'can hardly become a popular & is much more likely to be a starving one'.[31]

By 1846 we find William Allingham preaching Tennyson to the clerks in the Belfast Customs Office, and reciting parts of 'Locksley Hall', the poem which Charles Kingsley later considered to have 'had most influence on the minds of the young men of our day'.[32] In any event four editions of the *Poems* had been published by the end of that year, each of them slightly larger than its predecessor. In 1850 Kingsley was not only to comment on 'the absolute idolatry with which every utterance of [Tennyson's] is regarded by the cultivated young men of our day, especially at the universities', but also to indicate the widening diffusion of his work by making his Alton Locke, 'Tailor and Poet', discover in those two volumes 'the embodiment of thoughts . . . which I had concealed, because I fancied them peculiar to myself', an accurate description of the feelings with which a sensitive young reader encounters the work of an important new poet. When we remember that fewer than a thousand copies of the earlier volumes had been sold by the time when the larger collection appeared we realise that Tennyson had moved much closer to the centre of the literary scene; yet his sales remained inconsiderable when set beside those of Scott and Byron a decade or two earlier, to say nothing of the recent astonishing circulation of *Pickwick Papers*, *Nicholas Nickleby* and *The Old Curiosity Shop*.[33]

No feature of the reviews is more striking than the frequency with which they refer to the women in Tennyson's poems, and whereas Leigh Hunt described his nymphets as 'a sort of poetical milliners, or artificial idealisms full dressed',[34] the *Christian Teacher* was much more representative when it praised his 'keen and unslumbering perception of the Pure, the Graceful, the Lofty and the Lovely in Womanhood'.

'Godiva' evoked particular admiration. John Forster greeted it with 'rapture', and it was reprinted in the *Morning Post*, the *Monthly Review*, the *Morning Herald* and (for that matter) the *Sheffield and Rotherham Independent*. While we no longer condescend to the Victorians, while we are more and more impressed by the achievements of that remarkable age, we need not allow either admiration or familiarity to lead us to take for granted the extraordinary change of manners which occurred between the time when Byron was found shocking (indeed), yet was undoubtedly the best-selling poet of the day, and this time, only

127

twenty years later, when the least hint of overt sexuality had become too shocking for poetry. There were historical and sociological reasons for the change, and in some ways it was no doubt necessary and beneficial – but not for poetry. The Victorian chastity belt had already been designed, and Tennyson owed no small part of his success to a temperament which made it easier for him than for many men to write in the manner demanded by the age. A young Queen had come to the throne, a woman who was as much a product of her upbringing as Charles II had been of his, and Tennyson was soon to be as solicitous to write verses which would meet with her approval as Dryden had been to please a King who shared his own liking for '*broad Allusions*'.[35]

But that is to anticipate. The careful selection and brilliantly painstaking revision which produced the first volume of the *Poems* of 1842 were almost wholly beneficial. The omission of 'The Hesperides', the poem from which T.S. Eliot quoted at length to illustrate Tennyson's mastery of metre,[36] is almost the only instance in which we can say that he allowed the censures of the reviewers to lead him astray. Deeply as he had been wounded by one or two of them, they had helped him to 'purge and sublimate' his work and so to render it suitable for the admiration of a larger circle of readers than had cared for his earlier volumes. The new poems in the second volume, which included 'Morte d'Arthur', 'Ulysses', 'Locksley Hall' and 'Break, break, break', as well as the first group of English Idyls, were of the highest quality without being beyond the capacity of his audience. He had remembered his readers without truckling to them. *The Princess* was another matter.

The Princess appears to have been written directly to increase his reading public. As early as 1831 a reviewer had insisted that 'There is not a greater moral necessity in England than that of a reformation in female education',[37] and before the end of the decade Tennyson was discussing a poem on the subject with Emily Sellwood. It is not surprising, therefore, that when a remark of Sterling's discouraged him from attempting an Arthurian epic he decided to turn to very different subject-matter and write a long poem perhaps to be called *The University of Women*. Had he not been urged to deal with contemporary issues, and to become a Teacher? Was it not obvious that readers were now more at home with narrative than with any other form of poetry except the simplest of lyrics? Was there not a woman on the throne?

The weakness of *The Princess* is due to Tennyson's uncertainty about the issue which is supposed to inform the story. He simply plunged ahead and wrote a narrative in a highly 'poetical' style and hoped for the best. The sub-title, 'A Medley', suggests that he was uneasy from the first. 'My Book is out and I hate it', he wrote to FitzGerald, 'and so no doubt will you.'[38] It was a sign of the growth of his reputation in the previous five years that the poem was widely reviewed, but it is not surprising that the reviewers were divided. One praised him as a poet who 'studies the spirit of the time', another expressed the remarkable view that 'a great philosophical thesis' is discussed, ' . . . and satisfactorily settled', while a third, without a hint of irony, wrote that *The Princess* contains 'something more instructive than "the Corsair", more philosophical than "the Lay of the Last Minstrel" '.[39] More perceptive critics recognised that the new work did not fulfil the expectations aroused by the best of his previous poetry.

The revisions in the third edition are different in kind from the revisions of his earlier poems for the edition of 1842, and they are singularly revealing. He now seeks to cover his traces by having one of the poet's friends ask him to dress the story up 'poetically'. The poet wonders 'What style could suit?', and wavers between 'The sort of mock-heroic gigantesque' with which he had originally teased little Lilia and the 'true-heroic–true-sublime' preferred by the women:

> And I, betwixt them both, to please them both,
> And yet to give the story as it rose,
> I moved as in a strange diagonal,
> And maybe neither pleased myself nor them.[40]

It is an extraordinary admission, as if Pope had written *The Rape of the Lock* without being able to decide whether he was writing a heroic or a heroi-comical poem. Tennyson's verse-mill has run out of control, and he is merely producing passages of 'poetry', some good, some bad, all a jumble and more muddle than medley.

The other most interesting revision was the addition of the six rhymed lyrics now placed between the sections of the poem. Only the third of these – 'The splendour falls on castle walls' – can compete with the splendid unrhymed lyrics present from the first edition onwards, yet the new lyrics – added to emphasise the importance of the child – were particularly suited to the taste of the time. In the first a married couple make up a tiff and weep together over the grave of a child: in the second a woman who is awaiting her husband's return from the sea hums a lullaby: in the fourth a warrior gains strength from the thought of his wife and children: the fifth describes the comfort afforded a newly widowed young woman by her child: while in the last a woman accepts, with every possible modesty, the love of a good man. Nothing could have appealed more directly to Tennyson's audience than such blameless lyrics of domestic life, so much less interesting than the unrhymed lyrics which had been present from the first: their addition was a shrewd move.

From the first there was no doubt about the verdict of the general public. The first edition, of perhaps two thousand copies, was followed within a few weeks by a second; and no fewer than seventeen editions, two of them illustrated, appeared within a period of thirty years. *The Princess* became one of the best-known volumes of Victorian poetry, and it is not hard to see why. A poem that told a story, and such a story, was easier for readers primarily accustomed to novels than any collection of miscellaneous poems. The subject is presented in a manner that could offend only the most hidebound of conservatives or the wildest of progressives. The narrative is broken up by lyrics, and there is a happy ending of the sort to which readers had become accustomed. Tennyson had won a much wider popularity than could derive from the greatly superior poetry which he had published five years before.

But he had won it at a price. He had compromised his integrity. In a sense the most severe critique of *The Princess* appeared in the preface to Matthew Arnold's *Poems* in 1853.[41] Rejecting the fashionable view that the poet 'must leave the exhausted past, and draw his subjects from matters of present import, and *therefore* both of interest and novelty', Arnold argues 'The poet . . . has in the first place to select an excellent action', irrespective of the time at which it is supposed to have taken place; and secondly that modern poets should emulate the Greeks, who 'regarded the whole' while moderns 'regard the parts':

With them, the action predominated over the expression of it; with us, the expression predominates over the action . . . their expression is so excellent because it is so admirably kept in its right degree of prominence; because it is so simple and so well subordinated; because it draws its force directly from the pregnancy of the matter which it conveys.

It is hard not to believe that *The Princess* was one of the modern poems of which Arnold was thinking, and certainly there could be no clearer illustration of 'the all-importance of the choice of a subject; the necessity of accurate construction; and the subordinate character of expression'. Writers conversant in the great writers of antiquity, Arnold insists,

do not talk of their mission, nor of interpreting their age, nor of the coming poet; all this, they know, is the mere delirium of vanity; their business is not to praise their age, but to afford to the men who live in it the highest pleasure which they are capable of feeling. If asked to afford this by means of subjects drawn from the age itself, they ask what special fitness the present age has for supplying them. They are told that it is an era of progress, an age commissioned to carry out the great ideas of industrial development and social amelioration. They reply that with all this they can do nothing.

The judgment that Tennyson usually wrote best when he was not writing for a large audience finds support in the history of *In Memoriam*. When he began 'the elegies' in October 1833, the month in which the news of Hallam's death had reached him, there is no doubt that he was writing for his own solace. The extreme simplicity of the verse form, which he had already used in a number of political poems, must have enhanced the tranquillising effect of the work. While other of his poems owe their origin to the same bereavement, it was to this growing collection of lyrics that he kept returning, and at times when he could write nothing else – as when he was awaiting the reviews of the *Poems* of 1842, and during his emotional breakdown two years later – he found that he could still add a few more stanzas. Since he was never at his ease planning a long poem the method of aggregation over a long period suited him admirably. It is hard not to be reminded of Housman's notion that a poem may, like a pearl, be 'a morbid secretion'.[42]

No doubt he began, as he said later, with no thought of publication, but that possibility must have occurred to him at an early point. By Christmas 1841 Edmund Lushington had noted that 'the number of the memorial poems had rapidly increased . . . Some I heard him repeat before I had seen them in writing, others I learnt to know first from the book itself which he kindly allowed me to look through without stint.'[43] In April 1842 Tennyson read Aubrey de Vere 'some beautiful Elegies', and by the summer of 1845 we find that the marriage of Edmund Lushington and Cecilia Tennyson, which occurred three years earlier, had been introduced. By 1847, when he told an aunt that he had 'no wish to send them out yet', we have the impression that he merely wished to be reassured and nudged towards publication; while by early 1849 he had promised de Vere 'to *print* at least his exquisite Elegies, and let his friends have a few copies'. When he described them to Moxon as 'some things that the public would have no interest in' he found that the publisher took a very different view and offered him a large sum of money for them straight away. That same year Tennyson read some of the elegies to Palgrave, and the following January he was planning to have 'about twenty-five copies' printed, to lend (not give) to a few friends. Since in April Coventry Patmore believed that he had 'one of the *only* half-dozen copies', it is possible that fewer than twenty-five were in fact distributed. By this time, in any event, Tennyson was preparing the collection for publication. The prologue, dated 1849, seems to have been written for the trial printing, no doubt partly to please Emily Sellwood, whose doubts about marrying Tennyson now disappeared.

When he told his son that he had not written the elegies for publication Tennyson also said that he had originally had no 'view of weaving them into a whole'.[44] The rearrangement of the lyrics in a quasi-narrative sequence, so that he could describe the whole as 'a kind of *Divina Commedia*, ending with happiness', led Tennyson to conceive of his work as a poem rather than 'an actual biography', with the result that he could state that ' "I" is not always the author speaking of himself, but the voice of the human race speaking through him.' He emphasised that 'There is more about myself in *Ulysses* . . . [which] was more written with the feeling of his loss upon me than many poems in *In Memoriam*', the latter being 'very impersonal . . . as well as personal'. While such analyses as that of Bradley, and that preserved by James

Knowles, who tells us that he had it from the poet himself, are of considerable value, perhaps we come closest to Tennyson when we read or remember *In Memoriam* as a collection of lyrics expressing the 'different moods of sorrow'. If we read it in that way we shall be less disconcerted by his unexpected remark that 'It's too hopeful, this poem, more than I am myself', and his observation that he was thinking of 'adding another to it, a speculative one, . . . showing that all the arguments are about as good on one side as the other'.

In the event the quasi-narrative structure and the generalised tone of the mourning combined with the inspired simplicity of the title (Emily's suggestion) to render the poem supremely suited to the taste of the age. It satisfied, in a characteristically oblique manner, the principal desiderata of his friends and reviewers. He had been challenged to write a long poem: he had done so by stringing together a great many short poems: he had been asked to deal with the problems of the age: what he had done was to consider them in relation to death, which is the problem of every age. He had been urged to be more philosophical: he complied by raising some of the problems of religion and metaphysics without attempting to provide any dogmatic answers. While we may be surprised that hardly anyone objected to the vagueness of the references to Christianity in the body of the poem (for all the prominence of the season of Christmas), we also notice the absence of subject-matter likely to occasion debate or dissension: the element of satire, so common in elegy, hardly appears: there is nothing political except a belief in progress so vaguely worded that few could have objected: while the marriage with which the poem ends is a poetical version of the happy ending demanded by the novel-readers of the day.

While one or two contemporary reviewers were uncertain whether *In Memoriam* would prove popular, the proprietor of Mudie's Select Library can have had few doubts: he bought fifty copies at once, and they were all in circulation on the day of publication. More than one reviewer contrasted the simplicity of this new work with the ornate style of many of the earlier poems. The English quality of the elegy appealed to everyone, while the fact that so many of the lyrics deal with the universal experience of loss and regret rather than Hallam himself led to the poem's becoming, as G.H. Lewes prophesied, 'the solace and delight of every house where poetry is loved'. Sixty thousand copies were sold within a few months. The reviewer in *The Globe* expressed his belief that 'For one genuine reader of Wordsworth there are thousands who relish Tennyson.'[45]

Since that great poet had been in his late seventies when Tennyson was preparing his work for publication, it is difficult to believe his grandson's statement that the offer of the Laureateship came as a complete surprise. It was natural that the Queen should enquire whether Tennyson was of a suitable character, unsurprising that she should receive a reassuring answer. Yet Tennyson's own reaction was characteristic: he wrote one letter accepting the honour, and another refusing it, and waited for a day before deciding which to despatch. He was in two minds about this, as he had been and was to be about so many other problems. His ambiguous feelings about the 'establishment' of the day, traceable in part to the belief that his father had been disinherited while his uncle became a man of wealth and influence, was no doubt a factor. Inevitable as it now seems that it should have been the letter of acceptance that was sent off, he had in fact good reason to hesitate: as Poet Laureate he was bound to be constantly aware of his influence throughout the nation: he was committed to being a public man.

When he received his pension in 1845 he had been comforted by Peel's insistence that he 'need not . . . be fettered in the public expression of any opinion', so that – in his own words – 'if I take a pique against the Queen or the court, or Peel himself, I may, if I will, bully them with as much freedom tho' not perhaps quite so gracefully, as if I were still unpensioned'.[46] He was now being ushered further down the same triumphal drive, and as Bernard Martin observes he believed that he was 'morally obliged . . . not to oppose the Queen, either publicly or privately.'

While he proved a most successful Laureate, Tennyson must have been disappointed by the reception of his first separate publication after his appointment, the 'Ode on the Death of the Duke of Wellington'. The subject suited him: Wellington had always made a deep appeal to his imagination; and the Ode contains some splendidly eloquent verse. While 10,000 copies were

printed for sale on the day of the funeral, however, the verse-
form was too difficult for the common reader – who was of course
without the advantage of hearing the rich modulations of the
poet's voice – and the critics themselves were divided. Sir Henry
Taylor shrewdly remarked that while the poem would be
admired by 'many thousands at present' it would be admired by
'many hundreds of thousands' in the future.[47] By way of contrast
'The Charge of the Light Brigade', about which Tennyson was
later to express reservations, is in a simple metre which rendered
it suitable for a wide audience. A chaplain at Scutari wrote to say
that half of his men were singing it, and that they wanted copies
of their own. When 2,000 copies were despatched, the chaplain
assured Tennyson, in his letter of acknowledgement, that 'The
poet can now make heroes, just as in days of yore, if he will.'

The reception of the first long poem of his Laureate period
was deeply troubling. While it is not surprising that *Maud* should
have been more widely reviewed than any of the previous volumes, it is understandable (at least in retrospect) that more of
the reviews were unfavourable than favourable. The description
of Maud's odious but successful brother, contrasted with 'the
poor . . . hovelled and hustled together, each sex, like swine',[48]
and the bitterness which informs the poem as certain harsh
colours and shapes inform the unforgettable paintings of Edvard
Munch – these were found profoundly disconcerting. This was
not what critics who had urged Tennyson to be contemporary
had had in mind. George Eliot was shocked by the rejoicing of
the unnamed speaker that 'the long, long canker of peace is over
and done'.[49]

Tennyson's reply was of course that the poem was dramatic.
It would have helped if he had entitled it *Maud or the Madness*, as
he had at one time intended: the sub-title, 'A Monodrama', was
too late when it was added in 1875. As Walter Bagehot complained, 'He seemed to sympathize with the feverish railings, the
moody nonsense, the very entangled philosophy, which he put
into the mouth of his hero. There were some odd invectives
against peace, against industry, against making your livelihood,
which seemed by no means to be dramatic exhibitions of represented character, but, on the contrary, confidential expo-
sitions of the poet's own belief.' While Tennyson revised the
line which had offended George Eliot, that was the only con-

135

cession he made. It took even Gladstone many years to come round to the poem.

The whole affair makes it clear that Tennyson still had great difficulty in relating to the large readership which was now to be his. The fact that *Maud* was the poem which he most often read aloud to visitors is not merely a reminder of the importance which he attached to the sound of his verse, not merely a parent's fondness for a neglected child, but also an implicit acknowledgement that the poem requires stage-directions and explanations with which the reader is not provided. As it happens we now know more about the biographical genesis[50] of the poem than did Tennyson's contemporaries, and what we know confirms the sense that there is more that is personal in it than he was willing to admit. The incomplete success of *Maud* is due to a failure of technique which makes it only too obvious that the poet is using his poem to cleanse his bosom of some perilous stuff. It is not surprising that its first readers felt uneasy and bewildered.

In sharp contrast, one of the shorter poems in the volume received unanimous praise. 'When we read his poetry in this kind', Coventry Patmore wrote of 'The Brook', 'we wish that he might "ever do nothing but that" . . . Mr. Tennyson never wrote anything more wholesome, sweet, and real than this Idyl, which seems as if it had been expressly composed to refresh the spirits and restore us to a sense of life and nature after the feverish dreams of "Maud." '[51] While the volume reached a fifth edition in four years, that was due to the position which Tennyson had now attained and to the popularity of the shorter pieces, and not to the principal poem. He cannot have felt encouraged to further bold experiment, and a number of critical comments helped to drive him in a very different direction. Soon he was thinking again of his Arthurian scheme. He proceeded with caution, having six trial copies of a volume called *Enid and Nimuë* printed in 1857 to enable him to collect the opinions of a few friends. Further trial printings preceded the appearance of *Idylls of the King*, a volume containing *Enid*, *Vivien*, *Elaine* and *Guinevere*, two years later.

Christopher Ricks has emphasised the vacillation characteristic of Tennyson's approach to the whole scheme and suggested that what had hurt him most about the comments of

John Sterling on 'Morte d'Arthur' in 1842, which he held responsible for his not having proceeded with the 'whole great poem' on Arthur a quarter of a century earlier, was that they confirmed his own underlying uncertainty.[52] Tennyson was in two minds throughout the composition of the *Idylls*: a period coterminous with the greater part of his poetic career. While he was eager to write a major long poem, he assured his American publishers that it would be madness to attempt an epic 'in the heart of the 19th Century',[53] and in the end he stumbled on a compromise, a series of instalments written as the mood took him and rearranged to form the twelve 'Books' of a non-epic, the double 'l' being intended to distinguish the poems from the ordinary pastoral idyls usually spelt with one 'l'.

The principal feeling expressed by most reviewers of the *Idylls* was relief. Bagehot was glad that Tennyson had 'sided with the world', after *Maud*, which had appealed only to 'Tennysonians'.[54] Although there might be less subtlety now than in his earlier work that was a price Bagehot was very willing to pay. Although he sees the deficiency in dramatic power he yet welcomes what he regards as the maturity of a great poet, and classes Tennyson with Shelley, Coleridge, Keats and Wordsworth as one of 'the intellectualised poets', concluding that he is to be ranked 'as inferior in the general power of the poetic imagination' to Shelley alone – an over-estimate which demonstrates yet again the extreme difficulty of assessing one's contemporaries in relation to the great writers of the past.

The attempt at scrupulous assessment in Bagehot's review is less evident in Gladstone's salute to the poet's 'greatest exploit' by far.[55] What England needed was the presentation of 'Lofty example', and for this the Arthurian romance offers incomparable scope: 'It is national: it is Christian.' He hopes that Tennyson will achieve 'a full-formed epic' and so produce 'by far the greatest poetical creation' of the century in any language. One of Gladstone's most striking observations is his assertion that it is 'one of Mr. Tennyson's brightest distinctions that he is now what from the very first he strove to be . . . the poet of woman. We do not mean, nor do we know, that his hold over women as his readers is greater than his command or influence over men; but that he has studied, sounded, painted, woman in form, in motion, in character, in office, in capability, with rare devotion, power and skill; and the poet who best achieves this end does also most and best for man.'

The terms in which Gladstone makes the assertion render it slightly less astonishing. He surely cannot mean that Tennyson 'has studied, sounded, painted, woman' as Chaucer and Shakespeare had done. He means that Tennyson has studied and depicted the ability of Woman, and of the virtuous passion which she should inspire,

> Not only to keep down the base in man,
> But teach high thought, and amiable words.[56]

While we print women in lower case, and in the plural, Tennyson has Woman in upper case, and in the singular. The fact that 'the wily Vivien' is given to 'dainty gambols', to writhing and sliding and clinging 'like a snake', warns the careful schoolgirl reader that she is no better than she should be – the same reader who may be imagined nodding assent to what is surely the limpest of all *sententiae*:

> Let never maiden think, however fair,
> She is not fairer in new clothes than old.[57]

We can understand how such nonsense provoked Swinburne to his protest that 'It would seem . . . as though to publish a book were equivalent to thrusting it with violence into the hands of every mother and nurse in the kingdom as fit and necessary food for female infancy.'[58] While the lines just quoted are exceptionally weak, it is also instructive to consider the fine passage in which Guinevere addresses Arthur after he has magnanimously forgiven her:

> Then she stretched out her arms and cried aloud
> 'Oh Arthur!' there her voice brake suddenly,
> Then – as a stream that spouting from a cliff
> Fails in mid air, but gathering at the base
> Re-makes itself, and flashes down the vale –
> Went on in passionate utterance.

This is much less impressive than the single line given to Cresseid by Robert Henryson when as a leper she is told that the knight who has just thrown her a purse of gold is the Troilus whom she has betrayed:

> Nane but my self as now I will accuse.[59]

It is penetrating simplicity like that which reminds us of Homer's only comment on the beauty of Helen – when he makes the old men who watch her passing along the wall of Troy remark that it is no wonder that a war is being waged for such a woman – and not the brilliant virtuosity of a latter-day poet who too often allowed himself to become a gentleman writing for ladies.

Of the 40,000 copies of the *Idylls* printed as a first edition a quarter were sold in the first week, in spite of the high price of seven shillings. Even *Blackwood's* did not forbear to cheer. Prince Albert asked Tennyson to inscribe a copy for him, and when the Queen wished her Laureate to 'idealize' the Prince after his death Tennyson could not have done a more fitting thing than to dedicate the *Idylls* to his memory, 'since he held them dear, Perchance as finding there unconsciously Some image of himself'.

One of the most illuminating comments on the *Idylls* was made not by a professed literary critic but by a clever old woman writing her reminiscences many years later:

Nothing brings back those long-ago days like the thought of those little green volumes and the feelings they once aroused; yet how impossible to-day to recover the rapture with which one entered that fairyland of marvellous, impossible people, those knights in armour, with their lofty ideals, their tournaments and jousts, their hope and aim 'to love one maiden only, cleave to her and worship her by years of noble deeds'. It all belongs to the dreams of youth, to the thoughts of a schoolgirl lying in the grass in an orchard, and eating an apple or a piece of chocolate as she read, while far away in London the four-wheelers and hansom cabs thundered over the cobblestones, and the little green books lay on velvet-covered tables and were read by our mothers.[60]

The first *Idylls of the King* were followed five years later by what was to prove the most popular of all Tennyson's volumes. He thought of calling *Enoch Arden, etc.* 'Idyls of the Hearth' or 'Idyls of the People', and the greater part of the book consists of three long poems of the same type as 'The Gardener's Daughter' and 'Dora' (another English Idyl also published in 1842). The distinction of many of the descriptive passages in these poems may be exemplified by the opening of *Enoch Arden*:

> Long lines of cliff breaking have left a chasm;
> And in the chasm are foam and yellow sands;
> Beyond, red roofs about a narrow wharf
> In cluster; then a mouldered church; and higher
> A long street climbs to one tall-towered mill.

'Aylmer's Field' begins and ends finely, but much of the narrative itself is inferior, while the banal conclusion of *Enoch Arden* is often remembered. The mood which made these poems popular is more fairly illustrated by the end of 'Dora':

> So those four abode
> Within one house together; and as years
> Went forward, Mary took another mate;
> But Dora lived unmarried till her death.

The modern reader is likely to prefer the prose original, a story by Mary Russell Mitford,[61] and may further reflect that George Eliot's *Scenes of Clerical Life* achieve much more successfully some of the aims which Tennyson seems to have had in mind. 'Dora' lacks the metaphysical dimension which makes Wordsworth's 'The Leech Gatherer' more than a simple story. The 'Idyls' might be described (in Mario Praz's terms) as 'very Biedermeier',[62] and they hit the taste of the time to perfection. One of the two dramatic monologues in the same collection, 'Northern Farmer', makes one wish that Tennyson had more often written in dialect, since doing so enabled him to bring into his verse something of the 'broad, coarse and grotesque' which often appeared in his conversation.

The publishing history of the first major poem after *Enoch Arden*, recently studied in detail by Edgar Shannon,[63] shows that the poet's own scrupulosity was sometimes exceeded by that of his advisers. The monologue 'Lucretius' is based on the story that the poet's wife, resenting his neglect of her, gave him a love-potion which led him to madness and self-destruction. As Lucretius describes his amorous dreams we hear of 'Naked Hetairai, curious in their art, Hired animalisms': the word 'Naked' was excised, however, and we notice that it occurs remarkably seldom in Tennyson's work, except metaphorically or in relation to innocent 'babes'. But the passage which proved most debatable was another dream in which Lucretius sees a satyr pursuing an oread:

> how the sun delights
> To glance and shift about her slippery sides,
> And rosy knees and supple roundedness,
> And budded bosom-peaks.

Today these lines seem unremarkable, if undistinguished: we are reminded of Leigh Hunt, or of the painter William Etty, and we pass on. Tennyson knew his public, however, and when he asked Macmillan, in whose *Magazine* they first appeared, whether they should be omitted he was advised that they should. Such was also the view of David Masson, who worried about 'what the blatant beast, the public, might say about the longer form of the passage'. Tennyson told the editor to please himself but 'send the full passage to America', where 'They are not so squeamish as we are.'

Such prudence was rewarded by a writer in the *Pall Mall Gazette* who congratulated Tennyson on writing about sex 'so that not even the most feverish libertine might find a line for *his* enjoyment'; while another critic contrasted Tennyson's chaste treatment of the subject with the 'pruriency' which might have characterised Swinburne's: a reminder that *Poems and Ballads* had appeared two years before. Although another reviewer, who had seen a Canadian printing of the poem, considered that the English public had had a 'narrow escape', in fact there was little or no unfavourable comment when the fuller version was published in *The Holy Grail And Other Poems*. It is remarkable how readers accepted the poem as a daring excursion by the Poet Laureate and congratulated themselves on their broad-mindedness.

The fear of sexuality which informs 'Lucretius' is one of a number of fears which become particularly evident in Tennyson's later work, but which may readily be traced in the earlier. It is not surprising that in 1883 he should have taken up 'Tiresias', a poem partly written fifty years before. In an unpublished version of the dedication he expressed his feelings directly, complaining

> Of faded faiths and civic crimes,
> And fierce transition's blood-red morn,
> And years with lawless voices loud.[64]

It is to be regretted that he had a low opinion of satire as a poetic mode, for there is power in this poem, as in the earlier attacks on the marriage-market and the growing commercialism of the epoch in 'Locksley Hall' and *Maud*. In *Locksley Hall Sixty Years After* the element of autobiography is unmistakable, as Gladstone and others perceived: we hear the secret voice of Tennyson, and look into the dark places of his imagination. It is not one of his best pieces, yet there is a pathos about it which commands our respect. It was not only that his melancholy seemed to him to have been justified by experience: it was also that he remained a simple man at heart, and fiercely patriotic. He was profoundly troubled by the state of England, which already afforded a glimpse of what we term modern civilisation:

When was age so crammed with menace? madness? written, spoken lies?[65]

If the first half of Tennyson's career is the story of his conquest of the English reading public, the second half is the story of the reading public's conquest of Tennyson. His principal weakness, a weakness of character rather than of intellect, was increased by constant worry about the reactions of his readers. He seriously considered removing 'Northern Farmer' from the *Enoch Arden* volume because someone feared that the old man's attitude to the Almighty might offend religious susceptibilities, he was afraid that the publication of 'The Revenge' might inflame public opinion against Russia at a critical time, he was harassed by Temperance enthusiasts and Little Englanders who objected to his exhortation to 'drink a health' in 'Hands all round' – a lyric set to music by Lady Tennyson and sung throughout the country in celebration of the Queen's birthday in 1882.[66] It is easy for us to laugh, but 'To all this', in the words of Swinburne, ' . . . there is a grave side':

The question at issue is wider than any between a single writer and his critics, or it might well be allowed to drop. It is this: whether or not the first and last requisite of art is to give no offence; whether or not all that cannot be lisped in the nursery or fingered in the schoolroom is therefore to be cast out of the library; whether or not the domestic circle is to be for all men and writers the outer limit and extreme horizon of their world of work. For to this we have come; and all students of art must face the matter as it stands. Who has not heard it asked, in a final and triumphant tone, whether this book or that can be read aloud by her mother to a young girl? whether such and such a picture can properly be exposed to the eyes of young persons? . . . In no past century were artists ever bidden to work on these terms; nor are they now, except among us.[67]

This cannot be swept aside as Swinburnian hyperbole. 'On one occasion', to quote again from Laura Troubridge's memories of Tennyson, 'he said that his great aim had been never to write a single word that an Eton boy could not read aloud to his sister.'[68] When every allowance is made for the fact that Tennyson was talking to a very young woman, that surely remains one of the strangest remarks ever made about his audience by a major poet.

In his later years he suffered not merely from the waning powers common to most elderly poets, but also from a sense of

142

responsibility greater than is good for any poet. Nothing could be more revealing than his repeated observation that he would have given 'all his own writings to be able to produce a spontaneous lyric like Lovelace's "Althea" or the simple, exquisite songs of Burns'.[69] His lyric genius enabled him to write 'To Virgil' in his seventies and 'Crossing the Bar' at the age of eighty, but his circumstances too often denied him the possibility of the spontaneous and the simple. He once told the Queen that he was deeply aware of 'the power of literature in this age of the world',[70] and we can now see that it was greater then than it had ever been before and greater than it is ever likely to be again. The man whose verse had become, in the words of Henry James, 'part of the civilization of his day', suffered from greater constraints than his peers in earlier times. He had too large an audience, and before the end he realised as much. 'Tennyson says that as a boy he had a great thirst to be a poet', his son recorded, 'and to be a *popular* poet . . . but that now he is inclined to think popularity is a bastard fame, which sometimes goes with the more real thing, but is independent of and somewhat antagonistic to it. He appears to shrink from his own popularity.'

VI · YEATS
Always an Irish writer

WHEN he first visited Oxford Yeats immediately noticed 'How very unlike Ireland this whole place is – like a foreign land (as it is).'[1] The reminder is timely: Yeats is the only foreign poet considered in this book – and that is appropriate, since he is the only representative of a century in which the greatest poetry in English has been written by poets who have not been born in England. As soon as we open *The Wanderings of Oisin* we find poems that must primarily have been written for an Irish audience: the reader is expected to know who Caolte and Conan and Fin were, 'With Bran, Sgeolan, and Lomair', and to understand the significance of 'passionate Maeve' and 'the Firbolgs' burial-mounds'. In 'The Madness of King Goll' the speaker recalls how his word 'was law from Ith to Emain'. In 'The Ballad of Father O'Hart' we encounter the words 'shoneen' and 'sleiveens'. 'If it comes to lightening the ship', Yeats wrote to a friend when the need to shorten the volume arose, 'I will hardly know what to throw overboard . . . The Irish poems must all be kept, making the personality of the book – or as few thrown over as may be.'[2]

In retrospect we can see that his position was a highly favourable one. His father was of Anglo-Irish stock, an unworldly painter who talked well, loved poetry, and wrote (as we can verify for ourselves) quite admirable letters. When Yeats looked back on his life he realised that perhaps his greatest advantage had been the education he gained in his father's studio. As the second-rate painter Benjamin Robert Haydon had stimulated Keats and exemplified for him the life of genius, so his father provided Yeats with the spectacle of a man courageous enough to live for his art. The very suggestion that his son should contemplate some ordinary career seemed an outrage to this unusual father, who early told his son about Rossetti and Blake and gave him their poetry to read. It was perhaps as well that J.B. Yeats also provided his son with an example of fecklessness against which he could react: it may be that his lack of finishing power helped to make his son one of the greatest of all revisers.

It is said that the poet's mother never entered her husband's studio, and Yeats himself tells us, in a vivid page of his *Autobiographies*, that she 'read no books, but she and the fisherman's wife would tell each other stories that Homer might have told'.[3] She was Irish-Celtic, a daughter of the Pollexfens, 'a little patriarchal society' as Joseph Hone called them,[4] prosperous merchants from the west of Ireland who combined worldly ability with an essentially intuitive approach to life. Yeats's early memories were of their home in Sligo, a place which was always to mean a great deal to his imagination. 'All the well-known families had their . . . legends', he wrote of his earliest childhood, 'and I often said to myself how terrible it would be to go away and die where nobody would know my story. Years afterwards, when I was ten or twelve years old and in London, I would remember Sligo with tears, and when I began to write, it was there I hoped to find my audience.'[5] A rhetorical question later in the *Autobiographies* evokes the affectionate interest with which his earliest verses had been received: 'Does any imaginative man find in maturity the admiration that his first half-articulate years aroused in some little circle; and is not the first success the greatest?'[6] He tells us that one of his schoolfellows would never believe that he had fulfilled the promise shown in some rough verses he had written before the age of eighteen. He was greatly taken with Keats's phrase about leaving 'great verse unto a little clan', and it soon became his modest ambition to do for Sligo what William Allingham had done for Ballyshannon.

His destiny was to be very different, and it is clear that his parents' habit of moving from London to Dublin, and from Dublin to Sligo – an itinerant mode of life which he himself was to follow until his late marriage at the age of fifty-two – helped equip him to write Irish poetry which would soon appeal to readers in England as well as in Ireland, and in America as well as in England. As we trace his early footsteps we are bound to be struck by the skill with which he utilised to the full the favourable circumstances of his early life as he began to find an audience for his poetry.

When the family moved to London in 1887 Yeats met William Morris and came under new influences, but he remained essentially Irish and continued to dream of 'bring[ing] the halves together' – uniting Catholic Ireland and Protestant Ireland – by means of 'a national literature that made Ireland beautiful in the memory, and yet had been freed from provincialism by an exacting criticism, a European pose'.[7] He found the Young Ireland movement uncongenial because it 'sought a nation unified by political doctrine alone, a subservient art and letters aiding and abetting': there were too many people 'who would have felt it inappropriate to publish an Irish book that had not harp and shamrock and green cover, so completely did their minds move amid Young Ireland images and metaphors'.[8] He cherished the thought of returning to Ireland some day to begin a movement less immediately political. 'I feel more and more that we shall have a school of Irish poetry', he told Katharine Tynan, ' – founded on Irish myth and history – a neo-romantic movement.'[9] He was impressed by Matthew Arnold's lectures *On the Study of Celtic Literature*, and may have been struck by the coincidence that the first of them had been delivered in the year of his birth.

In the earliest of all his letters (only a pencil draft survives) we find Yeats, in a mood of bravado very different from that which led him to compare himself with Allingham, telling a girl called Mary Cronan that she may not like the verses he is sending her, 'not being used to my peculiaritys which will never be done justice to until they have become classics and are set for examinations'.[10] He knew that his initial audience must be a small one. Like *Mosada*, reprinted from the *Dublin University Review* as a small book, *The Wanderings of Oisin* was published by subscription. The friend who did most to promote the subscription was John O'Leary, the head of the Fenian Brotherhood. This high-principled old man, who had been converted to nationalism by the poetry of Thomas Davis, and who had spent five years in prison and fifteen in exile, took to the fastidious young poet who was no more in favour of violence than he was himself.

Yeats was astonishingly clear-sighted about the book and its limitations. Before it appeared he told a friend that 'All seems confused, incoherent, inarticulate', but immediately added: 'Yet this I know, I am no idle poetaster . . . Some day I shall be articulate, perhaps . . . this book . . . may make a few friends, perhaps, among people of my own sort.'[11] Except for the wish to make a little money', he was soon to write of his brief novel, *John Sherman*, 'I have no desire to get that kind of fussing regard a book wins from the many. To please the folk of few books is one's great aim. By being Irish, I think, one has a better chance of it.'[12] We know that a hundred copies of *The Wanderings of Oisin* remained unsold in 1891–2: if the original printing was 500, that would indicate a circulation of 400, which may be compared with the 250 copies of the first edition of *The Cenci*. Yeats was delighted that Morris liked the book, and his practical shrewdness is evident yet again when he writes that 'The people of my own age are in the long run most important. They are the future.' He knew that he would reach a larger audience at some future time: 'I shall sell but not yet. Many things, my own and others, have to grow first.'

Through the Rhymers' Club – which Yeats himself, the Great Founder, as someone was to call him, was largely responsible for organising – Yeats saw a good deal of Lionel Johnson, Ernest Dowson, John Davidson, Arthur Symons and others, and gradually widened an audience which was still largely Celtic. Richard Ellmann shrewdly guesses that while he was in London Yeats stressed the importance of a heroic and nationalist subject-matter, in the manner of his Dublin friends, and that while he was in Ireland he made much of the insistence of the Rhymers on the importance of technique.[13] 'We poets continued to write verse and read it out at "The Cheshire Cheese" ', he was to write later, 'convinced that to take part in [political] movements would be only less disgraceful than to write for the newspapers.'[14] He reflected constantly on the dilemma of the Irish intellectual: when Parnell died he hoped it would turn the imagination of young men away from politics and towards matters of permanent importance.

He could not have accomplished so much if he had not moved frequently from London to Dublin, and from Dublin to Sligo; while his visit to Paris in 1894 is further evidence of his desire to avoid the merely parochial. He met Verlaine and returned with a deepened interest in symbolism. We immediately notice a more determined cosmopolitanism, as when he insisted that 'as long as the Irish public knows nothing of literature Irish writers must be content to write for countries that know nothing of Ireland'.[15] When a writer in *United Ireland* attempted to use Walt Whitman in support of the thesis that English critical opinion was of little importance, Yeats counter-attacked by pointing out that the English had acknowledged Whitman's genius while his fellow-countrymen were still preoccupied with attacks on his morality:

> The truth is that the public of America was, and the public of Ireland is, uneducated and idle, and it was often necessary for an original American writer, and it is often necessary for an original Irish writer, to appeal first, not to his countrymen, but to that small group of men of imagination and scholarship which is scattered through many lands and many cities, and to trust to his own influence and the influence of his fellow-workers to build up in the fullness of time a cultivated public in the land where he lives and works. The true ambition is to make criticism as international, and literature as National, as possible.[16]

We recognise the reader of Matthew Arnold when Yeats observes that

> chance has hitherto decided the success or failure of Irish books; for one half Ireland has received everything Irish with undiscriminating praise, and the other half with undiscriminating indifference. We have founded the National Literary Society and the Irish Literary Society, London, to check the one and the other vice and to find an audience for whatever is excellent in the new or the old literature of Ireland. Political passion has made literary opinion in Ireland artificial.[17]

It is to be noticed how early he had taken the centre of the stage: he was scarcely exaggerating when he told Edward Garnett that he himself had 'practically planned and started this whole Irish literary movement'.[18] He saw clearly that a great critical effort was a necessary part of the movement. In England, he wrote, a proper respect for craftsmanship could be expected, but not in Ireland, where a librarian had published 'a dictionary of the Irish poets, containing, I think, two thousand names'.[19] Yeats reminded the editor of *United Ireland* that Whitman had appealed, 'like every great and earnest mind, not to the ignorant many, either English or American, but to that audience, "fit though few", which is greater than any nation, for it is made up of chosen persons from all'.[20]

The fact that he had for ever to walk a tightrope becomes particularly evident in a letter he wrote Katharine Tynan about an anthology she was compiling:

> A book such as you are doing should be Irish before all else. People will go to English poetry for 'literary poetry' but will look to a book like your collection for a new flavour as of fresh-turned mould . . . every poem that shows English influence in any marked way should be rejected.

148

No poetry has a right to live merely because it is good. It must be The Best of its Kind.[21]

His advice that Davis, Ferguson, Allingham, Mangan and Moore should be her mainstay, inevitable as it was, comes as something of an anti-climax.

In the preface to *The Countess Cathleen* Yeats expressed the hope that one day his country might 'make for herself a great distinctive poetic literature', and we recognise in the 'Legends and Lyrics' which accompanied it a courageous attempt to contribute to such a renaissance:

> I would, before my time to go,
> Sing of old Eire and the ancient ways:
> Red Rose, proud Rose, sad Rose of all my days.

He proclaims his aim in the poem 'To Ireland in the Coming Times', which is given a prominent place in the volume:

> Know, that I would accounted be
> True brother of a company
> That sang, to sweeten Ireland's wrong,
> Ballad and story, rann and song.

Once or twice Irish names are placed beside classical, as if to introduce to English readers the unfamiliar in the company of the familiar:

> Troy passed away in one high funeral gleam,
> And Usna's children died.

Although we find a few lyrics which require no knowledge of Ireland on the part of the reader – 'A Cradle Song', for example, and 'When you are old and gray and full of sleep' – the texture and colouring of the collection as a whole is essentially Irish.

About the turn of the century his sense of duty to his own people was as strong as ever. He planned to write a book called *What to read in Irish Literature*, and sent the Dublin *Daily Express* a list of Irish books 'that no gentleman's library should be without'.[22] He had a strong sense that 'our Celtic movement is approaching a new phase' and clearly saw the importance of an élite if the progress was to be real and permanent: 'Our instrument is sufficiently prepared as far as Ireland is concerned, but the people are less so, and they can only be stirred by the imagination of a very few acting on all.' He described his collection of stories, *The Secret Rose*, as 'at any rate an honest attempt towards that aristocratic esoteric Irish literature, which has been my chief ambition', adding: 'We have a literature for the people but nothing yet for the few.' Such comments provide an appropriate background to *The Wind among the Reeds*. Nothing could be more Irish, or more romantic, than the opening poem, 'The Hosting of the Sidhe':

> The host is riding from Knocknarea
> And over the grave of Clooth-na-Bare;
> Caoilte tossing his burning hair,
> And Niamh calling *Away, come away*.

While we find the occasional poem in a colloquial tradition – 'The Fiddler of Dooney' is a good example – the volume derives its character from such poems as 'The Song of Wandering Aengus', 'He remembers Forgotten Beauty' and 'The Secret Rose'. In spite of doubts on the part of reviewers about the notes and the symbolism, the collection enjoyed a measure of success in England as well as in Ireland. Our sense that Yeats knew exactly what he was doing is borne out by *In the Seven Woods: being poems chiefly of the Irish Heroic Age*, which was to be published at Dundrum in 1903 in an edition of 325 copies. Preceding the play in this little book we find a note drawing attention to the possibility of a change in his writing 'that may bring a less dream-burdened will into my verses'. He was referring to the influence of the dramatic verse which had been occupying most of his time for the last few years.

No part of Yeats's career throws more light on his search for an audience than the decade during which he was almost exclusively concerned with the theatre. Although in his youth he had dreamed of taking plays round Ireland in a wagon, he had little early experience of theatre-going, and it is revealing to find him, in 1891, describing 'the dramatic' as 'far the pleasantest *poetic form*'.[23] Soon he began *The Countess Cathleen*, which was based on a story he had found when he was collecting his *Fairy and Folk Tales of the Irish Peasantry* and intended for Maud Gonne to act in Dublin, but before that production took place he wrote a one-act play, *The Land of Heart's Desire*, which enjoyed a considerable success when it was acted in London with Shaw's *Arms and the Man*. In a letter to the editor of the Dublin *Daily Chronicle* at the beginning of 1899 he described the sort of audience he hoped might be attracted to Irish plays:

We will . . . gradually draw to us no great audience indeed, but one drawn from different classes, which will add to a true understanding of drama an interest in the life and in the legends on which our plays are founded so deep that it will give us that freedom to experiment, that freedom to search for the laws of what is perhaps a lost art, which even the most cultured London audience, with its half-conscious disbelief in the theatre, would not be able to give us. I know these people upon whom I rely, for I have worked with them and lived with them, and though I have heard them discuss what would seem to most Englishmen hopes and beliefs too wild even for laughter, I have not heard them exalt material above immaterial things, or claim any foundations for the arts but in moral and spiritual truths.[24]

When the play was performed, he found reality very different from aspiration. The actors

had to face a very vehement opposition stirred up by a politician and a newspaper, the one accusing me in a pamphlet, the other in long articles day after day, of blasphemy because of the language of the demons or of Shemus Rua, and because I made a woman sell her soul and yet escape damnation, and of a lack of patriotism because I made Irish men and women, who, it seems, never did such a thing, sell theirs. The politician or the newspaper persuaded some forty Catholic students to sign a protest against the play, and a Cardinal, who avowed that he had not read it, to make another, and both politician and newspaper made such obvious appeals to the audience to break the peace, that a score or so of police were sent to the theatre to see that they did not.[25]

Yeats remained optimistic, however, reporting that 'the stalls, containing almost all that was distinguished in Dublin, and a gallery of artisans alike insisted on the freedom of literature'.

The gallery was important to him because it was his ambition to use the drama to 'unite literature to the great passion of patriotism and ennoble both thereby'.[26] As he was to insist many years later, 'A nation should be like an audience in some great theatre – "In the theatre", said Victor Hugo, "the mob becomes a people" – watching the sacred drama of its own history.'[27] He was eager that the audience should be 'drawn from different classes' because he wished to see the theatre 'a national power', a focus of intellectual life and not merely a place for amusement, as the English theatre habitually was. At the same time, reflecting that even a play of Ibsen's could not be made to 'run for more than a few afternoons', he realised that he must depend to a great extent on 'that small public which cares for literature and the arts'.[28]

The patriotic nature of his dramatic ambitions is illustrated by *Cathleen ni Houlihan*, a play about Ireland and its struggle for independence first produced in 1902 and then revised and destined to become a central text for Sinn Fein and the republican movement.

When the following year the Irish Dramatic Company produced three of his plays in London, to an audience composed in large part of Irish exiles, Yeats wrote to John Quinn to thank him for the production:

I remember very well that when I first began to write plays I had hoped for just such an audience. One wants to write for one's own people, who come to the playhouse with a knowledge of one's subjects and with hearts ready to be moved. Almost the greatest difficulty before good work in the ordinary theatres is that the audience has no binding interest, no great passion or bias that the dramatist can awake . . . My work is, I am afraid, too full of a very personal comment on life, too full of the thoughts of the small sect you and I and all other cultivated people belong to, ever to have any great popularity.[29]

He adds that if he were offered one wish he would reply: 'Let my plays be acted, sometimes by professional actors if you will, but certainly a great many times by Irish societies in Ireland and throughout the world. Let the exiles, when they gather together to remember the country where they were born, sometimes have a play of mine acted to give wings to their thought.' It is significant that he refers to Burns when he remarks that he would 'like to help the imaginations that are most keen and subtle to think of Ireland as a sacred land'.

O'Leary had told Yeats that 'a man must have upon his side the Church or the Fenians, and you will never have the Church'.[30] It is not surprising that he had a short alliance with the militant nationalists, among whom Maud Gonne was one of the most prominent. Arthur Griffith had ruled that every intelligent Irish person must read Yeats, because he was 'Irish literature and Irish belief, and Irish faith, hope and aspiration', and had led a group of men from the Dublin Quays when *The Countess* had been performed, telling them to 'applaud everything the Church would not like'.[31] Griffith regarded the Irish National Theatre 'primarily as a means of regenerating the country', and believed that it could be 'a powerful agent in the building up of a nation'. It was a view close to that of Yeats himself, yet divided from it by a great chasm. When Griffith attacked Synge's play *In the Shadow of the Glen* as 'decadent cynicism' which had nothing to do with Ireland Yeats was soon moved to make their difference explicit:

Literature is always personal, always one man's vision of the world, one man's experience, and it can only be popular when we are ready to welcome the visions of others . . . I am a Nationalist, and certain of my intimate friends have made Irish politics the business of their lives . . . But if some external necessity had forced me to write nothing but drama with an obviously patriotic intention instead of letting my work shape itself . . . I would have lost, in a short time, the power to write movingly upon any theme. I could have aroused opinion, but could not have touched the heart.[32]

He concluded that he would sooner the theatre failed 'through the indifference or hostility of our audiences than gained an immense popularity by any loss of freedom'.

Although Yeats wished the Abbey Theatre, which opened in 1904, to limit itself to Irish plays initially, he continued to oppose those who regarded drama merely as a form of political propaganda, and one can only be impressed by the combination of courage and practical ability which he displayed both as manager and as dramatist. He modified his dramaturgy, including less mystical material in his plays and developing the skill of writing fine dramatic prose. If at times we are tempted to regard him as the Don Quixote of the Irish theatre, it is only because he persisted in the hope that Catholic and Nationalist sheep might turn into an intelligent and disinterested theatre-going public.

It was not that he lacked candid friends. 'You spoke once to me of two courts of appeal', George Russell wrote, 'the "popular" and the "intellectual". Neither one nor the other have awarded you any other position than as a writer of beautiful verse, and I think it is a mistake which later on you may regret that you should lose time managing a business, bringing endless annoyance with no added influence. As a poet you could and would exercise an immense influence on your contemporaries, as a dramatist you lose influence. The few dozen people who come to the Abbey Theatre are a poor compensation for the thousands who would read another *Wind among the Reeds* or another *Usheen*.'[33]

As we consider the numerous references to the audience in his letters it is often difficult to know to what extent Yeats was merely whistling to keep his courage up. In February 1905 he insisted on regarding *The Well of the Saints* as a success, although he had to admit that it had attracted only 'thin audiences'.[34] In October he told Florence Farr that he had 'a small genuine following as a dramatist', though he knew he would never have the support of the political clubs. 'I am trying for the general public', he told George Russell a little later, ' – the only question with me . . . is whether I should attack the clubs openly. Our small public at the theatre is, I am glad to say, almost entirely general public.' 'Small as our audiences are', he wrote to Katharine Tynan, 'they are Irish and well pleased. We had an audience at Longford that would have stirred your imagination – shopkeepers and lads of the town, who smoked and were delighted, I think.' Yet only Miss Horniman's subsidy kept the ship afloat, and it was soon evident that it was not enough. 'Last winter we played to almost empty houses', Yeats told a friend in 1906–7, 'a sprinkling of people in pit and stalls'; but his habitual optimism shines through when he reports 'big Saturday audiences'. When an unexpected legacy enabled Miss Horniman to open a repertory theatre in Manchester Yeats was not to be persuaded to move to England:

I am not young enough to change my nationality – it would really amount to that. Though I wish for a universal audience, in play-writing there is always an immediate audience also. If I am to try and find the immediate audience in England I would fail through lack of understanding on my part, perhaps through lack of sympathy. I understand my own race and in all my work, lyric or dramatic, I have thought of it. If the theatre fails I may or may not write plays – but I shall write for my own people – whether in love or hate of them matters little.

It is a courageous affirmation, and may be read with a letter to Quinn written a few months later:

The Abbey has been doing very well lately; for the last three months or so it has even been paying, and if it can keep on like this, which I doubt, we'll be able to do without a subsidy. The curious thing is that in spite of all the attacks upon us we have nothing but a pit and that is always full now. The stalls won't come near us, except when some titled person or other comes and brings guests. All the praise we have had from the most intellectual critics cannot bring the Irish educated classes, and all the abuse we have had from the least intellectual cannot keep the less educated classes away. I suppose the cause of it all is that, as a drunken medical student used to say, 'Pitt decapitated Ireland.'

The losing battle consumed an immense amount of Yeats's time. In November 1910 he told his father that he had been on a provincial lecture tour in England in which one of his aims had been 'to help the theatre to audiences when it goes on tour',[35] and mentioned the details of a patent application he was making

on behalf of the Abbey. More than a year later he admitted that
he had 'done nothing but theatre for months now'. A letter from
Synge must have been disappointing: 'We had "The Shadowy
Waters" on that stage last week, and it was the most *distressing*
failure the mind can imagine – a half-empty room, with growling
men and tittering females.'

It is hardly surprising that he later came round to the conception of 'a form of drama which may delight the best minds of my
time',[36] a drama for the intellectual élite. Of his brief play, *At the
Hawk's Well*, he wrote to Quinn that if 'Balfour and Sargent and
Ricketts and Sturge Moore and [Augustus] John and the Prime
Minister and a few pretty ladies will come to see it, I shall have
a success that would have pleased Sophocles. No press, no
photographs in the papers, no crowd. I shall be happier than
Sophocles. I shall be as lucky as a Japanese dramatic poet at the
Court of the Shogun.' Later still be wrote in his essay on 'A
People's Theatre':

I want to create for myself an unpopular theatre and an audience like a
secret society where admission is by favour and never to many . . . a mode
of drama Shelley and Keats could have used without ceasing to be themselves, and for which even Blake in the mood of *The Book of Thel* might not
have been too obscure . . . I seek, not a theatre but the theatre's anti-self, an
art that can appease all within us that becomes uneasy as the curtain falls
and the house breaks into applause.[37]

When he looked back on his dramatic experience, towards the
end of his life, Yeats contrasted the fortune of his 'famous
theatre' with the fortune it might have enjoyed if it had been
established in Poland, in Sweden, or in 'some Balkan State'.[38]
There (he mused) it would not have been so small (the Abbey
contained only 536 seats), it would have attracted larger audiences, and it would have been supported by the government. In
Ireland, by way of contrast, 'our upper class cares nothing for
Ireland except as a place for sport', while 'the rest of the popu-
lation is drowned in religious and political fanaticism'. As a
result, 'men of letters live like outlaws in their own country',
while the Abbey had to rely mainly on a pit audience consisting
of 'boys and girls out of the shops and factories' who 'come again
and again to a favorite play', while 'all others are casual or
uncertain, except some old adherents who have lasted out the
thirty years, and a few students from the National University'.

When we remember that Yeats belonged to the people which

had produced Goldsmith, Sheridan, Wilde, Shaw, O'Casey and
Synge, and which has since produced Samuel Beckett, we are
bound to notice that he did not write one play which holds the
stage, and may therefore be judged to have contributed nothing
to the repertory of the major English drama. Yet the Noh plays,
begun in 1913 or 1914, are the work of a most brilliant innovator,
and T.S. Eliot was moved to particular admiration of the last
play, *Purgatory*, in which (as he pointed out) Yeats 'solved his
problem of speech in verse' and 'laid all his successors under
obligation to him'.[39]

Yet Eliot seems to owe more to *Purgatory* in *Four Quartets* than
in his plays, and the most important thing about the plays of
Yeats for the student of his work as a whole is that he emerged
from the theatre a stronger man as well as a stronger poet. His
most important poetry, like that of Dryden, is the expression of
a poet who had enjoyed the advantage of hearing his verse
spoken by a variety of trained speakers, and who had reflected
deeply on the potential of poetry as speech.

While writing for the theatre is of value to any poet, it was of particular value to Yeats because his original conception of lyric
verse had been cripplingly romantic. And it occurred at the right
moment in his career. Whereas Tennyson (juvenilia aside)
attempted poetic drama too late, Yeats turned to it before he had
discovered the road to great poetry. His experience in the
theatre played a vital part in transforming the writer of 'The
Lake Isle of Innisfree' into the poet of *The Tower* and *Last Poems*.
He had always regarded verse as language that must be spoken
or chanted, believing that silent reading is 'an error, a part of the
fall';[40] but now he had learned a great deal more about the acous-
tic qualities of language. 'Some of my friends', he observed, 'and
it is always for a few friends one writes, do not understand why
I have not been content with lyric writing. But . . . to me drama
– and I think it has been the same with other writers – has been
the search for more of manful energy, more of cheerful acceptance of whatever arises out of the logic of events, and for clean
outline, instead of those outlines of lyric poetry that are blurred
with desire and vague regret.'[41]

I have already quoted an important note from the volume *In
the Seven Woods*: in the year of its publication Yeats told Lady

Gregory that he was 'full of new thoughts for verse' and that his work had become 'far more masculine' and had 'more salt in it'.[42] He exemplified his approach to a new style in 'Adam's Curse', but the fact that he is believed to have written only one lyric between 1902 and 1908 makes it clear that it is to his plays – the new plays, and the revisions of the old plays – that we are to look for his new manner. He told Florence Farr that he was surprised to find how bad much of *The Shadowy Waters* now seemed, and commented that the performance had enabled him to see it with a fresh eye. 'The very temper of the thing is different', he told another friend, referring to his comprehensive revision. 'It is [now] full of homely phrases and of the idiom of daily speech.' He was pleased to have brought 'creaking shoes' and 'liquorice-root' into 'what had been a very abstract passage', and added that he was more and more convinced that 'the element of strength in poetic language is common idiom'.

As he realised, Yeats was now much more widely known than he had been at the beginning of the century. 'I think this new book should sell very well', he wrote of *Poems: A New Series, 1899–1905*, 'for it will be the first big mass of verse that I have published for years, and will get a constant advertisement from the plays at the Abbey Theatre.'[43] The generous patronage of Miss Horniman enabled him to publish his *Collected Works* three years later, in an edition in eight volumes. He explained that he was 'insistent upon . . . revisions etc. in this expensive edition' because he wished to 'get my general personality and the total weight of my work into people's minds, as a preliminary to new work'. In an exceptionally perceptive review Walter de la Mare pointed out that Yeats desired 'to hark back through the written tradition, the poetry that is of the artist and of the narrow cultivated class, to the unwritten tradition, the poetry of the people':[44] a view which shows an understanding of one aspect of Yeats's work. De la Mare also suggested that there was nothing in the plays or poems 'that the English mind and taste are incapable of appreciating'.

It is appropriate that a group of his friends, no doubt aware of his new interest in the poet, should have given Yeats a copy of the Kelmscott Chaucer for his fortieth birthday: it came at the right moment, and may serve as a symbol for the transition from his William Morris period to that in which he was to write as frankly of human nature and its desires as the author of *The Canterbury Tales*. He told A.H. Bullen, who had asked him to write an essay on Shakespeare, that he was getting 'so deep in Chaucer' that he could not plunge his imagination 'into any other well for the present'.[45] A comment prompted by a poem of Lionel Johnson's enables us to measure the distance he had travelled since the days of the Rhymers' Club: 'The danger of the Psaltery is monotony. A thing the ancients were more alive to in all arts than we are – Chaucer for instance follows his noble "Knight's Tale" with an unspeakable tale told by a drunken miller. If Morris had done the like – everyone would have read his *Earthly Paradise* for ever. By the by Chaucer . . . calls a certain young wife "white and small as a weasel". Does it not bring the physical type clearly to the mind's-eye? I think one wants that sort of vivid irresistible phrase in all verse to be spoken aloud.'

If there is no phrase as vivid as that in the transitional volumes he published in the next few years, which serve as stepping stones to the work of his maturity, a markedly satirical vein is apparent, and with it a colloquial idiom very different from that of his early poems. In *The Green Helmet and other Poems* Yeats contrasts his youthful conception of poetry, sung with 'Such airs That one believed he had a sword upstairs' with the more sober notion of the craft at which he had now arrived. Reflecting on the Abbey period, he complains that the audience is never pleased:

> When we are high and airy hundreds say
> That if we hold that flight they'll leave the place,
> While those same hundreds mock another day
> Because we have made our art of common things.

His impatience with his 'blind bitter land' and with the people for whom he had worked and written is even more noticeable in *Responsibilities*, where the Abbey Theatre is hardly mentioned. While many of us may find it as impossible to take an interest in 'The Two Kings', a long poem on Irish history, as did Ezra Pound – who remarked that it was as devoid of interest as 'the "Idylls" of another'[46] – there is much more vitality in the poems about beggars, who are romanticised as free men who are to be preferred to clerks and shopkeepers. The new enterprise of 'walking naked' is exemplified by the description of one of them 'skelping his big brawling lout' and of another cursing 'the . . . devil that is between my thighs'.

In the most intelligent review of the volume Pound acknowledged that 'a lot of his admirers will be rather displeased with
the book', but added: 'That is always a gain for a poet, for his
admirers nearly always want him to "stay put", and they resent
any signs of stirring, of new curiosity or of intellectual uneasi-
ness'. In reply to critics who ask whether Yeats is 'in the movement' Pound replies that he is a great poet whose work is
'becoming gaunter, seeking greater hardness of outline'.

At times Yeats feared that his readers would not understand
what he was about; apart from the development of his style,
which many were bound to find disconcerting, those who knew
only about 'some contest with Irish opinion' might fail to understand that his work had been 'done in every detail with a deliber-
ate Irish aim'.[47] He himself had no doubts, however: he told
Joseph Hone that his house was still unfinished, but that in the
end it would contain 'many rooms and corridors' and that he was
still building upon foundations laid long before.

Most of the poems in *The Wild Swans at Coole*, published at
London in 1919, had appeared in a volume of the same name
published at Dundrum two years earlier. At no point is the
reader more acutely aware that Yeats was not English. While the
First World War raged he bought a tower in Galway, proposed to
Maud Gonne and then to her daughter Iseult, and married
Georgie Hyde-Lees. The only poems in this highly personal collection which relate to the war are those dealing with the death
of Lady Gregory's nephew, a young airman portrayed as going to
his death without hate for those against whom he is fighting and
without love for those whom he is guarding. In other poems we
find that the poet is still angry with the people of Dublin for their
'daily spite': in 'The Fisherman' we find him creating 'In scorn
of this audience' the sort of man for whom he would have liked
to write,

> A man who does not exist,
> A man who is but a dream.

It was a difficult volume to assess, and a critic as intelligent as
Middleton Murry, disconcerted by a phrase in the preface about
'the phantasmagoria' through which alone Yeats could express
his 'convictions about the world', concluded that he was a poet
'whose creative vigour has failed him when he had to make the
highest demands upon it'.[48] We may assume that Murry's tone

would have been very different if he had known 'Easter, 1916', the manner of whose publication is of particular interest. It was written within a few months of the rising, and printed in an edition of twenty-five copies, which were not for sale. After the war, in 1920, it appeared in *The New Statesman* and *The Dial*, periodicals read only by the intelligentsia on either side of the Atlantic; the following year it was included in the Dundrum printing of *Michael Robartes and the Dancer*, a little book which went virtually unnoticed; only in 1922 was it included in a volume published at London, *Later Poems*. The poem deals with an event which was to prove of cardinal importance to Yeats. The rising helped him to escape from too great a concern with his 'mythological people', and presented him with the very different problems of political verse.

It was during this period after the war that Yeats emerged from the regimen which had cured his 'romantically Celtic'[49] phase and presented himself as a European poet to an international reading public whose attitudes had been profoundly modified between 1914 and 1919. The *Michael Robartes* volume contains that great poem, 'The Second Coming', which includes a sentence which characterised a generation and which retains to this day its sombre relevance:

> The best lack all conviction, while the worst
> Are full of passionate intensity.

Yeats reprinted the collection at the end of *Later Poems* in 1922, as if to make it clear to what an extent he was a different poet from the author of the *Poems* of 1895 and the *Collected Works* of 1908. In the preface he points out that he has omitted 'nearly all the long notes which seemed necessary before the work of various writers, but especially of my friend Lady Gregory, had made the circumstantial origins of my verse, in ancient legend or in the legends of the country side, familiar to readers of poetry'. He was now in a position to expect of his readers some knowledge of Ireland, as part of the common background of the cultivated public. The élite who read Pound and Eliot – an élite gradually increasing in numbers as the years passed – found Yeats less difficult than much of their work, while a steadily increasing public bought his later volumes, even if they sometimes found that they preferred his earlier lyrics. If he had received the acclamation due to a great poet somewhat prematurely, he was now proceeding to write poems which justified his reputation. In the words of a fine poet of our own day, Yeats had 'found at last that noble, candid speech In which all things worth saying may be said'.[50]

The contrast between the exoteric and the esoteric in Yeats is evident in two aspects of his work at this time. Throughout his life he had practised the art of public speaking – 'we are what we are', he wrote of himself and other Irish poets of the period, 'because almost without exception we have had some part in public life'[51] – and now he spoke in the Senate. He was the 'sixty-year-old smiling public man', appointed as one of the first Senators of the Irish Free State at least as much because he had once been a member of the Irish Republican Brotherhood as because of his eminence as a poet. It is tempting to attribute something of the assurance of his later poetry to his experience of affairs, which was greater than that associated with the running of the Abbey Theatre, considerable as that had been. He was as far as possible from being an introvert, and he accepted (as Browning had not, and Eliot would not) the inevitable fact that readers of his poetry would be interested in the details of his life, since 'poetry is no rootless flower but the speech of a man'.[52]

On the other hand an esoteric thread runs through his life, from an early time. From the day when his father read him *The Lay of the Last Minstrel* he saw the poet as a magician, no less than as a public figure. He told O'Leary that he could not have done his work on Blake if he had not 'made magic [his] constant study', adding: 'The mystical life is the centre of all that I do and all that I think and all that I write.'[53] He had been a member of various theosophical and mystical societies, and not the least of the gifts brought him by his wife was her automatic writing, which led him to feel for the first time that he understood human life. *A Vision*, privately printed in 1926, grew directly from these new experiences. 'I write very much for young men between twenty and thirty', he told Olivia Shakespear, 'as at that age, and younger, I wanted to feel that any poet I cared for – Shelley let us say – saw more than he told of, had in some sense seen into the mystery . . . The young men I write for may not read my *Vision* – they may care too much for poetry – but they will be pleased that it exists . . . I have constructed a myth – but then one can believe

161

in a myth – one only assents to philosophy.' Here we have a poet profoundly esoteric by instinct who is yet constantly aware of the likely reactions of his readers.

When we turn the pages of *The Tower*, published in 1928 and mainly consisting of recent poems, we find a poet who is writing for an international highbrow audience, and see how appropriate it had been that James Joyce should have been the first friend to telegraph his congratulations on the award of the Nobel Prize, five years before. 'Nineteen Hundred and Nineteen' is a great sequence, but it was little likely to please the majority of Irish nationalists or of any other organised group. This is proud poetry which demands of its readers not merely understanding but at least a temporary suspension of hatred and partisanship. Irish mythology has all but disappeared, to be replaced by phantasmagoric imagery which is only partly explained in *A Vision*. An illuminating comment on the energy of the verse is provided by Yeats's observation in a letter that the weakness of much poetry since Wordsworth is due to 'the lack of natural momentum in the syntax'.[54] There is a remarkable variety of style, from passages of great simplicity to the relative obscurity of 'All Souls' Night'. The contrast between the pedestrian opening of 'Among School Children' and the astonishing conclusion:

> O chestnut-tree, great-rooted blossomer,
> Are you the leaf, the blossom or the bole?
> O body swayed to music, O brightening glance,
> How can we know the dancer from the dance?

is the work of a great poet who has mastered his art until it seems to have the inevitability of nature, and who knows that he can rely on his readers to make the necessary effort to understand him. *The Tower* sold 2,000 copies in the first month, the largest sale of any book by Yeats so far on its first appearance.[55]

'I too have tried to be modern', Yeats was soon to write in the introduction to *The Oxford Book of Modern Verse*,[56] with more than a suggestion of irony. Nothing could more clearly mark the 'modernity' of *The Winding Stair and other Poems* than the notes at the end, which draw attention to 'a quotation from somewhere in Mr. Ezra Pound's "Cantos" ', a passage from Macrobius 'found for me by Dr. Sturm, that too little known poet and mystic', and 'Byzantine mosaic pictures of the Annunciation', as well as 'gyres in Swedenborg, and in Thomas Aquinas and certain classical authors'. It is illuminating to juxtapose these notes with those in some of his early volumes, or with the colophon to the Dundrum edition of *In the Seven Woods* thirty years before: 'Here ends In The Seven Woods' it reads, 'written by William Butler Yeats, printed, upon paper made in Ireland, and published by Elizabeth Corbet Yeats at the Dun Emer Press, in the house of Evelyn Gleeson at Dundrum in the county of Dublin, Ireland, finished the sixteenth day of July, in the year of the big wind 1903.' The poet who had written in the tradition of William Morris was writing for a very different public thirty years later.

Yet it remained his deepest instinct to write for 'a few friends', as he acknowledged when he dedicated his *Autobiographies* 'To those few people mainly personal friends who have read all that I have written'. When, in 'Coole Park, 1929', he presents us with 'A scene well set and excellent company', we realise that the fascination of the Country House for Yeats lay not only in his sense of tradition and beauty – of the stillness in the midst of the chaos of modern times – but also in his delight at having men and women he could converse with and who would understand the esoteric allusions of some of his finest poetry. Coole Park had been his Appleton House.

Not that all the poems in *The Winding Stair* are difficult. The volume contains simple lyrics which Yeats described as 'all emotion and all impersonal'[57] as well as esoteric poems which yet contain lines as direct and unforgettable as 'No man has ever lived that had enough Of children's gratitude or woman's love.' Beside 'Byzantium' and 'Veronica's Napkin' we find a lyric, 'I am of Ireland', which is 'developed from three or four lines of an Irish fourteenth-century dance song'.[58] He was becoming more and more aware of the value of the dramatic mode which had been described by Browning when he observed that the poems in his 'Dramatic Lyrics' were 'so many utterances of so many imaginary persons, not mine'.[59] In a letter referring to some prose stories written in the persona of 'Michael Robartes' he remarked that, 'Having proved, by undescribed process, the immortality of the soul to a little group of typical followers, he will discuss the deductions with an energy and a dogmatism and a cruelty I am not capable of in my own person.'[60] As a result we have the sequence called 'A Woman Young and Old', poems accessible to any reader, and 'Words for Music Perhaps', which include the Crazy Jane poems which have shocked some readers but perplexed few:

> But Love has pitched his mansion in
> The place of excrement.

One of the advantages of not writing for the theatre was that he did not have to worry about the Church.

In 'Remorse for Intemperate Speech' Yeats had confessed that although he had at last found 'Fit audience', his 'fanatic heart' still tempted him towards the old ranting of his youth. When Lady Gregory died in 1932 and 'the great house died too' his creative impulse flagged for a while, and it was political passion which brought him back to verse. In *Reveries over Childhood and Youth* he had described how the recitation by John F. Taylor of some political verse by Thomas Davis at a Young Ireland meeting had early given him 'a conviction of how great might be the effect of verse, spoken . . . at some moment of intensity'.[61] As early as 'Easter, 1916', with its unforgettable line, 'A terrible beauty is born', he had discovered his own potential as a political poet – a potential the implications of which troubled him, as well they might.

A remarkable instance of his setting out to write exoterically on a political theme is provided by 'Three Songs to the Same Tune'. Yeats tells us how, appalled by the 'growing disorder, the fanaticism that inflamed it like some old bullet imbedded in the flesh', in 1933 he desired 'for the first time in [his] life . . . to write what some crowd in the street might understand and sing'.[62] Accordingly he wrote the first song to an old march tune, 'O'Donnell Abu': then he 'tired of its rhetorical vehemence, thought that others would tire of it unless [he] found some gay playing upon its theme, some half-serious exaggeration and defence of its rancorous chorus', and wrote the second song, and then the third. He read the songs to friends, 'they talked to others, those talked, and now companies march to the words "Blueshirt Abu", and a song that is all about shamrocks and harps or seems all about them, because its words have the particular variation upon the cadence of "Yankee Doodle" Young Ireland reserved for that theme'. In reaction, Yeats increased the 'fantasy' of his songs, 'their extravagance, their obscurity, that no party might sing them'. Having given way to a natural desire to write for a wide audience in a manner calculated to have an immediate political effect, he had quickly recoiled from what he had done and had revised the songs until they became poetry. Having ventured too far into the merely local and partisan, he drew back. We may recall 'The Man and the Echo', written in 1938, which seems to have been inspired by a comment of Stephen Gwynn's on a performance of *Cathleen ni Houlihan*: 'I went home asking myself if such plays should be produced unless one was prepared for people to go out to shoot and be shot.'[63]

He had been similarly roused by the discovery of the forgery of the Casement Diaries in 1936. 'I long to break my rule against politics and call these men criminals . . . ', he wrote to Ethel Mannin. 'Perhaps a verse may come to me, now or a year hence. I have lately written a song in defence of Parnell . . . a drinking song to a popular tune and will have it sung from the Abbey stage at Xmas. All my life it has been hard to keep from action.'[64] In the event he wrote two Roger Casement poems, and the first of them has a direct force that recalls 'The Mask of Anarchy':

> I say that Roger Casement
> Did what he had to do.
> He died upon the gallows,
> But that is nothing new.

Whereas he had never enjoyed true popular success in the theatre, he found that the circulation of this poem, 'as direct and natural as spoken words',[65] as he said himself, could not be stopped: people had copies, and in any case he did not want to suppress the poem. When his wife went shopping one day she was surprised at the deference shown her in buses and shops until she discovered that the ballad had been printed in the morning paper. Yeats was thanked by De Valera's political secretary and others, an 'old revolutionist', Count Plunkett, called it 'a ballad the people much needed', and copies were sent – of course – to America. His own verdict, which was remarkably just, was that 'These ballads of mine though not supremely good are not ephemeral, the young will sing them now and after I am dead.' 'I do the old work of the poets', he added, 'but I will defend no cause.'

No feature of his later poems is more striking than the versatility which they display. 'This difficult work', he wrote to Dorothy Wellesley about certain poems in *The Faber Book of*

Modern Verse, ' . . . is being written everywhere now (a professor from Barcelona tells me they have it there), [it] has the substance of philosophy and is a delight to the poet with his professional pattern; but it is not your road or mine, and ours is the main road, the road of naturalness and swiftness, and we have thirty centuries upon our side.'[66] In his last years he wrote 'endless ballads to music', and no doubt aspired to have them sung by girls working in the fields, as he had so often heard the Gaelic songs of Douglas Hyde sung in his youth. Yet he also wrote difficult poems which are among his supreme achievements, such as the great poems in *ottava rima* which may be spoken of in the same breath as the Odes of Keats. The first-written, 'The Municipal Gallery Revisited', was initially printed in an edition of seventy copies,[67] and it, like 'The Statues', is evidence of a concern with Ireland that grew rather than slackened. The question

> When Pearse summoned Cuchulain to his side,
> What stalked through the Post Office?

is not merely audacious in defying the censure that it is prosaic, it also demonstrates his confidence that his readers now knew something of the 'circumstantial origins' of his work. The poem is highly abstract and philosophical, and can at first have been accessible only to that fit audience, though few, which formed the inner circle of his readers. Even 'The Circus Animals' Desertion' is for a reader well acquainted with his work: one who will not be 'thrown' by the title and who will understand the reference to the absence of his old 'ladder' as he decides that he must lie down

> where all the ladders start,
> In the foul rag-and-bone shop of the heart.

If one compares the life and circumstances of Yeats with those of the other poets considered in this study one can only conclude that he was remarkably lucky, though it took all his genius to exploit the luck to the full. His parentage fitted him to become the first great poet of modern Ireland. He was as fortunate in his failure to marry Maud Gonne, 'A proud woman not kindred of his soul',[68] as in his success in marrying a wife who introduced order into his life and brought him metaphors for poetry. At all times he had understanding friends and was greatly helped by women who have put us in their debt by preserving his letters, as he no doubt knew they would: Lady Gregory and Miss Horniman are reminders that patronage had not died in the eighteenth century, or the nineteenth, and that patronage inspired by personal affection and understanding will always be a different thing from official patronage because it is warmer and less inhibiting.

Yet he enjoyed official patronage as well. In his thirties such a possibility had already been mentioned, and on the second occasion that the offer was made, as he told Ethel Mannin, 'it was explained to me that it implied no political bargain. I said "Am I free to join an Irish insurrection?" The answer was "Yes, perfectly." '[69] From 1910, therefore, he had been free from 'the one thing I have always dreaded, that some day I might have to think of the prejudices or convictions of others before I wrote my own': 'free to do only the work [he] was most fitted for'. During the First World War, in which he took so little interest, he told his sister Lily that he had been offered a knighthood by the British government: an offer he refused in order to retain his own unfettered scope.[70] Such a degree of freedom has been the lot of few writers in any country or in any age. In our own day the political systems of a great part of the world make the idea seem no more than a cruel joke. Politics apart, as a contemporary of D.H. Lawrence and of Joyce, Yeats could write of love with a freedom inconceivable in the century into which he had been born, while as a contemporary of Pound and Eliot he could write difficult poetry in the knowledge that it would be studied with the respect due to a classical text.

His deep patriotism was not a constraint. Two observations about a collection of Irish songs he was making for Macmillan towards the end of his life are particularly revealing. First he insists that 'The Irish race – our scattered 20 millions – is held together by songs', and adds that 'we must get the young men who go to the American universities as well as those in factories and farms'; then he provides a comment on his insistence: 'That is what I say to Irish Americans in justification of all my work, and to our own Government and politicians generally. But in reality I am more anarchic than a sparrow.'[71] Insistence and comment are both sincere: neither cancels out the other.

In response to Archibald MacLeish's regret that such a master of 'public' language should not have written more often about politics, Yeats wrote the poem 'Politics', with its memorable opening:

> How can I, that girl standing there,
> My attention fix
> On Roman or on Russian
> Or on Spanish politics?

It is significant that nothing is here said of Irish politics: for all his impatience with the ignorance and prejudice of the mass of his countrymen Yeats remained as irrevocably an Irishman as he was a poet. 'I have always written as an Irish writer', he comments in a letter, 'and with Ireland in my mind.'[72] As an old man he took a justifiable pride in the success of the movement in which he played so prominent a part, a pride tempered by awareness of the murderous excesses of the zealots. 'The work of Irish poets, quite deliberately put into circulation with its music thirty and more years ago, is now all over the country', he wrote. 'The Free State Army march to a tune called "Down by the Salley Gardens" without knowing that the march was first published with words of mine, words that are now folklore.'

No poet better illustrates Wordsworth's remark that 'every author, as far as he is great and at the same time *original*, has had the task of *creating* the taste by which he is to be enjoyed'.[73] Yeats created the taste by which his poetry is enjoyed, and as he did so he did a great deal to bring Ireland and its tragic history into the consciousness of Europe and of the world. He had educated his audience, and the text-book is the volume of his poems.

Conclusion

Friends have asked me the 'thesis' of my book. It has no thesis. My aim is descriptive, not prescriptive: exploratory, not exhortatory. What interests me is how certain good poems came to be as they are.

For those who desire dogmatic statements, there is no shortage. We are told that the poet should be at the king's side, that he should be the upholder of religion, that he should write for the cultivated few, for the proletariat, for the public at large, or for posterity. Such pronouncements belong to realms other than that of literary criticism.

Like exhortations, generalisations have as a rule only a limited validity, and tend to throw light on the writer who formulates them and not on poetry in general. One of the few exceptions remains Wordsworth's remark that the poet 'is a man speaking to men'.[1] That sounds a truism, yet we have only to remember John Stuart Mill's claim that 'eloquence is *heard*, poetry is *over*heard', with its rider that 'Eloquence supposes an audience; the peculiarity of poetry appears to . . . lie in the poet's utter unconsciousness of a listener',[2] to realise that Wordsworth's statement – which has the same splendidly obvious quality as certain observations in the *Poetics* – recalls us to a deeper and truer understanding. Mill's view is hopelessly 'romantic', betraying a complete failure to consider the facts of the case, the actual history of poetry. Any empirical enquiry is likely to lead to the conclusion that a good poet is almost always conscious of his audience – of the audience, at least, to which he wishes to address his verse – and that what he writes is influenced by his assessment of that audience.

It is true that there have been good poets who have written with virtually no audience.[3] They have not been numerous, and in almost every instance the lack of an audience appears to have been a handicap, the achievement a triumph won in the face of extreme difficulty. Gerard Manley Hopkins, who told Robert

Bridges that he did not write for the public – 'You are my public'[4] – was a remarkably gifted poet, and a handful of his poems are amongst the most moving in the language; yet I believe that Bridges was right when he singled out 'Oddity and Obscurity' as blemishes in much of his work. When Alfred Domett, on reading *Sordello*, concluded that Browning was 'difficult on system', Browning hastened to contradict him: 'No, really – the fact is I live by myself, write with no better company, and forget that the "lovers" you mention are part and parcel of that self, and their choosing to comprehend *my* comprehensions but an indifferent testimony to their value . . . I wish I had thought of this before.'[5] A poet who has hardly any readers – unlike Browning, Blake and Emily Dickinson remained in this condition throughout their lives – is likely to exhibit some of the eccentricities of a man or woman too much in the habit of living alone. He becomes accustomed to speaking to himself, elliptically, and often has great difficulty in communicating.

A poet without an audience may also be betrayed into faults of tone – an aspect of poetry which is, as I.A. Richards long ago pointed out, too easily overlooked. In *Practical Criticism* he observed that 'poetry, which has no other very remarkable qualities, may sometimes take very high rank simply because the poet's attitude to his listeners – in view of what he has to say – is so perfect'.[6] Citing Dryden and Gray, he suggested that 'many of the secrets of "style" could, I believe, be shown to be matters of tone, of the perfect recognition of the writer's relation to the reader in view of what is being said and their joint feelings about it'. I am happier with Dryden as an example than with Gray – how much can we in fact deduce about Gray's 'attitude to his listeners' in the *Elegy*? I suspect that sureness of tone is characteristic of more good poetry than Richards seems to acknowledge, and I would suggest that some good poetry – *Don Juan* immediately comes to mind – owes its success less to 'joint feelings' than to the skill with which the poet, aware as he is of his audience, delights in teasing or perplexing his readers. Yet the observation remains important and suggestive.

While we may agree that it is good for a poet to be conscious of an audience, the size of the audience is another matter. We have seen that some of the best poetry – that of Byron and Tennyson, for example – has reached a very large audience during the poet's lifetime; but it is equally true that some of the best poetry (like that of Shelley) fails to find any considerable audience, and that there have been poets (Donne and Marvell are outstanding examples) who have made no attempt to gain a wide readership. Pindar's description of himself as φωνᾶντα συνετοῖσι has been quoted or alluded to by a great many poets, of every level of ability. It is clear that the size of a poet's contemporary audience is no indication of his poetic merit.

What seems more important is that it should have a sound core. If he is not to find himself in desperate straits, a poet needs an inner circle of 'Understanders' – they may sometimes be as few as half-a-dozen or even two or three – who form his initial audience, comprehend his poetic aims, and are in a position to provide him with the blend of praise and criticism which suits his particular temperament. We have seen how important a few friends were to Pope, both early and late, and how eagerly Byron awaited the verdict of Murray's '*knowing ones*'. We know how much Ezra Pound helped Eliot with *The Waste Land*, and how John Hayward suggested 'improvements of phrase and construction' in *Four Quartets*.

Helped (if he is fortunate) by such friends, the poet must work out his own salvation. He may live in an age when poetry is highly regarded, or in an age like our own when it retains little significance for the greater part of the reading public. He may belong to a culture in which he is free to write as he pleases – it is instructive to compare the situation of Yeats with that of Dryden – or to a culture in which certain topics – religious, political or moral – are more or less taboo. It is for him, as a man speaking to men, to reach out towards some sort of audience. While he will sometimes think of posterity, it will be the audience of his contemporaries which is most likely to influence his poetry. It is (after all) the poet's contemporaries who influence the very way in which he sees himself – for it is a fallacy to suppose that a poet's personality is something fixed and immutable, a *donnée* from the moment when he sets out on the long journey to his best work. On the contrary the personality which he forges as he creates his poems will be very different from the personality which would have been his if he had continued, as small poets do, to write in the manner in which he began.

171

Notes

The place of publication is London or Oxford unless otherwise stated.

Introduction

1 See for example A.V.C. Schmidt, in *The Review of English Studies*, n.s., 34 (February 1983), 52–3.
2 Ben Jonson, 'To Lucy, Countesse of Bedford, with M. Donnes Satyres', line 6.
3 *Prologue Spoken at the Opening of the Theatre in Drury-Lane 1747*, lines 53–4.
4 'In my Craft or Sullen Art', lines 12ff.

I Dryden: Servant to the King

Quotations from poems and prefatory matter to poems are from *The Poems of John Dryden*, ed. James Kinsley (4 vols., 1958). Quotations from plays and attendant matter are, where possible, from the relevant volumes of the California Edition of *The Works* (Berkeley and Los Angeles, 1961–   ). References to essays in George Watson's useful Everyman edition, *Of Dramatic Poesy and Other Critical Essays* (2 vols., 1962), are added in brackets ('W. i', 'W. ii').'Malone' indicates references to *The Critical and Miscellaneous Prose Works*, ed. Edmond Malone (3 vols. in 4, 1800).

1 *Memoir of Richard Busby D.D.*, by G.F. Russell Barker (1895), p. 16.
2 *Works*, viii. 99 (W. i. 6).
3 Quoted in *The Poems of John Cleveland*, ed. Brian Morris and Eleanor Withington (1967), p. lxx.
4 The first of several reprints by enemies appeared in 1681, 'published to shew the Loyalty and Integrity of the POET'.
5 *Lives of the English Poets*, ed. George Birkbeck Hill (3 vols., 1905), i. 334.
6 *Astraea: The Imperial Theme in the Sixteenth Century* (1975), p. 33.
7 *Contexts of Dryden's Thought* (Chicago and London, 1968), pp. 21ff.
8 I agree with the California editors (i. 255) that this poem was probably written early in 1663. Charles told Clarendon that 'whosoever I find to be My Lady Castlemaine's enemy . . . I do promise on my word to be his enemy as long as I live': see *England in the Reign of Charles II*, by David Ogg (2 vols., 1934), i. 188.
9 *The Diary of Samuel Pepys*, ed. Robert Latham and William Matthews (11 vols., 1970–83), iv. 56; *Works*, viii. 3 (W. i. 131).
10 *The Diary of John Evelyn*, ed. E.S. de Beer (6 vols., 1955), iii. 465. Evelyn adds that the theatres are 'fowle & undecent; Women now (& never 'til now) permitted to appeare & act, which inflaming severall young noblemen & gallants, became their whores, & to some their Wives', mention-

ing several noblemen as well as 'another greater person' who is obviously the King. Women had acted regularly from 1661, if not earlier.

11 *Works*, viii. 283. By marrying Lady Elizabeth Howard in 1663, Dryden gained access to the Court, an advantage of which he made good use. As a friend suggests to me, he seems almost to have shamed courtiers into reading and so to have continued his effort to make the aristocracy conscious of their role as arbiters of taste.

12 *The Indian Queen* (*Works*, viii), II. i. 32, III. i. 161, V. i. 231, V. i. 274.

13 *Works*, ix. 23; Malone, II. 214.

14 *Works*, ix. 15 (W. i. 123).

15 *Poems*, i. 44; (W. i. 94); *Paradise Lost*, ix. 28–9.

16 *Paradise Lost*, vii. 31.

17 The Duke of Buckingham noted, in his 'Character of Charles II', that 'the great and almost only pleasure of mind he appeared addicted to, was shipping and sea-affairs; which seemed to be so much his talent both for knowledge, as well as inclination, that a war of that kind was rather an entertainment, than any disturbance to his thoughts': *The Works of John Sheffield . . . Duke of Buckingham* (2 vols., 3rd edn, 1740), ii. 77. At the end of 'An account of the ensuing Poem' Dryden states that its 'Argument' was the choice of Sir Robert Howard. Cf. Milton's remark, in *Reason of Church Government*, that 'Tasso gave to a prince of Italy his choice whether he would command him to write of Godfrey's expedition against the infidels, or Belisarius against the Goths, or Charlemagne against the Lombards': *Milton on Himself*, ed. John S. Diekhoff (edn of 1965), p. 9.

18 *The Diary of Pepys*, viii. 40.

19 Ibid., vii. 55.

20 *The Diary of John Evelyn*, iii. 457; *Annus Mirabilis*, lines 949–50.

21 *History of the Royal Society* by Thomas Sprat, ed. Jackson I. Cope and Harold Whitmore Jones (Saint Louis, Missouri, 1958), pp. 120, 362, 404, 151, 408.

22 *Poems*, i. 43.

23 W. i. 44, 76, 78, 86, 116, 120.

24 I. ii. 86–9.

25 *Works*, xi. 215–16 (W. i. 180–1).

26 W. i. 191. The quotations in the following paragraph are from Malone, I. ii. 416, 427.

27 IV. i. 133.

28 *An Account of the English Dramatick Poets* (1691), p. 130.

29 Quoted in *Works*, ii. 302–3.

30 *Works*, ii. 306–7.

31 David M. Vieth, 'The Discovery of the Date of *Mac Flecknoe*', in *Evidence in Literary Scholarship: Essays in Memory of James Marshall Osborn*, ed. René Wellek and Alvaro Ribeiro (1979).

32 *Works*, ii. 226, 227.

33 Ed. Godfrey Davies (Los Angeles, 1950), 12–13.

34 *Works*, ii. 236–7.

35 *Lives of the Poets*, i. 373.

36 Joseph Spence: *Observations, Anecdotes, and Characters of Books and Men*, ed. James M. Osborn (2 vols., 1966), i. 28–9.

37 *Lives of the Poets*, i. 442.

38 *Works*, xviii. 7, 17.
39 Dedication of *King Arthur* (1691), in Malone II. 206ff.
40 Line 382.
41 *Poems*, ii. 468, 469.
42 *The Life of St. Francis Xavier, of the Society of Jesus . . . Written in French by Father Dominick Bohours* (1688); *Britannia Rediviva* (1688): lines 30 and 223 are quoted.
43 *The Times Literary Supplement*, 10 April 1953, p. 244.
44 *Poems*, ii. 584.
45 Lines 363ff.
46 *Poems*, iii. 1424 (W. ii. 259).
47 *Poems*, i. 399, ii. 651, 654 (W. ii. 31, 132, 135).
48 *Poems*, ii. 669–70 (W. ii. 154–5).
49 The First Satyr, line 122; Argument of the Third Satyr.
50 'perierunt tempora longi / servitii; nusquam minor est iactura clientis' (lines 124–5): 'all my long years of servitude go for nothing. Nowhere is it so easy as at Rome to throw an old client overboard.'
51 It would be an amusing and instructive study in social history and racial prejudice to see what becomes of Juvenal's Greek parasite in translations into the various modern European languages.
52 See the end of the Argument to the third satire. The compliment to Busby is in large and emphatic type, perhaps for the benefit of an old man's eyes.
53 Charles Tomlinson, in the introduction to *The Oxford Book of Verse in English Translation* (1980), p. xvii.
54 George Stepney to Leibniz, quoted in 'Some suppressed verses in Dryden's translation of Juvenal VI', by W.B. Carnochan, *The Times Literary Supplement*, 21 January 1972, pp. 73–4, from which I take my other MS quotations.
55 *Poems*, ii. 668 (W. ii. 153).
56 Preface to *Ovid's Epistles*: *Poems*, i. 186 (W. i. 273).
57 *Poems*, ii. 617 (W. ii. 92).
58 *The Letters of John Dryden*, ed. Charles E. Ward (Durham, North Carolina, 1942), p. 64.
59 Spence, *Anecdotes*, i. 27.
60 Prologue to *Aureng-Zebe*, line 21.
61 *Letters*, p. 93. While most of the plates show a hooked nose, the original moustache being deleted, there are several where it is not visible.
62 *Letters*, pp. 85–6. In his courteous letter of acceptance Chesterfield stated that 'the greatest men are desirous of being distinguished by some marks of your esteem': p. 87.
63 *Poems*, ii. 869, iii. 1003 (W. ii. 216–17, 223).
64 On this interesting but difficult matter see (in particular) George Watson, 'Dryden and the Jacobites', *The Times Literary Supplement*, 16 March 1973, pp. 301–2.
65 *Letters*, p. 94.
66 Whereas Charles E. Ward estimates that 'All in all, he probably received close to £1,400' (*The Life of John Dryden*, North Carolina and London, 1961), p. 273, John Barnard suggests a maximum of £1,075 in his 'Dryden, Tonson, and subscriptions for the 1697 *Virgil*': *The Papers of the*

Bibliographical Society of America 57 (New York, 1963), p. 150. I owe the quotation from Blackmore to Barnard's article.

67 Malone prints the agreement in *Prose Works*, I. i. 560–1.

68 *Poems*, iv. 2070.

69 *Poems*, iv. 1445, 1450, 1447, 1462, 1463 (W. ii. 271, 277, 273, 293, 293–4).

70 It is worth noticing that Dryden had told Lord Latimer that 'the King . . . is parcell poet with me in the plott' of *The Kind Keeper*: 'one of the designes being a story he was pleased formerly to tell me': *Letters*, pp. 11–12.

71 *Poems*, iv. 1443, followed by iv. 1460 (W. ii. 290). Elsewhere in the preface (iv. 1455–6, W. ii. 285) Dryden mentions that he has confined his choice 'to such Tales . . . as savour nothing of Immodesty', adding: 'If I had desir'd more to please than to instruct, the *Reve*, the *Miller*, the *Shipman*, the *Merchant*, the *Sumner*, and above all, the *Wife of Bathe*, in the Prologue to her Tale, would have procur'd me as many Friends and Readers, as there are *Beaux* and Ladies of Pleasure in the Town. But I will no more offend against Good Manners: I am sensible as I ought to be of the Scandal I have given by my loose Writings; and make what Reparation I am able, by this Publick Acknowledgment.'

72 *Poems*, iv. 1445, 1453 (W. ii. 271, 281–2). It is noteworthy that the 1670 Patent confirming Dryden as Poet Laureate and appointing him Historiographer gives and grants him 'all and singular the rights, privileges, benefits, and advantages, thereunto belonging, as fully and amply as Sir Geoffery Chaucer, Knight, Sir John Gower, Knight, John Leland, Esquire, William Camden, Esquire, Benjamin Johnson, Esquire, James Howell, Esquire, Sir William D'Avenant, Knight, or any other person or persons having or exercising the place or employment of Poet Laureat or Historiographer, or either of them, in the time of any of our royal progenitors': Malone, I. i. 557.

II Pope: No man's slave

Quotations are from *The Poetical Works*, ed. Herbert Davis (1966), and *The Correspondence*, ed. George Sherburn (5 vols., 1966). Frequent reference is also made to the Twickenham Edition of the *Poems* (11 vols., 1939–69), to Joseph Spence, *Observations, Anecdotes, and Characters of Books and Men*, ed. James M. Osborn (2 vols., 1966), and to *Pope: The Critical Heritage*, ed. John Barnard (1973).

1 *Correspondence*, iii. 361. Cf. Pope's criticism of a book by Dr Delany: 'the whole book, tho' he meant it *ad Populum*, is I think purely *ad Clerum*' (ibid., iii. 276).

2 Robert M. Schmitz, *Pope's Windsor Forest 1712: A Study of the Washington University Holograph* (Saint Louis, Missouri, 1952), p. 7.

3 *Correspondence*, i. 59.

4 Lines 542–3, 550, 553.

5 'The function of criticism at the present time', *The Complete Prose Works of Matthew Arnold*, iii (*Lectures and Essays in Criticism*, ed. R.H. Super, Michigan, 1962), 270.

6 Spence, i. 60.

7 Isaac Kramnick, *Bolingbroke and his Circle* (Cambridge, Mass. and London, 1968), p. 217.

8 *Correspondence*, i. 128. Mr Foxon mentions that the poem 'took at least eighteen months to sell a thousand copies, and the so-called "third" and "fourth" editions suggest an attempt to encourage poor sales'. The quotation in the text makes it clear that Pope realised that a *succès d'estime* was more likely than a wide sale. Earlier in the sentence he offers to make some revisions, in deference to Caryll, 'in case of a Second Edition, – which I yet think the book will never arrive at'.

9 *The Spectator*, ed. Donald F. Bond (5 vols., 1965), i. xxvi. Pope told Steele that he had passed part of Christmas 'with some honest Country Gentlemen, who have . . . no manner of Relish for criticisme or polite writing, as you may easily conclude when I tell you they never read the Spectator': i. 139. The previous year he had told a friend that he had 'not quoted one Latin author' since arriving in the country, 'but have learn'd without book a Song of Mr Tho: Durfey's, who is your only Poet of tolerable Reputation in this Country': p. 81.

10 Twickenham, i. 130 and note, supplemented by information from Mr Foxon.

11 iv. 176, v. 67–70.

12 *An Essay on the Genius and Writings of Pope* (5th edn, 2 vols., 1806), i. 235.

13 *Correspondence*, i. 211.

14 *The Prose Works of Alexander Pope*, ed. Norman Ault, (all pub., 1936), i. 176; followed by *Trivia*, ii. 563.

15 *Critical Works of John Dennis*, ed. E.N. Hooker (2 vols., Baltimore, 1939, 1943), i. 325.

16 *Correspondence*, i. 175.

17 Ibid.

18 *Correspondence*, i. 282–3.

19 Spence, i. 83. The agreement between Pope and Tonson is described in Twickenham x. 606.

20 See John Nichols, *Literary Anecdotes of the Eighteenth Century* (9 vols., 1812–15), i. 400n.

21 *Correspondence*, i. 226.

22 Ibid., i. 233.

23 Spence, i. 87; *Correspondence*, i. 267.

24 Carnarvon subscribed for twelve sets; Buckingham, Halifax, Bolingbroke and Lansdowne for ten each. It is doubtful whether such men would have taken all the sets to which they were entitled. Burlington and the Duke of Leeds subscribed for no fewer than fifty copies of Gay's *Poems on Several Occasions*, 1720. Gay wrote to Addison: 'I have sent you only two Copys of my Poems though by your Subscription you are entitled to ten, whatever Books you want more Tonson or Lintot upon your sending will deliver': *The Letters of John Gay*, ed. C.F. Burgess (1966), pp. 5–6.

25 George Sherburn, 'Letters of Alexander Pope, chiefly to Sir William Trumbull': *Review of English Studies*, n.s., 9 (1958), 398.

26 *Correspondence*, ii. 164.

27 Ibid., ii. 156–7.

28 Ibid., ii. 265.

29 Ibid., ii. 275–6.
30 Ibid., ii. 279.
31 Quoted in Charles Chenevix Trench, *George II* (1973), pp. 159–60.
32 In his poem, 'Mr Popes Welcome from Greece'.
33 *The Second Epistle of the Second Book*, lines 68–9.
34 Twickenham, v. 12.
35 The first quotation is from the poem Broome appended to his Observations on the Twenty-fourth Book of the *Odyssey*, the second from *Correspondence*, ii. 219.
36 *The Correspondence of Jonathan Swift*, ed. Harold Williams (5 vols., 1963–5), iii. 110.
37 *Correspondence*, ii. 472, followed by *Correspondence of Swift*, iv. 53.
38 *A Tale of a Tub*, ed. A.C. Guthkelch and D. Nichol Smith (2nd edn 1958), p. 4.
39 Twickenham, v. xxii.
40 *Correspondence of Swift*, iii. 293.
41 *Correspondence*, iii. 61.
42 *Characteristicks* (3 vols., 1711), i. 264.
43 *Correspondence*, i. 242.
44 Twickenham, v. 50–1 and 60n.
45 'Discoveries', in the Works, ed. C.H. Herford and Percy and Evelyn Simpson (11 vols., 1925–52), viii. 601; *Characteristicks*, i. 213.
46 *Eighteenth Century Essays on Shakespeare*, ed. D. Nichol Smith (Glasgow, 1903), pp. 50–1.
47 *Some Materials Towards Memoirs of the Reign of King George II*, by John, Lord Hervey, ed. Romney Sedgwick (3 vols., 1931), i. 261.
48 *George II*, p. 139.
49 See George Sherburn, 'The *Dunciad*, book IV', in *Essential Articles for the Study of Alexander Pope*, ed. Maynard Mack (rev. edn, Hamden, Connecticut, 1968), for example, p. 737.
50 *Memoirs*, ii. 382. Maynard Mack has revealed that 'in a manuscript of rejected passages from the early *Dunciad* George II himself probably figured as the Arch-Dunce': see Howard Erskine-Hill, *Review of English Studies*, n.s., 30 (February 1979), 93.
51 *Correspondence*, ii. 502, followed by iii. 26.
52 'To my dear Friend Mr. Congreve', line 48.
53 *Correspondence of Swift*, iii. 326.
54 *Correspondence*, iii. 367; iv. 5; *Correspondence of Swift*, iv. 547 (italics added). Remarkable efforts were made to persuade Pope to join the Court of the Prince of Wales: 'Don't complain of your being Useless to him', Lyttelton wrote in an important letter in 1738; 'a Friend is never so, especially to a Prince . . . If that Sacred Fire, which by You and other Honest Men has been kindled in his Mind, can be Preserv'd, we may yet be safe; But if it go out, it is a Presage of Ruin . . . For the Age is too far corrupted to Reform itself; it must be done by Those upon, or near the Throne, or not at all': *Correspondence*, iv. 138–9. 'You ask me how I am at Court?', Pope wrote to Swift a few months later. 'I keep my old Walk, and deviate from it to no Court. The Pr. shews me a distinction beyond any Merit or Pretence on my part': ibid., iv. 178.
55 *Correspondence*, iv. 6. 'Lord Bolingbroke is something superior to anything

I have seen in human nature', Pope told Spence. 'You know I don't deal much in hyperboles: I quite think him what I say': Spence, i. 121.

56 *Correspondence*, iii. 77.

57 Spence, i. 129. The best account of the whole plan is to be found in *Alexander Pope's 'Opus Magnum' 1729–1744*, by Miriam Leranbaum (1977).

58 Preface to *The Excursion*, 1814; *Essay on Man*, Argument to Epistle I.

59 Spence, i. 135.

60 *Correspondence of Swift*, iv. 263; *Heritage*, 295.

61 *Heritage*, 321, 279.

62 *Correspondence*, iii. 433, 364.

63 See, for example, Robert Shackleton, 'Pope's *Essay on Man* and the French Enlightenment', in *Studies in the Eighteenth Century II*, ed. R.F. Brissenden (Canberra, 1973).

64 *Correspondence*, iii. 354; Joseph Trapp, *Lectures on Poetry . . . Translated from the Latin* (1742), p. 189n.

65 Spence, i. 134.

66 Dr Howard Erskine-Hill draws my attention to the Morgan MS, which shows that Pope considered 'honest Sh[ippen]' instead of 'Marcellus', and 'W[alpole]' instead of 'Caesar'. (William Shippen was the Jacobite leader in the Commons.) See *Alexander Pope: An Essay on Man: Reproductions of the Manuscripts*, with an introduction by Maynard Mack (1962), p. xxxiii. Bentley's comment may be found in *Heritage*, p. 323.

67 *Correspondence*, iii. 37; iii. 433; iii. 354.

68 *Correspondence of Swift*, iv. 135. Swift would have liked to have had an Epistle addressed to him: 'I have the ambition and it is very earnest . . . to have one Epistle inscribed to me while I am alive, and you just in the time when wit and wisdom are in the height. I must once more repeat Cicero's desire to a friend. *Orna me*': ibid., iv. 382.

69 Cf. Swift's remark about Bolingbroke, made in 1738: 'He began in the Queen's time to be my Patron, and then descended to be my Friend': *Correspondence of Swift*, v. 119.

70 *Correspondence*, i. 338; *Anecdotes of Painting in England*, ed. Horace Walpole (ed. Ralph N. Wornum, 3 vols., 1849), iii. 773; Berkeley's observation was quoted by R. Wittkower in 'That great luminary of architecture', *The Listener*, 24 December 1953, p. 1080.

71 *Correspondence*, i. 347.

72 *Poetical Works*, p. 3; *Correspondence*, i. 417–18; ibid., iii. 413 ('actually' no doubt in the French sense of 'at the moment'); ibid., ii. 185.

73 *The Spectator*, ed. Donald F. Bond (5 vols., 1965), v. 113 (no. 618); *The Critical Works of John Dennis*, ed. Edward Niles Hooker (2 vols., Baltimore, 1939, 1943), ii. 219: Shaftesbury, *Characteristicks*, i. 266; *Correspondence*, iii. 366. Cf. my *Augustan Satire* (1952), ch. vi.

74 *Horace's Satires, Epistles, and Art of Poetry, Done into English, with notes*, S. Dunster (5th edn, 1739), p. 117.

75 *Correspondence of Swift*, iii. 373, v. 58; 'A letter to a noble lord', in *The Works of Alexander Pope*, ed. Warburton (9 vols., 1751), viii. 279.

76 *Correspondence*, iii. 417, 420.

77 See, for example, André Dacier's *Remarques critiques sur les oeuvres d'Horace* (Paris, 1689), ix. 308. On Dryden and Pope in general, and the *Imitations*

of Horace in particular, see Howard Erskine-Hill, *The Augustan Idea in English Literature* (1983).

78 *Correspondence*, iv. 112.

79 *The Yale Edition of Horace Walpole's Correspondence*, (1948), xiii. 248–9.

80 *The Garden and the City* (Toronto and London, 1969), p. 136; *Correspondence of Swift*, v. 119–20.

81 Mack, p. 138.

82 Twickenham, iv. 330, 334.

83 *Heritage*, p. 242 (cf. J.V. Guerinot, *Pamphlet Attacks on Alexander Pope 1711–1744*, 1969, 254ff.); *Heritage*, p. 247. Many country gentlemen were of course strongly opposed to Walpole, and that probably explains how Aaron Hill was able to tell Pope, in the very month of the poem's publication, that he had found a copy of the Second Dialogue of the *Epilogue to the Satires* 'at an old fashioned country gentleman's, who lives in a hole at the foot of a hill, and a wood, like the cave of some captain of Banditti': *Correspondence*, iv. 112.

84 *The Whitehall Evening-Post*, no. 1485, 16–19 March, pp. 1727–8. I owe this reference to Dr Robert Inglesfield. It is noteworthy that 'the *Fair Sex*' were seldom thought of as *purchasers* of books – particularly (one supposes) expensive books. Dr Foxon draws my attention to an agreement between Benjamin Motte and Charles Bathurst about a proposed collection of Pope's prose writings, dated 24 February 1736. The publishers agreed 'not to sell the said Books of Letters &c. at a less Price than Eighteen Shillings per Book to Booksellers or one Guinea per Book to Gentlemen in Sheets for the Quarto or large Folio; or at a less Price than Eight shillings and six Pence to Booksellers and half a Guinea to Gentlemen in Sheets for the small Folio'. No mention is made of Ladies.

85 *Heritage*, p. 340.

86 *Correspondence of Swift*, iv. 546.

87 *Poetical Works*, p. 703. 'I heard the dying swan talk over an epick plan a few weeks before his decease': Edward Young, *Works* (1770), iv. 285, cited in *Lives of the English Poets*, by Samuel Johnson, ed. George Birkbeck Hill (3 vols., 1905), iii. 189n.

III Byron: Too sincere a poet

Verse quotations are from *The Complete Poetical Works*, ed. Jerome J. McGann, i–iii (1980–1 [to April 1816]); *The Works . . . Poetry*, vols. iv–v, ed. E.H. Coleridge (1922, 1924); and *Byron's Don Juan: A Variorum Edition*, ed. Truman Guy Steffan and Willis W. Pratt (4 vols., Austin, Texas, and Edinburgh, 1957). The letters are quoted from *Byron's Letters and Journals*, ed. Leslie A. Marchand (12 vols., 1973–82). Where possible quotations from the Reviews are from *Byron: The Critical Heritage*, ed. Andrew Rutherford (1970). Also referred to are *Byron: A Biography*, Leslie A. Marchand (3 vols., 1957); *Lady Blessington's Conversations of Lord Byron*, ed. Ernest J. Lovell, Jr (Princeton, New Jersey, 1969); *His Very Self and Voice: Collected Conversations of Lord Byron*, ed. Ernest J. Lovell, Jr (New York, 1954); and *A Publisher and his Friends: Memoir and Correspondence of . . . John Murray*, Samuel Smiles (2 vols., 1891).

1 *Letters*, ix. 43, i. 49; *Biography*, i. 165, 169; Pope, preface to *The Works*, 1717.

2 *Letters*, i. 97. McGann is the first editor to include this poem in a collected edition: i. 132–5.

3 *Letters*, i. 103, 111, 112, 118.

4 *Letters*, i. 125, 126 (Crosby was a London bookseller who had a consignment of *Hours of Idleness* for sale in the capital and the provinces), 130, 131, 132, 158–9; *Biography*, i. 148. The *Edinburgh Review* for January 1808 appeared about 27 February, eight months after the publication of Byron's volume.

5 *Biography*, i. 149, 179; *English Bards*, lines 917–18, preface.

6 Lovell, p. 39; *Letters*, ii. 75, ii. 90–1.

7 For the stanzas on Wellington see McGann, ii. 42n, for the Cintra passage ii. 19n–20n, and for the stanza on Beckford, 18n. The stanzas on Elgin are in McGann, ii. 48n, the 'hypothetical' stanza is II. viii, while the reference to 'boyish minions' is in McGann at ii. 63n.

8 Lovell, p. 47; *Biography*, i. 335; *Letters*, iii. 230; Lovell, p. 54; *Blessington*, p. 12; *Biography* i. 330n; *Blessington*, p. 12; *Letters*, ii. 180.

9 *Heritage*, pp. 48, 40; *Childe Harold*, II. 514, I. 609.

10 *Letters*, iii. 34, 63, 70.

11 'Advertisement'; *John Bull's Letter to Lord Byron*, ed. Alan Lang Strout (Norman, Oklahoma, 1947), p. 80; *Persuasion*, ch. xi; *Letters*, iii. 168, 194.

12 *Letters*, iii. 161, 196.

13 *The Corsair*, i. 173–4; *Biography*, i. 442n; Smiles, i. 223, 225.

14 *Letters*, iv. 53–4.

15 In the Venetian period, however, Byron became deeply interested in the profits of his poems, as his letters make abundantly clear.

16 *Letters*, iv. 47; *Biography*, ii. 677.

17 *Heritage*, pp. 90–1; the omitted lines in *The Prisoner of Chillon* stand between lines 378–9 in the MS; Smiles, i. 424.

18 Smiles, i. 388; *Biography*, ii. 699; *Heritage*, pp. 111, 117. It is interesting, as Mr T.A.J. Burnett points out to me, that in the diaries and other memoranda of Byron's friends at the time of the separation references to homosexuality are represented by a dash, while incest is written out in full, an indication that the taboo against the latter was apparently less strong.

19 *Letters*, v. 170, ix. 36, viii. 119.

20 *Letters*, v. 267, vi. 25.

21 *Letters*, vi. 15. It should be noted that a letter usually took between two and three weeks to reach England, however, so that Byron had to make a determined effort to keep in touch with England and English affairs.

22 *Letters*, vi. 193.

23 *Letters*, vi. 36, 67–8, 76–7.

24 *Recollections of a Long Life*, ed. Lady Dorchester (6 vols., 1909–11), ii. 107, quoted in *Variorum*, i. 17; ibid., i. 17–18; *Biography*, ii. 763, 764–5. It seems that only Hobhouse, Scrope Davies, Kinnaird and Frere saw the MS: a less literary group than that which customarily considered Byron's MSS. For a while Byron agreed to suppress *Don Juan I* in order not to damage Hobhouse's election chances.

25 *Letters*, vi. 94 (*The New Bath Guide* was by Christopher Anstey: 'Thomas Little' was Moore's *nom de plume*); 'a dry Bob' refers to copulation without emission. In the event the dedication was not printed at this time.

26 *Letters*, vi. 95; Lovell, pp. 268–9; *Letters*, vi. 105–6.
27 *Letters*, vi. 99, vii. 61; *Memoirs of Thomas Moore*, ed. Lord John Russell (8 vols., 1853–6), ii. 260; *Letters*, vi. 123.
28 *Variorum*, ii. 9ff. and 29; *Letters*, vi. 107; Smiles, i. 401.
29 II. 1096 (referring to Admiral John Byron's *Narrative . . . of the great distresses suffered by himself and his companions on the coast of Patagonia . . .* , 1768).
30 *Biography*, ii. 804; *Letters*, vi. 237; *Biography*, ii. 840; *Heritage*, p. 258; Smiles, i. 405.
31 *Heritage*, pp. 166ff. ('we are aware, that very few of our Northern readers have seen it': p. 169); Smiles, i. 404; *Heritage*, p. 163; *Letters*, vi. 237, 238, x. 36, vi. 207–8.
32 *Letters*, vi. 232, vii. 162, viii. 85, viii. 147–8; *John Bull's Letter*, pp. 83–4, 91, 95–6.
33 *Letters*, viii. 65, 148; Canto IV. 33–4 and 775–6; Smiles, i. 413.
34 *Letters*, viii. 78, 229, ix. 125; Lovell, p. 267.
35 *Letters*, ix. 100, 136.
36 *Letters*, viii. 219 ('Send me *six*', he told Moore, 'and distribute the rest according to your own pleasure'); *Byron, Shelley, Hunt, and 'The Liberal'*, by William H. Marshall (Philadelphia, 1960), p. 100.
37 *Letters*, ix. 187–8, x. 12, x. 58; *Biography*, iii. 1040.
38 Canto VI. 736.
39 Lovell, p. 327; *Letters*, x. 69.
40 *Heritage*, pp. 199–200; *Letters*, x. 42, 58, 69, 68.
41 *Letters*, x. 81, 90; *Blackwood's Magazine*, 7, (December 1822), 710; *Letters*, x. 145.
42 Canto XI. 679–80, 440; Canto XI. lviii and lines 687–8. For an account of the 'Fashionable Novels' see my *English Literature 1815–1832* (1963), pp. 247–52.
43 Cantos XIII. 386, XIV. 71–2, 146–7, 567–8, XV. 544.
44 *Poetry*, ed. E.H. Coleridge, iv. 479; Marshall, *Byron, Shelley, Hunt*, p. 205; Hobhouse, quoted in *The Late Lord Byron*, by Doris Langley Moore (1961), p. 46, the modern study which gives the best account of the history of the Memoirs.
45 *Blessington*, pp. 97–8; *Letters*, iii. 217; *Biography*, iii. 1052; Lovell, p. 451; *Letters*, ix. 41; Lovell, p. 398.
46 *Blessington*, p. 85; 'To the Rev. J.T. Becher', lines 17–18 (McGann i. 178); *Letters*, iii. 217–18, vi. 229; preface to *Julian and Maddalo*.
47 Lovell, p. 465.
This chapter was completed before the publication of Philip W. Martin's interesting study, *Byron: A Poet Before His Public* (1982). It has not seemed useful to attempt to record agreements and disagreements.

IV Shelley: The unacknowledged legislator

Quotations are from *The Complete Poetical Works*, ed. Thomas Hutchinson (1905, reprinted 1947). Reference has also been made to the first two volumes (1972, 1975) of the edition by Neville Rogers. Where possible early reviews are quoted from *The Unextinguished Hearth*, by Newman Ivey White (Durham, North Carolina, 1938). Other works frequently cited are *Shelley: the Pursuit*, by Richard Holmes (1974, reprinted 1976); *The Letters of Percy*

Bysshe Shelley, ed. Frederick L. Jones (2 vols., 1964); and *Shelley's Prose or The Trumpet of a Prophecy*, ed. David Lee Clark (Albuquerque, New Mexico, 1954).

1 *Letters*, i. 55, ii. 71.
2 *Letters*, i. 5–6, 20, 40, 130n.
3 *Letters*, i. 16; *The Wandering Jew*, ed. Bertram Dobell (Shelley Society, 1887), xvi; *Letters*, i. 348.
4 *Letters*, i. 22, 23.
5 *Letters*, i. 27n, 27, 25.
6 *Letters*, i. 52. Shelley instructed Graham in the same sentence to 'Cut out the title page.'
7 *Letters*, i. 151, 229, 235.
8 'Advertisement' on the title-page (*Prose*, 39n); *Letters*, i. 234 (cf. 239); *Letters*, i. 235, 258 (cf. p. 256: 'The style . . . is adapted to the lowest comprehension that can read); *Prose*, p. 59; *Letters*, i. 263, 256.
9 *Letters*, i. 263, 265, 263.
10 *Letters*, i. 282, 296, 319.
11 *Letters*, i. 201, 324, 350, 352–3. With reference to 'the chosen few' it is relevant to remember that when Burdett was being tried for seditious libel for having sent to the press an open letter 'To the Electors of Westminster' the judge instructed the jury in these words: 'If you find in [it] an appeal to the passions of the lower orders of the people, and not having a tendency to inform those who can correct abuses, it is a libel.' As Holmes comments (p. 539), 'if such a composition as Burdett's was addressed to the ruling classes, it was allowable; if it was addressed to the working classes, it was libellous'. It will be seen that it was safer to express revolutionary ideas in verse than in prose. We know that in 1819 there were seventy-five prosecutions for seditious or blasphemous libel.
12 Clark does not mention this, as he should, in *Prose*, p. 118.
13 *Letters*, i. 361. The book is in fact an octavo. The following quotation is from *Letters*, i. 348.
14 *Letters*, i. 361, 368n.
15 Holmes, p. 280. Another prose work, *A Refutation of Deism*, which was privately published in 1814, was also printed in *The Theological Inquirer*.
16 *Nightmare Abbey*, ch. ii.
17 Rogers, i. 380; Holmes, p. 201.
18 *Letters*, i. 438; *The Examiner*, 1 December 1816; *Letters*, i. 517.
19 *Letters*, i. 517, 552; Holmes, p. 309; *Letters*, i. 530, i. 552.
20 *Prose*, p. 162; Holmes, p. 365; *Letters*, i. 533.
21 *Letters*, i. 557.
22 *Letters*, i. 563–4.
23 *Letters*, i. 571; *Peacock's Memoirs of Shelley*, ed. Brett-Smith (1909), p. 61; *Letters*, i. 579–80.
24 *Letters*, i. 586 and n., 585, 582.
25 *Letters*, i. 594.
26 See White, pp. 117–24.
27 *Letters*, ii. 118.
28 Hutchinson, p. 271.
29 *Letters*, ii. 200, 174, 388.
30 *Letters*, ii. 102, 108,116–17, 102–3, 120.
31 *Letters*, ii. 102; i. 340.

32 Shelley had written this 'with the idea of offering it to the Examiner' (*Letters*, ii. 108), knowing that the familiar style would appeal to Leigh Hunt, but found it was too long. In the end Mary Shelley printed it in the *Posthumous Poems*.

33 Preface.

34 *Byron: The Critical Heritage*, p. 117.

35 *Letters*, ii. 128, 163 (cf. 178), 190.

36 *Letters*, ii. 178. Jones comments that either this is a slip for Covent Garden or it had been refused by both theatres.

37 Ibid.

38 White, pp. 167ff.

39 *Letters*, ii. 116. With characteristic malice the *Quarterly* had contrived to find one of the copies of *Laon and Cythna*, which it reviewed with *The Revolt of Islam* in vol. 21 (April 1819, actually published in September). 'I send you a most extraordinary Poem by Godwins now Son-in-law', Murray wrote to Croker, ' – pray keep it under Lock & Key – it is an avowed defense of *Incest* – the author is the vilest wretch in existence – living with Leigh Hunt – The Book was published & he is now endeavouring to suppress it': *The Quarterly Review Under Gifford*, by Hill Shine and Helen Chadwick Shine (Chapel Hill, North Carolina, 1949), p. 66. The reviewer, John Taylor Coleridge, praised some passages of the poem, but essentially the 'review' is an intemperate attack, and Shelley was deeply hurt by it, supposing it to be the work of Southey. For evidence of the misery which he suffered as a result of the reviewers, see 'Lines to a Critic', 'Lines to a Reviewer', and 'Fragment of a Satire on Satire' (Hutchinson, pp. 550, 625, 625).

40 Hutchinson, p. 271.

41 *The Correspondence of Leigh Hunt, edited by his Eldest Son* (2 vols., 1862), i. 163. The line quoted from *Prometheus Unbound* is IV. 235.

42 *Letters*, ii. 174, 219, 221, 262, 263.

43 *Letters*, ii. 152.

44 *Letters*, ii. 152n.

45 On Shelley as a classicist see in particular Timothy Webb, *The Violet in the Crucible* (1976). It is interesting to notice that in 'A Defence of Poetry' Shelley pointed out that through Jesus Christ 'Christianity, in its abstract purity, became the exoteric expression of the esoteric doctrines of the poetry and wisdom of antiquity' (*Peacock's Memoirs*, p. 44).

46 *Letters*, ii. 119; Hutchinson, p. 345; lines 5–8.

47 *Letters*, ii. 136–48.

48 *Letters*, ii. 164.

49 As Lockhart commented, 'Poor Mr. Shelley cannot publish a wicked poem which nobody ever read, or was likely to read, but the whole band were up in arms against him . . . But not so with the noble Don': *John Bull's Letter to Lord Byron*, ed. Alan Lang Strout (Norman, Oklahoma, 1947), p. 83.

50 *Letters*, ii. 191.

51 *Letters*, ii. 196, 213, 258.

52 *Letters*, ii. 263; 363. Cf. the prefatory note to the 1633 edition of Donne's *Poems*: 'The Printer to the Understanders'.

53 *Letters*, ii. 300–1, 298, 305, 302; Holmes, pp. 208–9, 660. On Carlile see

E.P. Thompson, *The Making of the English Working Class* (1963, revised edn, 1968).

54 *Letters*, ii. 299, 294, 299, 349 (italics added).

55 *Letters*, ii. 375n; *Peacock's Four Ages of Poetry, Shelley's Defence of Poetry, Browning's Essay on Shelley*, ed. Brett-Smith (1921), p. 19; *Letters*, ii. 245n.

56 *Letters*, ii. 323, 331, 368.

57 *Letters*, ii. 354, 363–4.

58 *Letters*, ii. 364, 382, 423, 436.

59 *Letters*, i. 214, 277, 507, 577; ii. 206–7, 310.

60 Brett-Smith, *Four Ages of Poetry*, p. 31; Hutchinson, p. 388; 'An Exhortation', lines 1–2.

V Tennyson: Laureate to Victoria

Quotations are from *The Poems of Tennyson*, ed. Christopher Ricks (1969). Where possible early reviews are quoted from *Tennyson: The Critical Heritage* (1967), ed. John D. Jump. Other works frequently cited are *Alfred Tennyson*, by Charles Tennyson (1949); *The Letters of Alfred Lord Tennyson*, ed. Cecil Y. Lang and Edgar F. Shannon, Jr, (1982), i; *Tennyson: The Unquiet Heart*, by Robert Bernard Martin (1980); *Alfred Lord Tennyson: A Memoir*, by his son (2 vols., 1897); *Tennyson*, by Christopher Ricks (New York, 1972); and *Tennyson and the Reviewers*, by Edgar Finley Shannon, Jr, (Cambridge, Mass., 1952).

1 Ricks, p. 1.

2 C. Tennyson, p. 256.

3 Martin, p. 425, followed by C. Tennyson, p. 85.

4 *William Allingham: A Diary*, ed. H. Allingham and D. Radford (1907), p. 344.

5 Martin, p. 556.

6 C. Tennyson, p. 50; *Letters*, p. 7 (quoting *The First Epistle of the Second Book of Horace Imitated*, by Pope, line 305).

7 *The Letters of John Keats*, ed. Hyder Edward Rollins (2 vols., Cambridge, Mass., 1958), i. 218; 'The Ancient Sage', line 66; Martin, p. 88.

8 Edward Lytton Bulwer, *England and the English* (2 vols., 1833), ii. 107, 105–6.

9 Shannon, p. 42.

10 Martin, p. 574 (Edmund Gosse on Tennyson's reading of 'Boädicea', a late poem).

11 C. Tennyson, p. 149.

12 *Memoir*, i. 51.

13 I quote from the first edition. In 1842 'clearvoiced' acquired a hyphen: 'fledgling' was revised to 'callow' in 1853.

14 'Chorus, in an unpublished drama, written very early', stanza 2: *Poems*, p. 237.

15 οἱ ῥέοντες: *Poems*, pp. 257–8. The footnote reads: 'Argal – this very opinion is only true relatively to the flowing philosophers.'

16 *Heritage*, pp. 87–8.

17 *Heritage*, pp. 34ff.

18 *Heritage*, pp. 63, 50.

19 Martin, p. 155.

20 Later revised to ' . . . spirit, full and free'. For Trench's observation see *Poems*, p. 400.
21 *Letters*, p. 84; Tennyson deleted the words 'yet as popularity is not what I am particularly anxious for' from the middle of the passage quoted. For Hallam's comments see C. Tennyson, p. 129.
22 *Heritage*, p. 81.
23 'A Dream of Fair Women', lines 15–16.
24 *Heritage*, p. 174.
25 *Letters*, p. 95.
26 *Ars Poetica*, 386–9: 'put the parchments in the cupboard, and let them be kept quiet till the ninth year'.
27 *The Cambridge 'Apostles'*, by Frances M. Brookfield (1906), p. 268 (I have emended 'far more' to 'for more', as the context seems to require); Martin, p. 226 (original emphasis).
28 *Letters*, p. 204. The following quotation, 'I hate and shun the common herd', is from Horace's *Odes*, III. i.
29 *Edinburgh Review*, 20 (November 1812), 279–80; *Contributions to the Edinburgh Review*, 2nd edn (3 vols., 1846), ii. 325.
30 *Heritage*, pp. 137–8, 125, 152.
31 *A New Spirit of the Age*, ed. R.H. Horne (2 vols., 1844), ii. 5 (cf. Shannon, p. 82 and n53); Martin, p. 283.
32 *William Allingham: A Diary*, p. 31; *Heritage*, pp. 178, 173; *Alton Locke*, ed. Elizabeth A. Cripps (World's Classics, 1983), 97.
33 It should also be remembered that religious poetry had a large public. *The Course of Time*, by Robert Pollok (1827), sold 12,000 in some eighteen months: a fifteenth edition appeared in 1840, and by 1869 78,000 copies had been sold. *The Christian Year*, by John Keble, appeared in the same year and had sold 379,000 by 1873. *The Omnipresence of the Deity*, by Robert Montgomery, was published in 1828 and reached a twenty-eighth edition by 1855. In a class of its own, Martin Tupper's *Proverbial Philosophy* (1838) sold 200,000 by 1866 and reached a fiftieth edition in 1880. See Richard D. Altick, *The English Common Reader* (Chicago, 1957), pp. 386–7.
34 *Heritage*, p. 130; Shannon, pp. 74, 62–9.
35 *The Complete Works of George Savile First Marquess of Halifax*, ed. Walter Raleigh (1912), p. 198.
36 *Selected Essays* (3rd enlarged edn, 1951), pp. 329–30.
37 Shannon, p. 93.
38 *Letters*, p. 281.
39 Shannon, pp. 100, 105–6.
40 *The Princess*, 'Conclusion', lines 25–8.
41 *The Poems of Matthew Arnold*, ed. Kenneth Allott (1965), pp. 592–3, 595–6, 603, 604–5.
42 *The Name and Nature of Poetry* (Cambridge 1933), p. 48.
43 These allusions are usefully assembled in *Poems*, pp. 855ff. See also Martin, p. 324.
44 *Poems*, pp. 859–60.
45 *Heritage*, p. 7; Shannon, p. 151.
46 Martin, pp. 294, 352.
47 *Memoir*, i. 362; C. Tennyson, p. 288.
48 *Maud*, part I, line 34.

49 *Maud*, part III, line 50; *Heritage*, p. 219; see too Edgar F. Shannon, Jr, 'The critical reception of Tennyson's "Maud" ', *Publications of the Modern Language Association of America* 68 (1953), 397ff.

50 Ralph W. Rader, *Tennyson's Maud: The Biographical Genesis* (Berkeley and Los Angeles, 1963).

51 Quoted by Shannon in 'Tennyson's "Maud" ', p. 414.

52 Ricks, p. 265.

53 Ricks, p. 264.

54 *Heritage*, pp. 220, 216, 240.

55 *Heritage*, pp. 249, 250, 260, 244.

56 *Guinevere*, lines 477–8.

57 *Merlin and Vivien*, lines 5, 307, 237, 240; *The Marriage of Geraint*, lines 721–2.

58 'Notes on Poems and Reviews', in *Swinburne Replies*, ed. Clyde Kenneth Hyder (Syracuse, New York, 1966), p. 24.

59 *Guinevere*, lines 602–7; *The Testament of Cresseid*, line 574.

60 *Memories and Reflections*, by Laura Troubridge (1925), pp. 32–3. When Tennyson visited London about this time George Smith offered him 5,000 guineas 'for a volume of the same length as the *Idylls of the King*. In return for this he asked only the right to publish for three years. This was said to be the highest offer ever made to a poet up to that time': C. Tennyson, p. 322.

61 'Dora Creswell', in *Our Village*, (1828) iii.

62 See Part I ('Romanticism turns bourgeois') of *The Hero in Eclipse in Victorian Fiction*, by Mario Praz, translated Angus Davidson (1956).

63 See 'The publication of Tennyson's "Lucretius" ', by Edgar F. Shannon, Jr, *Studies in Bibliography* 34 (Charlottesville, Virginia, 1981), 146ff. 'Naked' (line 52) was revised to 'But girls' in all editions. The next quotation (lines 188–91) was revised to one line in *Macmillan's* – 'And here an Oread – and this way she runs'.

64 C. Tennyson, p. 483.

65 Line 108.

66 C. Tennyson, pp. 351, 442, 461.

67 *Swinburne Replies*, pp. 29–30.

68 *Memories and Reflections*, p. 30.

69 C. Tennyson, p. 206.

70 C. Tennyson, pp. 472, 436; *Memoir*, ii. 79–80.

VI Yeats: Always an Irish writer

Quotations from the poems are taken from *The Collected Poems* (2nd edn, 1950) or from the original editions, as appropriate. Also referred to are *The Letters of W.B. Yeats*, ed. Allan Wade (1954); and *W.B. Yeats: The Critical Heritage*, ed. A. Norman Jeffares (1977).

1 *Letters*, p. 135.

2 *Letters*, p. 66. It is interesting that Yeats changed the spelling to 'Usheen', to make the pronunciation clearer, in the *Poems* of 1895 (often reprinted). In *The Collected Poems* of 1933 and subsequently he reverted to 'Oisin'.

3 *Autobiographies*, by W.B. Yeats (1955), p. 61.

4 J. Hone, *W.B. Yeats 1865–1939* (1942), p. 15.

5 *Autobiographies*, pp. 17–18.

6 Ibid., p. 246.
7 Ibid., p. 102.
8 Ibid., pp. 204, 203.
9 *Memoirs: Autobiography – First Draft*, ed. Denis Donoghue (1972), p. 50; *Letters*, p. 33.
10 *Letters*, p. 30.
11 Ibid., p. 84.
12 Ibid., pp. 166, 111, 138.
13 R. Ellmann, *Yeats: The Man and the Masks* (1949, reprinted 1969), p. 147.
14 *The Oxford Book of Modern Verse 1892–1935 Chosen by W.B. Yeats* (1936), xi.
15 *Letters*, p. 238.
16 Ibid., pp. 238–9.
17 Ibid., pp. 250–1.
18 Ibid., p. 215.
19 *Autobiographies*, p. 208. The book exists, and must be most useful to librarians: *The Poets of Ireland A Biographical and Bibliographical Dictionary of Irish Writers of English Verse*, by D.J. O'Donoghue; Librarian of University College, Dublin (Dublin, 1912).
20 Ibid., p. 241.
21 *Letters*, pp. 205–6.
22 Ibid., pp. 246, 280, 286.
23 Ibid., p. 122 (italics added).
24 Ibid., p. 311.
25 *The Land of Heart's Desire* and *The Countess Cathleen* (Cabinet Library edn, 1925), pp. 160, 161.
26 'The Irish National Literary Society', in *Letters to the New Island* (1934, reprinted 1970), p. 155. The essay was published in 1892.
27 *The Variorum Edition of the Poems of W.B. Yeats*, ed. Peter Allt and Russell K. Alspach (New York, 7th printing, 1977), p. 836.
28 *Letters*, p. 310.
29 Ibid., pp. 406–7.
30 *Autobiographies*, p. 209.
31 James W. Flannery, *W.B. Yeats and the Idea of a Theatre* (New Haven and London, 1976), p. 324.
32 Ibid., pp. 332–3.
33 Hone, p. 209.
34 *Letters*, pp. 447, 464, 466, 476, 482, 500–1, 512.
35 Ibid., pp. 555, 567; *Heritage*, p. 58.
36 *Letters*, p. 610.
37 *Explorations*, selected by Mrs W.B. Yeats (1962), pp. 254–7.
38 *Variorum Edition*, pp. 835–6.
39 *Poetry and Drama* (1951), p. 20.
40 *Letters*, p. 354.
41 *Variorum Edition*, p. 849.
42 *Letters*, pp. 397, 453, 462.
43 Ibid., pp. 449, 498.
44 *Heritage*, pp. 23–4.
45 *Letters*, pp. 457, 456.
46 *Heritage*, pp. 188, 189, 188.
47 *Letters*, p. 605.

48 *Heritage*, pp. 218–19.
49 Ezra Pound's phrase: *Heritage*, p. 189.
50 A.D. Hope, 'William Butler Yeats'.
51 *The Oxford Book*, xv.
52 *Heritage*, p. 55 (from a lecture of 1910, 'Friends of my Youth').
53 *Letters*, pp. 211, 781.
54 Ibid., p. 710.
55 Hone tells us (p. 302) that until about 1915 Yeats seldom earned more than £200 per annum from his books, but within six years his royalties from the frequently reprinted *Poems* of 1895 were growing markedly. In 1925 *The Land of Heart's Desire*, now reprinted with *The Countess Cathleen*, sold 10,000 copies: a striking reminder that the majority of his readers were still preoccupied with his early work while he was moving on to his greatest achievements.
56 *The Oxford Book*, xxxvi.
57 *Letters*, p. 758.
58 *The Winding Stair*, p. 100.
59 'Advertisement' to *Bells and Pomegranates* (1842), iii.
60 *Letters*, pp. 769, 796.
61 *Autobiographies*, p. 99.
62 *Variorum Edition*, 543n–544n, 837. Cf. 'Three Marching Songs', pp. 613ff.
63 Quoted in *A Commentary on the Collected Poems of W.B. Yeats*, by A. Norman Jeffares (1968), p. 512.
64 *Letters*, pp. 867–8.
65 Ibid., pp. 871, 880, 881–2.
66 Ibid., pp. 853, 877.
67 In *A Speech and Two Poems* (seventy copies, not for sale).
68 'A Dialogue of Self and Soul', line 64.
69 *Letters*, p. 873.
70 *Letters*, p. 604. The late Professor F.S.L. Lyons informed me that Maud Gonne's son, Sean MacBride, told him that he remembered his mother and Iseult 'being vehement with Willie that he would never be admitted to the house again if he accepted'.
71 *Letters*, pp. 895–6.
72 Ibid., pp. 328, 841.
73 'Essay, supplementary to the preface', in *The Poetical Works*, ed. E. de Selincourt (1944), ii. 426.

Conclusion

1 Preface to the second edition of *Lyrical Ballads: The Poetical Works*, ed. E. de Selincourt (1944), ii. 393.
2 'Thoughts on poetry and its varieties', reprinted from *The Monthly Repository* (January 1833), in Mill's *Dissertations and Discussions* (4 vols., 1875), i. 71.
3 For an amusing treatment of the case of a painter with virtually no public, see Henry James's story, 'The Tree of Knowledge'.
4 *The Letters of Gerard Manley Hopkins to Robert Bridges*, ed. Claude Colleer

Abbott (1935), p. 46. For the criticism of Robert Bridges, see the preface to his Notes, here quoted from *Poems of Gerard Manley Hopkins*, ed. W.H. Gardner (3rd edn, 1948), p. 205.

5 *Robert Browning and Alfred Domett*, ed. Frederic G. Kenyon (1906), pp. 28–9.
6 *Practical Criticism: A Study of Literary Judgment* (1929, 5th impression, 1946), pp. 206–7.

Index

Some names (e.g. those of many of the subscribers to Dryden's *Virgil* and Pope's *Homer*, and those of modern editors) are excluded. Short poems are not listed separately.

Index

and Shelley, 99
Browne, James Hamilton: 88
Browning, Robert: influenced by
Shelley, 115; Tennyson on, 118;
Sordello, 125; on the dramatic
mode, 163; on his audience, 170
Brutus: 53, 88
Buckingham, John, Duke of: encouraged Pope, 38; on Charles II, 173
n. 17
Bulwer Lytton: 119
Bullen, A.H.: 158
Bunyan, John: 59
Burdett, Sir Francis: and Shelley, 91,
99, 182 n. 11
Burnett, T.A.J.: 180 n. 18
Burlington, Richard Boyle, 3rd Earl
of: and Pope, 48ff
Burns, Robert: Tennyson on, 143;
Yeats and, 152
Busby, Dr Richard: and Dryden, 4, 25
Byron, George Gordon, Lord: 3, 30,
60, *61–89*; and Pope, 60, 61; and
Shelley, 90, 98, 100, 103–4, 109,
113–15; and Tennyson, 119, 121,
123, 127, 170, 171; *Fugitive Pieces*,
61; *Poems on Various Occasions*, 62;
Hours of Idleness, 62–4, 67; *Poems
Original and Translated*, 63; *English
Bards and Scotch Reviewers*, 63–7;
Childe Harold's Pilgrimage, 64ff., 84,
89, 103, 115; *Hints from Horace*, 64;
The Curse of Minerva, 64; *The Giaour*,
66–7; *The Bride of Abydos*, 67–8; *The
Corsair*, 68–9, 107, 129; *Poems on his
Domestic Circumstances*, 69; *The
Prisoner of Chillon*, 70–1; *Manfred*, 71,
106; *Marino Faliero*, 72; *Beppo*, 72–4;
Don Juan, 73ff., 81ff., 89, 114; *The
Vision of Judgment*, 80–2, 86–7; *Cain,
Sardanapalus* and *The Two Foscari*, 81;
Werner, 81; *The Irish Avatar*, 82;
Heaven and Earth, 84; *The Age of
Bronze*, 85; *The Island*, 85; *Memoirs*,
87
Byron, Lady (Annabella Milbanke):
68, 69–70, 75

Caesar, Julius: 13, 47, 51, 88, 92
Cambridge University: Dryden and,
4, 29; Pope and, 39; Byron and, 52,
63; Tennyson and, 118–19
Campbell, Thomas: 65, 66, 87

Canning, George: 68
Carlile, Richard: defended by Shelley,
109; pirates *Queen Mab*, 112, 183–4
n. 53
Carlyle, Jane Welsh: on Tennyson,
118
Carnochan, W.B.: 174 n. 54
Caroline, Queen: Byron on, 80, 83
Caryll, John: 37, 47, 50, 176 n. 8
Casement, Roger: Yeats on, 165
Casti, G.B.: his *Novelle Galanti* quoted,
72
Castlemaine, Countess of: Dryden
and, 7–8
Castlereagh, Robert Stewart,
Viscount: Byron and, 75, 83, 89;
Shelley on, 109
Charles II: and Dryden, 3, 4, 6, 8,
11–13, 14, 15, 18–22, 26, 31, 33, 35,
75, 128, 172 n. 8, 173 n. 17, 175
n. 70
Charleton, Dr Walter: Dryden and, 7
Chaucer, Geoffrey: and his audience,
1; Dryden and, 30–1; Byron mentions, 75; contrasted with Shelley,
113; contrasted with Tennyson,
118, 126, 138; Yeats and, 157–8;
Dryden on, 175 n. 71
Chesterfield, Philip Stanhope, 2nd
Earl of: 28
Chesterfield, Philip Dormer
Stanhope, 4th Earl of: 58
Chetwood, Knightly: 27
Cicero: 52, 53
Clarendon, Edward Hyde, Earl of:
6–7, 8, 172 n. 8
Clark, William: 111
Clarke, Alured: 47
Clarke, Edward: 67
Clarke, Hewson: 64
Clermont, Mary Jane: 69
Cleveland, John: 4–5
Clifford, Lord: 28
Cobbett, William: 99
Cogni, Margarita: 73
Coleridge, John Taylor: on Shelley,
183 n. 39
Coleridge, S.T.: and Wordsworth, 46;
satirised by Byron, 63; and Tennyson, 137
Collier, Jeremy: and Dryden, 8, 17, 30
Congreve, William: and Dryden, 28;
and Pope, 37–8, 52, 60

Index

'Cornwall, Barry' (B.W. Procter):
Shelley on, 113
Cowper, William: 58
Crabbe, George: Jeffrey on, 125–6
Croker, Thomas Crofton: on Byron,
70; on Tennyson, 123–4; and
Shelley, 183 n. 39
Crosby, Ben: 62
Curll, Edmund: 52, 84

Dacier, André: 178 n. 77
Dallas, R.C.: 64, 65
Dante: and Shelley, 103, 110; and *In
Memoriam*, 132
Davenant, Sir William: on 'heroique
plays', 8
Davidson, John: 147
Davies, Scrope: 74, 180 n. 24
Davis, Thomas: 146, 149, 164
de la Mare, Walter: on Yeats, 157
Dennis, John: on drama, 36; on satire,
50–1
Denham, Sir John: 4
Derham, William: 46
de Vere, Aubrey: 132
Dial, The: 160
Dickens, Charles: 127
Dickinson, Emily: had hardly any
readers, 170
Domett, Alfred: 170
Donne, John: and love poetry, 61, 171,
183 n. 52
Dowson, Ernest: 147
Drama: Dryden and, 8–9, 13–17, 30;
and Pope, 36; and Byron, 71–2;
and Shelley, 104–8; and Tennyson,
156; and Yeats, 150–6
Dryden, John, 1, 3, *4–31*; plays, 8–9,
13–17, 31; and Pope, 32–7, 45, 48,
51, 52, 54; and Byron, 61, 75; and
Shelley, 113; and Tennyson, 128;
and Yeats, 156; 'tone' in, 170; see
also Poet Laureate; *Heroique
Stanza's*, 5, 111; *Astræa Redux*, 5–6,
10, 34; *To My Lord Chancellor*, 6;
Annus Mirabilis, 7, 10–13, 19; *Of
Dramatick Poesie*, 9, 13–14; *Mac
Flecknoe*, 16–17, 36–7, 41; *Ovid's
Epistles*, 26; *Absalom and Achitophel*,
3, 12, 15, 18–22, 35, 45; *The Medall*,
20; *Religio Laici*, 9, 20; *The History of
the League*, 21; *Threnodia Augustalis*,
21–2; *The Hind and the Panther*, 22; *A

Song for St. Cecilia's Day, 23; *The Life
of St. Francis Xavier*, 174 n. 72;
Eleonora, 23; *Britannia Rediviva*, 174
n. 42; *Discourse Concerning Satire*, 24,
26–7; *The Satires of Juvenal and
Persius*, 24–7; *The Works of Virgil*,
27–9, 36–8; *Fables*, 29–31
Dunster, S.: 178 n. 74
Durfey, Thomas: 176 n. 9

Eaton, Daniel: 97
Ebers's British and Foreign Circulat-
ing Library: 101–2
Eclectic Review: on *Don Juan*, 78; on
Alastor, 98
Edinburgh Review: on *Hours of Idleness*,
63, 123; on *Childe Harold's Pilgrim-
age*, I–II, 66; on *Beppo*, 74; on
Byron, 84; on Tennyson's *Poems*
(1842), 126
Edleston, John: 62, 65
Elgin, Lord: 65
Eliot, George: and *Maud*, 135; *Scenes of
Clerical Life*, 140
Eliot, T.S.: and 'The Hesperides',
128; on Yeats's *Purgatory*, 156; 160;
171
Elizabeth I: 12, 45
Ellmann, Richard: on Yeats, 147
Emerson, Ralph Waldo: 125
Erskine-Hill, Howard: 177 n. 50, 177
n. 66, 178–9 n. 77
Etherege, Sir George: 17
Eton College: 90, 94
Etty, William: 140
Euripides: 104
Evelyn, John: on Cleveland, 5; on the
Restoration theatres, 8
Examiner, The: on *The Revolt of Islam*,
102–3; *The Mask of Anarchy* intended
for, 108; Shelley writes to, 109,
111; *Julian and Maddalo* and, 183
n. 32

Faber Book of Modern Verse, The: 165–6
Farr, Florence: 153, 157
Fenton, Elijah: 38
Ferguson, Sir Samuel: 149
Fielding, Henry: 52, 59, 75
FitzGerald, Edward: on Tennyson,
124; Tennyson to, 125, 129
Fletcher, John: 30, 75
Ford, John: 75

192

Index

Fortescue, William: 47

Fox, W.J.: 121

Foxon, David: 176 n. 8, 176 n. 10, 179 n. 84

Franklin, Benjamin: 88, 95

Frere, John Hookham: 68, 71–4

Galignani: 85, 115

Galt, John: 68

Gamba, Count Pietro: 88

Garth, Samuel: 28, 37, 38, 52

Gascoigne, George: 45

Gay, John: Pope's epitaph on, 32; on *The Rape of the Lock*, 35; *The What D'ye Call It*, 36; *The Beggar's Opera*, 40, 44; and Burlington, 49; *Poems on Several Occasions*, 176 n. 24

George I: 39, 43

George II: 43ff., 51, 54ff., 57

George III: 80–1, 86, 177 n. 54

George IV: 66, 76, 79, 86

Gifford, William: 65, 68, 70, 71, 84, 87

Gisborne, John: 110, 112, 114

Gladstone, William Ewart: and Tennyson, 126–7, 137–8, 141

Godwin, Fanny: 99

Godwin, William: 104, 115, 183 n. 39

Goldsmith, Oliver: 156

Gonne, Iseult: 159

Gonne, Maud: 152, 159, 166

Gosse, Sir Edmund: 184 n. 10

Granville, George, Baron Lansdowne: 52

Gray, Thomas: 58, 59, 170

Griffith, Arthur: 152

Gregory, Lady: 156–7, 159, 160, 164, 167

Guiccioli, the Contessa: 79, 80, 89

Gwynn, Stephen: 165

Halifax, Lord: 37, 38

Hallam, Arthur Henry: 120ff., 131, 133

Handel, George Frederick: 49

Harley, Edward, 2nd Earl of Oxford: 39, 48

Harrow School: 63

Hastings, Lord: 4

Harth, Phillip: 7

Haydon, Benjamin Robert: 144

Hayward, John: 171

Heber, Richard: 68

Hemans, Mrs: 125

Henryson, Robert: 138

Herrick, Thomas: 4

Hervey, Lord: 43, 44

Hill, Aaron: on Pope, 56, 179 n. 83

Hitchener, Elizabeth: 94, 95, 115

Hobhouse, John Cam (Baron Broughton): 63, 74, 79, 180 n. 24

Hodgson, Francis: 68

Hogarth, William: 45

Holland House: 65ff., 84

Holland, Lord and Lady: 65, 87, 99

Holmes, Richard: 97, 99, 182 n. 11

Homer: 15; Pope and, 29, 37ff.; on Helen, 138–9

Hone, Joseph: 145, 159, 188 n. 55

Hone, William: 99

Hookham, Thomas: 91, 95, 96, 99, 106

Hope, A.D.: on Yeats, 161

Hopkins, G.M.: on his audience, 169–70

Horace: and Dryden, 20, 24, 26; and Pope, 48, 50ff.; Byron's *Hints from Horace*, 64; 124, 125

Horniman, Miss: 154, 157, 167

Horne, R.H.: 126

Howard, Lady Elizabeth: 173 n. 11

Howard, Sir Robert: 8, 173 n. 17

Housman, A.E.: 131

Hugo, Victor: on the theatre, 151

Hume, David: 93

Hunt, 'Bristol': 89

Hunt, John: 81, 86–7

Hunt, Leigh: on John Murray, 83–4; Byron on, 84–5; Shelley to, 90; on Shelley, 98; Shelley and, 99; on Shelley, 102–3; and Shelley, 105–9; Shelley to, 114; on Tennyson, 121, 127, 140; Shelley and, 183 n. 32, 183 n. 39

Hyde-Lees, Georgie: see Yeats, Mrs W.B.

Ibsen, Henrik: 151

Incest: and *The Bride of Abydos*, 68; and *Manfred*, 71; and *Laon and Cythna*, 101–2; and *The Cenci*, 105–6; 180 n. 18

Indicator, The: 107, 108

Inglesfield, Robert: 179 n. 84

James II: 21–3, 28

James, Henry: on Tennyson, 143, 188 n. 4

193

Index

Index